# IN THE NAME OF DEMOCRACY

# IN THE NAME OF DEMOCRACY

U.S. POLICY TOWARD LATIN AMERICA
IN THE REAGAN YEARS

THOMAS CAROTHERS

UNIVERSITY OF CALIFORNIA PRESS
BERKELEY   LOS ANGELES   OXFORD

University of California Press
Berkeley and Los Angeles, California
University of California Press
Oxford, England
Copyright © 1991
by The Regents of the University of California
Printed in the United States of America
1  2  3  4  5  6  7  8  9

Library of Congress Cataloging-in-Publication Data

Carothers, Tom H.
  In the name of democracy : U.S. policy toward Latin America in
the Reagan years / Thomas Carothers.
     p.    cm.
  Includes bibliographical references (p.     ) and index.
  ISBN 0-520-07319-3
  1. Latin America—Foreign relations—United States.  2. United
States—Foreign relations—Latin America.  3. United States—
Foreign relations—1981–1989.  4. Latin America—Politics and
government—1980–  5. Representative government and
representation—Latin America—History—20th century.  I. Title.
F1418.C295   1991
327.7308—dc20                                             91-19947
                                                              CIP

*To my mother and father*

# CONTENTS

# PREFACE

Shortly after joining the Office of the Legal Adviser of the U.S. Department of State in 1985, I was assigned on an interagency detail to a recently created office in the Latin America bureau of the Agency for International Development (AID) called the Office of Administration of Justice and Democratic Development. There I worked on a variety of assistance projects designed to promote democracy in Latin America and the Caribbean, in particular the administration of justice project, a program to help Latin American countries develop their judicial systems. The democracy assistance projects carried out by AID were only one very small part of the Reagan administration's overall Latin America policy. My work, however, brought me into contact with the general policy-making process on Latin America and allowed me to travel to numerous countries in the region and serve temporarily in several U.S. embassies, including those in El Salvador, Nicaragua, and Haiti.

From my position in the government, I was struck by the degree to which the concept of promoting democracy had penetrated the Reagan administration's policy toward Latin America. The administration had arrived at the point of unifying a tremendously disparate set of policies under the stated theme of promoting democracy, policies such as helping the Salvadoran government fight a civil war, pressuring President Augusto Pinochet of Chile to proceed with a fair plebiscite, and carrying out a vast paramilitary assistance program for the Nicaraguan contras. Moreover, much of the debate over Latin America policy between the administration and its critics focused on the question of how the United States should promote democracy in Latin America and whether U.S. policies were in fact serving that goal.

Having come into the government with a fairly high degree of skepticism about the relation between lofty moral constructs and day-to-day reality in U.S. foreign policy, I also could not help but be struck by the fact that promoting democracy was not just a rhetorical theme of the Latin America policy but a subject of genuine interest and concern among many U.S. officials. Contrary to the picture that sometimes was presented on the outside, U.S. officials behind closed doors did not wink and nudge each other when they spoke of promoting democracy in Latin America, nor for the most part did they maintain a consciously cynical attitude about what constitutes democracy in Latin America. At the same time, however, I was also startled by how little many U.S. officials seemed to know about political development in Latin America and the history of U.S. efforts to influence Latin American political development; I became aware of the strong tendency of officials confronted with the issue of promoting democracy abroad to resort to simplistic formulas based on ideas and assumptions derived solely from the U.S. national experience.

The further I got involved in the political development assistance programs and the policy-making process generally, the more ambiguous and confusing the issue of promoting democracy became. The web of rhetoric and reality surrounding the issue was very tangled within the government. U.S. officials had been talking about promoting democracy in Latin America so insistently and for so long that they had come to believe they were fully engaged in doing it even when particular policies corresponded very little to democratic norms or goals. I saw firsthand that there were real opportunities for the United States to promote democracy in Latin America and that at least in some cases, Latin Americans were eager for the United States to involve itself. On the other hand I also saw how easily a stated concern for promoting democracy shaded into political interference or outright interventionism and how rarely the impulse to promote political change was complemented by a sophisticated or subtle understanding of the foreign countries in question.

These experiences prompted me to write this book. I sought to disentangle the web of prodemocratic rhetoric and reality that surrounded U.S. policy toward Latin America in the 1980s, both to determine what the United States actually did to promote democracy and to assess the Reagan administration's far-reaching claim that it contributed significantly to the democratic trend in Latin America. I also wanted to extract from the Latin American experience some general lessons about promoting democracy and its proper place in U.S. foreign policy. The recent trend toward democracy in many areas of the world has raised the issue of promoting democracy to the top of the U.S. foreign policy agenda. I felt certain that the experience of a decade of democratic resurgence in Latin America and intense U.S. involvement in that region contained important lessons for the United States.

Although the book was stimulated by my experiences in the government, it is not in any sense a bureaucratic memoir. I participated directly only in very peripheral parts of the Latin America policy-making process and am not in a position to write a "tell-all" book even if I were so inclined. Nonetheless, working in the State Department and the Agency for International Development did permit me something of an insider's view. Above all, it helped me see below the surface of the policy to gain a sense of how policymakers were thinking about the issues they confronted and how they conceived of the policies they adopted. Much of the analysis in this book reflects that perspective. Being on the inside of the policy process also greatly aided my later efforts to interview policymakers when I began to do the formal research for this book. Much of the specific factual information about the policies described herein is based on numerous formal interviews and informal conversations with current and former U.S. officials.

I wrote most of this book while an International Affairs Fellow at the Council on Foreign Relations and a Guest Scholar at the Woodrow Wilson International Center for Scholars. I am deeply indebted to both institutions for their support; I particularly thank Kempton Dunn of the Council on Foreign Relations and Joseph Tulchin and Samuel Wells of the Wilson Center. I am also grateful to the Center for Strategic and International Studies, especially Georges Fauriol of the Latin American program, for hosting me during a good part of my time as a Council on Foreign Relations Fellow. I made much use of the libraries at the School of Advanced International Studies of Johns Hopkins University and the Council on Foreign Relations; the press clipping service of the Council on Foreign Relations library was a particularly valuable source. William Burns, Abraham

Lowenthal, and Joseph Tulchin provided valuable comments on the entire manuscript and a great deal of other types of assistance and support. I also thank Georges Fauriol, Robert Harris, and Viron Vaky for reading selected parts of the manuscript. Phebe Macrae did some useful research work in the final stages of the writing.

I owe Laura Bocalandro, my wife, more than can be expressed here for her love and companionship. Our first child, Christopher, born between the first and second drafts, helped put the book in useful perspective. My parents have always been an unswerving source of love and support; it is to them I dedicate this book.

# Introduction

The impulse to promote democracy has been a recurrent element of United States policy toward Latin America in the twentieth century. In the 1910s President Woodrow Wilson led a vigorous campaign to foster elected, constitutional governments in Latin America. In the second half of the 1940s, the United States actively supported the emergence of democratic governments in a number of Latin American countries. In the 1960s, President John F. Kennedy launched the Alliance for Progress, a massive aid program for Latin America of which one principal objective was promoting democracy. And in the late 1970s, President Jimmy Carter championed the cause of human rights and democracy in Latin America as part of his global human rights policy.

Although these recurring bouts of interest in promoting democracy in Latin America were to some degree an expression of the idealist, moral crusader streak in U.S. foreign policy, for the most part they were grounded in the practical belief that promoting democracy in Latin America was a way of advancing the United States's underlying economic or security interests in the region. Prior to World War II the United States's main concerns in Latin America were protecting U.S. business interests and upholding the Monroe Doctrine, that is, keeping extrahemispheric powers out of Latin America. Several U.S. administrations in this period saw promoting democratically elected governments as a way of preventing the sort of political instability and turmoil in Latin America that might lead to the emergence of governments hostile to U.S. business interests or might prompt other extraregional powers to intervene. After World War II the overriding concern of the United States in Latin America became fighting communism, or more specifically,

1

trying to prevent the emergence of left-leaning governments and seeking to oust ones that did emerge. During this latter period some U.S. administrations came to see promoting democracy as a solution. By opening up political participation and alleviating drastic economic inequalities, democratic governments in Latin America would undercut local pressures for leftist revolutionary change.

Just as the impulse to promote democracy has been a recurrent feature of U.S. policy toward Latin America, democracy itself has been an intermittent but persistent feature of Latin American political life in the twentieth century. Democracy has long been the formal organizing principle of Latin American political systems and the genuine aspiration of many Latin Americans. It has been consistently achieved, however, by only a few Latin American countries. In most countries of the region, democracy has been a precarious affair, with democratic governments rising and falling in episodic fashion. Scholars of the region commonly characterize Latin American politics of the twentieth century as a cycle of authoritarianism and democracy, with democratic peaks occurring in the 1920s, the late 1940s, the early 1960s, and the 1980s.

The periodic efforts by the U.S. government to promote democracy in Latin America and the cyclical achievement of democracy in most Latin America countries bear an uncertain interrelation. Little scholarly consensus exists as to the effects of U.S. policies of promoting democracy in Latin America. Some scholars maintain that the United States has on balance been a negative force, that its attempts to promote democracy have been too narrowly focused on formalistic political reforms and have in any case been outweighed by the significant periods of U.S. support for dictatorial governments and economic elites.[1] Others contend that the United States has often played a distinctly positive role in Latin America's political development by fostering political reforms and helping head off dangerous extremes.[2] And some observers hold to yet a different view, that the United States has not been a major factor, either positive or negative, in the changing fortunes of democracy in most Latin American countries.[3]

The 1980s offer a particularly vivid and important case for this unresolved debate. In the 1980s, Latin America experienced a widespread resurgence of democracy. Throughout both Central and

South America, military dictatorships fell and were replaced by elected, civilian governments. By the end of the decade, very few blatantly nondemocratic governments remained in Latin America and in numerous countries initial postdictatorship elected governments were already ceding power through orderly elections to "second generation" democratic governments. Democracy was by no means fully achieved in the 1980s in Latin America. In many countries the new democratically elected governments exercised only partial authority over societies still dominated by well-entrenched, undemocratic militaries and economic elites. The political change that had occurred in these countries represented merely the initiation rather than the fulfillment of a democratization process. Nonetheless, the resurgence of democracy in Latin America in the 1980s was of unquestionable significance and raised hopes in the region that had been dormant for decades.

During the same years that democracy was spreading through Latin America, the United States government made democracy the principal stated goal of its Latin America policy. Throughout the 1980s, in innumerable speeches and press conferences, President Reagan and his advisers declared that the United States was committed to promoting the emergence and maintenance of democratic governments throughout Latin America. All other U.S. policy goals, including anticommunism, economic development, and peace, were expressed as subsidiaries of the central goal of democracy promotion. U.S. assistance to the Salvadoran government's struggle against leftist rebels was a contribution to "the battle for democracy."[4] The contra war in Nicaragua was a struggle for "true democracy."[5] In Chile, the administration said, "U.S. Government policy . . . is straightforward and unequivocal: We support a transition to democracy."[6] In post-Duvalier Haiti, the administration explained, "Our purpose all along has been to help Haiti make a transition from dictatorship to democracy."[7] In Guatemala, "the primary U.S. objective . . . is the promoting of a democratic government."[8] And so forth around the region.

One can of course question how much this commitment to promoting democracy in Latin America was rhetorical and how much it was real. Yet its central place in the public formulation of the policy is unquestionable, as underlined by Elliott Abrams in one of his final speeches as assistant secretary of state for inter-American affairs, entitled "The Reagan Legacy in Latin America: Active Support for Democracy:"

> An extraordinary development has unfolded during the Reagan years. A democratic revolution is underway. One country after another has joined the ranks of democratic states. The political map of Latin America and the Caribbean has been transformed, and today more than 90 percent of the people in the region live in societies that are, or are moving to, democracy.
>
> Here was a rare opportunity for American statecraft to respond to a historic opening as it was happening. We in the Reagan Administration gave it our full support. No mere spectator in this revolution, we did more than just welcome the trend rhetorically. *Democracy became the organizing principle of our policy.* It encompassed the divergent interests of this country within a unifying and coherent framework (emphasis added).[9]

The concurrence of the resurgence of democracy in Latin America on the one hand and the strong stated emphasis in U.S. policy on promoting democracy on the other raises an obvious, important question: Did the United States contribute to the resurgence of Latin American democracy in the 1980s? The Reagan administration had few doubts about the value of its policies and did not shy away from taking credit. In 1988 Assistant Secretary Abrams proclaimed that the administration's Latin America policy had "met with extraordinary success in building democracy," and that in the 1980s, "the United States has led a historic expansion of democracy [in Latin America].[10] Secretary of State George Shultz put it in somewhat less expansive but still definite terms: "Our strategy has been to support reform and freedom, it has had substantial bipartisan support, and it has worked."[11] Reagan administration officials argued that U.S. policy had been essential to the emergence of "truly democratic governments" in El Salvador, Honduras, and Guatemala,[12] that the contras were on the verge of bringing democracy to Nicaragua before they were cut off by Congress,[13] and that the United States played a substantial positive role in the numerous democratic transitions in South America.[14] Critics of the administration, however, dismissed such claims out of hand, arguing that the administration's commitment to promoting democracy was purely rhetorical and that if anything, the administration's Latin America policy was a military-oriented, interventionist policy that on balance was harmful to the democratization of the region.

Neither the proponents nor the critics of the Reagan administration's Latin America policy attempted a comprehensive, systematic answer to the question of the effects of U.S. policy on the resurgence of democracy in Latin America during the 1980s. Most judgments on both sides were hurried salvos in the fierce war of words over Latin America that raged within the U.S. foreign policy community throughout the decade. With that decade over it is perhaps now possible, in a more detached and systematic fashion, to evaluate the Reagan administration's policy toward Latin America, particularly the crucial question of whether the United States helped or harmed the return of democracy to the region. Such an evaluation is the primary purpose of this book.

The book is organized into six chapters. Chapters 1 through 5 identify and analyze the four major policies the Reagan administration pursued in Latin America in the name of promoting democracy. In El Salvador, Honduras, and Guatemala, the Reagan administration attempted to prevent the spread of leftism through a multifaceted policy that combined military assistance, economic assistance, and efforts to promote elected civilian governments. This anticommunist policy was publicly cast as a democracy policy, with democracy to be achieved by gradualist, centrist transitions away from the clash of political extremes. Chapter 1 considers the main application of this policy, which was in El Salvador. Chapter 2 analyzes its application in Honduras and Guatemala, as well as the Reagan policy toward Costa Rica, which was a mix of military, economic, and political measures, presented as an effort to help preserve Costa Rican democracy. In Nicaragua and Grenada, the Reagan administration employed direct or indirect military force against leftist governments. Chapter 3 examines these anticommunist military campaigns, which were publicly portrayed as pro-democracy campaigns under a newly articulated doctrine of promoting democracy by the application of military force against leftist governments.

After an initial unsuccessful attempt to renew U.S. relations with the military governments of South America, the Reagan administration adopted a low-profile policy of diplomatic support for the emerging democratic governments of the region. Chapter 4 studies this policy evolution in South America, identifying the content of a policy the Reagan administration described as a policy of support for South American democracy, labeled here as promoting democracy by applause. In the later Reagan years, the United States exerted economic and diplomatic pressure against the remaining right-wing dictators in Latin America and the Caribbean—President Augusto Pinochet of Chile, President Alfredo Stroessner of Paraguay, General Manuel Antonio Noriega of Panama, and President Jean-Claude Duvalier of Haiti—to cede power and permit transitions to elected rule. Chapter 5 reviews this policy of pressure against right-wing dictatorships, under the heading of democracy by pressure. Interspersed among the various general policies elaborated by the Reagan administration were many specific U.S. assistance projects aimed at promoting democratic development in Latin America and the Caribbean, carried out by various U.S. government agencies, including the Agency for International Development, the State Department, and the United States Information Agency, as well as by the newly created National Endowment for Democracy. Chapter 6 provides a taxonomy and preliminary evaluation of this growing set of political development assistance programs.

In the course of evaluating the effects of U.S. policies on the resurgence of democracy in Latin America, the book also explores two related questions. Why did the Reagan administration adopt such a strong stance, whether rhetorical or real, toward promoting democracy in Latin America? The democracy theme of U.S. Latin America policy has in recent years come to be accepted as something of a given; it is important to remember that when the Reagan administration took power in 1981, most observers expected it to drop the Carter administration's emphasis on human rights and democracy and pursue a purely realpolitik, security-oriented policy. The incoming Reagan team was preoccupied with what it perceived as a Soviet-Cuban threat to all of Latin America and appeared intent on uncritically embracing right-wing dictators as part of an all-out anticommunist policy. Yet the goal of promoting democracy in Latin America was soon articulated by Reagan officials and by the end of

President Regan's first term had become the main stated theme of U.S. policy in the region. During the second Reagan administration that emphasis intensified and observers were surprised to see a conservative U.S. administration attempting to weaken or even undermine traditional authoritarian friends such as President Augusto Pinochet of Chile, President Alfredo Stroessner of Paraguay, and President Jean-Claude Duvalier of Haiti. This book examines and attempts to explain the causes of the growing reliance on the democracy theme by the Reagan administration.

The second question asks what the Reagan administration meant by *the phrase* democracy in Latin America. The Reagan administration invoked the term democracy so frequently and, in a sense, so indiscriminately, that it took on the quality of a refrain one often hears but rarely listens to. Within the government I was struck that U.S. officials constantly referred to democracy and its promotion in Latin America, but almost never discussed the specific meaning of the term. The meaning of the term democracy appeared to be anchored in a strong unstated consensus. In this book I explore what that consensus was as well as the assumptions about politics and about Latin America that lay behind it.

To analyze the effects of U.S. policy on the progress of democracy in Latin America, it is necessary of course to work from some definition of democracy. I do not wish to make definitional issues a major concern of this book and operate from the conventional conception of liberal or pluralist democracy used by Western political scientists who engage in comparative studies of democracy. That conception emphasizes representative governing institutions, free and fair elections, and an open, broad process of political participation. Juan J. Linz, a leading comparative scholar of democracy, offers the following criteria for a democracy:

> Legal freedom to formulate and advocate political alternatives with the concomitant rights to free association, free speech, and other basic freedoms of person; free and nonviolent competition among leaders with periodic validation of their claim to rule; inclusion of all effective political offices in the democratic process; and provision for the participation of all members of the political community, whatever their political preferences. Practically, this means the freedom to create political parties and to conduct free and

honest elections at regular intervals without excluding any effective political office from direct or indirect electoral accountability.[15]

A common feature of academic analyses of U.S. efforts to promote democracy abroad, and this book is no exception, is criticism of the U.S. government for employing too formal or narrow a conception of democracy, in particular for attaching too much importance to elections and the superficial forms of a country's governing institutions. It is very important to note that there are in fact two different such critiques, only one of which is pursued in this book. One critique, which tends to be set forth by a subgroup of U.S. political scientists and by a number of Latin American political scientists, holds that the conventional U.S. political science definition of liberal democracy is itself too narrow, that it is based on an inadequate conception of political participation. They argue that political participation should not be seen simply in terms of the exercise of political and civil rights but rather as a much broader process that includes economic and social activities. John Booth and Mitchell Seligson, for example, define political participation as "behavior influencing or attempting to influence the distribution of public goods,"[16] and contend, for example, that a road is a public good and therefore, "the efforts of citizens to build a road . . . would constitute political participation." This critique of the conventional Western political science definition of democracy is linked with the broader argument that democracy cannot be seen as a purely political phenomenon but must be defined to include economic and social factors, or more plainly, that economic and social justice must be criteria of democracy.

The other critique holds that in attempting to promote democracy abroad, the U.S. government tends to use an overly narrow version of the conventional Western political science conception of democracy that emphasizes elections at the expense of everything else. In this view, the U.S. government does not question whether an elected government genuinely exercises full authority or is simply a facade covering entrenched undemocratic structures. Moreover, according to this view, the U.S. government assesses political participation only by looking at voting and not by inquiring whether citizens are free on a day-to-day basis to oversee the full range of political and civil rights included in the conventional definition of democracy, such as free speech and free association.

The first critique assumes that the U.S. government is following the conventional definition of democracy and attacks that definition as being too narrow. The second critique accepts the conventional definition as valid and instead criticizes the U.S. government for adopting a formalistic version of that conventional definition. This book generally pursues the second critique rather than the first. The evaluation of the Reagan administration's policies of promoting democracy is an analysis of whether the Reagan administration promoted democracy in the conventional sense that democracy is understood in the United States; it is not an attempt to formulate a new definition of democracy for the Latin American context. I am not entirely unsympathetic to the critique of the conventional definition of democracy, but I have concentrated on the other level of analysis for two reasons. First, the book is an attempt to understand whether recent U.S. policies of promoting democracy in Latin America were at least effective in the terms that most Americans understand by the word "democracy." Second, attempting to evaluate particular policies of promoting democracy while simultaneously searching for a new definition of democracy is akin to shooting at a moving target from a nonstationary platform. This book concentrates on the target; I leave arguments about whether to move the platform to others.

A final word about the book's scope and style. Of all the areas of U.S. foreign policy in the 1980s, Latin America was the subject of the most heated debate within the United States. U.S. relations with other parts of the world, particularly the Soviet Union and Japan, captured more sustained and substantive attention; but more emotion, or at least higher peaks of emotion were expended over Latin America. Much of this emotional debate focused on just one country, Nicaragua, and on just one issue—whether the United States should fund the Nicaraguan contras in their war against the Sandinista government. The fixation on Nicaragua led to serious shortcomings in the administration's overall Latin America policy, as is discussed in the chapters that follow. It also, however, led to shortcomings in attempts by contemporaneous observers to understand and analyze the Reagan administration's Latin America policy.

To start with, the focus on Nicaragua has led to insufficient scrutiny of Latin American policy as a whole. Although President Reagan and his top advisers paid predominant attention to Nicaragua, the United States did have active policies in many other countries in Central and South America. Few off those policies have been written about in any detail or related to one another systematically. In addition, the focus on Nicaragua led many observers to see the whole of the Reagan administration's Latin America policy as a static, ideologically rigid policy controlled by conservative ideologues. That view was at least partially, or even substantially, wrong. The Reagan administration's Latin America policy was racked by continual divisions between conservative ideologues and relative moderates. Nicaragua was the sole Latin American issue over which the hardliners in the administration maintained rigid control over the duration of the Reagan years. The rest of Latin America policy was strongly influenced by the moderates and evolved significantly away from an early hardline approach. Finally, the Nicaraguan issue deeply divided and in a real sense wounded the U.S. policy community of Latin Americanists. The debate in the United States over Nicaragua degenerated into regrettable depths of discord and incivility, with participants on both sides putting passion ahead of reason and opinion ahead of fact. The writing and discussion on U.S. policy toward Nicaragua in the 1980s is noteworthy not simply for its extraordinary volume but for its exaggeration, bombast, and stridency.

This book attempts to steer clear of these shoals of recent debate on U.S. Latin America policy. In the first place, it covers many different areas of the Reagan administration's Latin America policy rather than focusing only on Nicaragua and El Salvador. In recognition of their dominant place in the policy, Nicaragua and El Salvador do receive more detailed treatment than other countries, but an effort is made to keep the focus wide. Although the book takes a survey approach, some selectivity was inevitably necessary. U.S. relations with Mexico are not considered. The Reagan administration pursued relations with Mexico almost on a separate plane from the rest of its Latin America policy and did not extend its promoting democracy theme to U.S.-Mexican relations. The Caribbean (including Cuba) is not analyzed, except for Haiti and Grenada.

Furthermore, the book seeks to explore the evolution of the Reagan administration's Latin America policy rather than simply to concentrate on the high-visibility fights and debates on Central America of the early 1980s. The policies of the second Reagan administration are given as much attention as those of the first administration, with a continual emphasis on the tendency of policy to evolve in response to events, but to be explained as an anticipation of events. Lastly, a concerted attempt is made to avoid an all-or-nothing style of evaluation. The Reagan administration's Latin America policy was not an extraordinary success as administration officials claimed. Nor, however, was it an unbroken string of embarrassing, costly failures launched by wild-eyed zealots, as some critics charged. As is almost always the case with U.S. foreign policy, in Latin America or elsewhere, the policies were far more complex in implementation than in conception and the results were not a black-and-white assortment of successes and failures. This book highlights the complexities of the policies and ambiguities of motivation and result, reflecting my broader conviction that only through such an approach to understanding U.S. relations with the world will we be able to go beyond our traditionally formulaic approach to international relations and develop policies whose sophistication and subtlety match the nature of the challenges they confront.

# 1

# DEMOCRACY BY TRANSITION (I)

## EL SALVADOR

When the Reagan administration took power in January 1981 it found Central America in a state of revolutionary ferment. Strong economic growth in the 1960s and 1970s had generated pressures for political and social change that the archaic ruling systems of the region, based on alliances between reactionary economic elites and repressive militaries, could not accommodate. The sharply inequitable nature of that economic growth, together with the continued repression of political reform movements, had increasingly polarized what were already deeply divided societies. Fueled by the emergence of Castro in Cuba, leftist rebel groups had multiplied in the 1960s and launched guerrilla campaigns. They were beaten back by brutal counterinsurgency campaigns but they regrouped in the 1970s and renewed their struggles. In 1979, President Anastasio Somoza Debayle of Nicaragua, the last representative of the Somoza family, which had ruled Nicaragua since 1937, fell to the Sandinista National Liberation Front. Leftist rebel groups in El Salvador and Guatemala escalated their attacks and moved their countries to the brink of all-out civil war. Honduras and Costa Rica, although relatively stable, began to be affected by the spillover of the revolutionary violence from their neighbors and watched the regional turmoil with growing nervousness.

The incoming Reagan administration, whose overriding foreign policy concern was the growing strength of the Soviet Union and the perceived decline of U.S. power, saw Central America as one theater, in fact the most urgent and dangerous one, of the global

12

conflict between the Soviet Union and the United States. The early Reagan administration believed that the armed conflicts in El Salvador and Guatemala were proxy wars fought by agents of the Soviet Union and Cuba and that the whole of Central America was a target of Soviet expansionism. In the words of Alexander Haig, President Reagan's first Secretary of State, the Soviet-Cuban penetration of Central America was "a four-phased operation": "First is the seizure of Nicaragua. Next is El Salvador, to be followed by Honduras and Guatemala."[1] President Reagan and his advisers envisioned the leftist subversion of Central America as the first step of a broader Soviet plan to destabilize Mexico in the north and threaten U.S. control of the Panama Canal in the south, leading to direct, dire threats to U.S. territorial security.

The Reagan administration committed the United States to preventing the spread of leftism, or what it saw as Soviet-sponsored Marxism-Leninism, in Central America and quickly developed a two-part policy to meet that objective. One part was bolstering the governments of El Salvador, Guatemala, Honduras, and Costa Rica to ensure that they did not fall to internal or external leftist aggression. The other part was pressuring the Sandinista government of Nicaragua, initially to stop it from supporting leftist rebels in neighboring countries, particularly El Salvador, and later to oust it altogether. Reagan officials framed both halves of this regional anticommunist policy as efforts to promote democracy. The Reagan administration described its anticommunist policies for El Salvador, Honduras, and Guatemala as the promotion of democratic governments by processes of centrist transition away from right-wing authoritarian rule. And the anti-Sandinista campaign in Nicaragua was characterized as an effort to force the Sandinistas to accept democracy. In this way, promoting democracy became the central stated goal of the Reagan administration's intensive involvement in Central America.

As will be seen in this chapter and the two subsequent chapters, the Reagan administration's stated emphasis on promoting democracy in Central America had only a partial relation to the reality of U.S. policy in the region. Furthermore, the political changes that did occur cannot be understood simply as transitions to democracy and U.S. policy had at best ambiguous and often contradictory effects.

## EL SALVADOR

For much of this century, El Salvador has been dominated by a reactionary economic oligarchy allied with a brutal, repressive military. Starting in the 1930s the oligarchy's hold on power was periodically but unsuccessfully challenged by a variety of reformist elements, including peasant groups, moderate civilian politicians, and occasional reform-minded junior military officers. In the late 1960s, the Christian Democratic party, allied with the Social Democratic party and the Communist party, mounted a major political challenge to the ruling military-oligarchy elite that culminated in an apparent victory for the Christian Democratic candidate, José Napoleón Duarte, in the 1972 presidential elections. The military intervened in the vote-counting process, declared the military candidate the winner, and arrested and tortured Duarte. The failure of this reform movement provoked a serious polarization of the already turbulent political process.

In the early 1970s a number of leftist guerrilla groups formed and began fighting the Salvadoran armed forces. At the same time, a number of popular movements, such as labor unions, teacher associations, and student groups, formed and began mobilizing to promote political and economic reforms. The stagnant Salvadoran military governments of the 1970s responded to this ground swell of political opposition in heavy-handed fashion, launching a violent counterinsurgency campaign based on indiscriminate rural and urban terror. A number of junior military officers were increasingly concerned by the rising civil conflict and the government's inflexible response. They saw an obvious parallel to Nicaragua, where a stagnant, corrupt dictator had fallen to a relatively small group of rebels who combined an armed insurgency with popular mobilization efforts. In October 1979 these junior officers in El Salvador overthrew the regime of General Carlos Humberto Romero and installed a civilian-military junta that incorporated political forces ranging from the moderate left to the right.

The Carter administration was in the midst of formulating a new Central America policy when the 1979 Salvadoran coup occurred. Alarmed by the rise of radical leftist guerrilla movements in Central America, the Carter administration had begun moving in

1978 away from its human rights policy to a policy more focused on combatting leftism. The new policy incorporated a dual military-political approach: the United States would renew assistance to Central American militaries, both to strengthen their capability to meet the guerrilla challenges and to gain political leverage over those militaries; and the United States would promote the emergence of centrist civilian governments committed to political and economic reforms as a means of alleviating the underlying causes of leftist revolutionary pressures.

The October 1979 coup in El Salvador was the opening the Carter administration needed to apply this new policy to a country it recognized was far down a dangerous path of political stagnation and polarization. The Carter team quietly welcomed the coup and committed itself to supporting the civilian-military junta, in the belief that it represented a nascent but legitimate political center that must be developed against the extremes of the left and right. In early 1980 the Carter administration renewed military aid to El Salvador, despite the worsening human rights situation there, arguing that the junta must have the means to defend itself against the rebels.[2] At the same time the State Department pushed the junta to adopt an ambitious set of economic reforms—most notably a broad land reform program and the nationalization of the country's commercial banks—that it believed would weaken the oligarchy's hold and improve the lot of the long-suffering Salvadoran peasantry.

The fledgling political center in El Salvador only barely held together in 1980. The reins of power passed from one weak, divided junta to another with each unable to assert any controlling authority over the Salvadoran military and economic oligarchy. The civil war intensified furiously. The rebels, who unified in 1980 as the Farabundo Martí National Liberation Front (FMLN), expanded their field of action and gained control over substantial areas of the Salvadoran national territory. The Salvadoran security forces responded with increasingly savage, indiscriminate attacks on villages and towns suspected of harboring the rebels, resulting in the deaths of thousands of Salvadoran civilians. The extraordinary political violence in El Salvador forced its way into the U.S. public's consciousness in December 1980 when four Americans, three nuns, and a Catholic lay worker, were murdered in cold blood by members of the Salvadoran security forces. On January 10, 1981, the

FMLN launched its "final offensive," with the aim of toppling the Salvadoran government and presenting the incoming Reagan administration with the *fait accompli* of a second leftist revolution in Central America. President Carter hurriedly restored U.S. military assistance (it had been suspended after the murder of the nuns) and approved an additional $5 million of military aid. The rebels fell short of victory but succeeded in making clear the very precarious state of affairs in El Salvador.

## The Reagan Administration Confronts the Crisis

The incoming Reagan administration wasted no time in sounding the alarm bells on El Salvador. For President Reagan and his top advisers, El Salvador was not a civil war in a small, remote country, but a geostrategic crisis of major proportions. It was the hottest flashpoint of the perceived Soviet-Cuban campaign to spread communism throughout Central America. As Secretary of State Alexander Haig said in February 1981, "Our problem with El Salvador is external intervention in the internal affairs of a sovereign nation in this hemisphere, nothing more, nothing less."[3] El Salvador was seen as a test of U.S. will on the order of the communist invasion of South Korea, the Berlin crisis, and the Cuban missile crisis. The Reagan administration quickly resolved that in El Salvador it would draw the line against Soviet expansionism. Just as it viewed the Salvadoran conflict in almost purely military (rather than political) terms, the incoming Reagan team was certain that the only possible solution was a military one. U.S. policy was to be directed toward all-out support for the El Salvadoran armed forces to help them achieve a quick total defeat of the FMLN.

The early Reagan team was not especially concerned by the nondemocratic character of the Salvadoran junta or the abysmal human rights record of the Salvadoran security forces. It was strongly influenced in this regard by the ideas of Jeane Kirkpatrick.[4] Kirkpatrick held that the only immediate political alternatives in much of the developing world were left-wing totalitarians and right-wing authoritarians, that no democratic middle ground alternative was feasible, at least in the short-term. In this view, the United States should recognize the need to choose between authoritarians and totalitarians, and choose the former because they are less repressive, more pro-U.S., and more likely to evolve toward democracy. The United States should not distance itself from shaky authoritarian regimes (as the Carter administration had done with the Shah in Iran and Somoza in Nicaragua) because the result would likely be leftist revolutions leading to governments inimical to U.S. interests. The early Reagan administration applied these ideas to El Salvador and resolved not to back away from and risk "losing" El Salvador simply because of some political shortcomings of the Salvadoran government and military.

During the first few months of 1981, President Reagan, Secretary of State Haig, U.N. Ambassador Kirkpatrick, and other high-level U.S. officials broadcast loudly and often the U.S. commitment to preventing a leftist takeover in El Salvador. In February, the State Department issued a report entitled "Communist Interference in El Salvador" that trumpeted evidence of Soviet bloc assistance to the rebels and concluded that El Salvador had become "a textbook case of indirect armed aggression by Communist powers through Cuba."[5] In March, the State Department announced an emergency grant of $25 million of military assistance for El Salvador and the sending of twenty additional U.S. military advisers to the country.[6] Although the $25 million would be dwarfed by the assistance levels of subsequent years, at the time it was a very large amount, greater than all previous U.S. military assistance to El Salvador from 1946 to 1980 *combined*, as well as more than the total U.S. military assistance to the rest of Latin America and the Caribbean in 1981.[7] The rapid, large grant of military assistance and the administration's high-temperature language on Soviet-Cuban intervention sparked a ferocious debate in the United States over the administration's intentions in El Salvador. Talk of El Salvador as "the next Vietnam" became common and administration officials were pushed in press conferences and before congressional committees as to whether the administration had any plans for sending U.S. combat troops to El Salvador.

Although by mid-1981 the Reagan administration's El Salvador policy appeared to be clearly launched on a hard-line path, in fact a debate was going on within the administration over the appropriate policy direction. The debate was between two groups that were just beginning to differentiate themselves but that would come to form a

dualist opposition that would define much of the Reagan administration's Latin America policy, particularly in Central America. On
the one hand were the hard-liners, the "Reaganaut" ideologues preoccupied with Soviet expansionism. In the early 1980s the hard-
liners dominated the top level of the foreign policy process with
Secretary of State Alexander Haig, Secretary of Defense Casper
Weinberger, U.N. Ambassador Jeane Kirkpatrick, CIA Director William Casey, National Security Adviser Richard Allen, and his successor William Clark. They were also well-represented in the middle
and upper tiers of the policy-making hierarchy in the first Reagan
administration by persons such as Under Secretary of Defense Fred
Iklé, National Security Council staff members Roger Fontaine, Al-
fonso Sapia-Bosch, and Oliver North, CIA National Intelligence Officer (and later NSC staff member) Constantine Menges, CIA officer
(and later Assistant Secretary of Defense) Nestor Sanchez, CIA officer Dewey Clarridge, and others. The hard-liners espoused the
East-West, crisis-oriented view of El Salvador described above and
were the force behind the high-profile policy of "drawing the line"
in El Salvador.

On the other hand were the moderates, a much less visible part
of the policy bureaucracy, but an important one, even in the early
Reagan administration. The moderates dominated the Bureau of
Inter-American Affairs of the State Department. The Reagan transition team did effect a rapid, exceptionally punitive housecleaning of
the State Department to rid officials (including career foreign service
officers) associated with Carter's Latin America policy. The housecleaning did not, however, convert the Bureau of Inter-American Affairs to the hard-liners' camp. The officials appointed to run the bureau, Assistant Secretary of State Thomas Enders and his two most
relied-upon deputies, Stephen Bosworth and Craig Johnstone, were
career foreign service officers who, while conservative, were by no
means Reagan ideologues. They were generally new to Latin American affairs and relied a good deal on the professional staff within
the bureau, a staff that had not been greatly affected by the Reagan
housecleaning. The various office directors and desk officers who
made up the staff, and who in conjunction with the U.S. embassy in
El Salvador were actually responsible for much of the day-to-day
implementation of the policy, ranged from liberal to conservative.
In the style of the foreign service, they were inclined toward a sort

of pragmatic moderation, particularly in response to a strong ideological blast from an incoming administration.

The moderates differed with the hard-liners over the causes of the Salvadoran conflict and the appropriate U.S. response. They believed the conflict stemmed from the glaring economic inequalities and repressive political structures of Salvadoran society. They shared the hard-liners' view that the Salvadoran rebels were receiving substantial support from outside communist powers, but saw that assistance as an aggravating factor rather than a cause of the conflict. With respect to policy, they agreed that the United States should step up assistance to the Salvadoran military. They were adamant, however, that a military policy alone would not succeed, that the United States must combine military assistance with an effort to encourage economic and political reforms, particularly a transition to elected civilian rule. The economic and political components were necessary both to undercut the "roots of revolution" in El Salvador and to gain the support of liberals in the U.S. Congress who were unlikely to approve large amounts of military assistance unless there were clear signs of political progress in El Salvador.

The moderates' outlook, with its emphasis on the need to combine political and economic reform with military assistance, was basically similar to the approach taken by the Carter administration subsequent to the October 1979 coup. There were some differences of emphasis. The Reagan moderates were less wary of working closely with the Salvadoran military and more supportive of a large-scale U.S. military assistance program. They were also more inclined to play an intensive, hands-on role in the Salvadoran political process than the Carter team had been, reflecting the prointerventionist attitude prevalent in the Reagan administration versus the general ethos of noninterventionism in the Carter administration. Overall, however, the moderates' outlook and the Carter outlook were more similar than different. Both were derivatives of the 1960s Alliance for Progress approach that had emphasized the pursuit of economic development and democratization as a means of inoculating Latin American countries against communism.

The hard-liners and moderates struggled for priority during the formal policy review process on El Salvador that took place in the first half of 1981. Their fight was not simply about El Salvador but also about how foreign policy should be made. The hard-liners were not interested in enlisting congressional support, they just wanted to push ahead with an all-out military policy. If Congress wanted to go along, fine; if not, Congress would just have to take the blame for losing El Salvador to the communists. The moderates were much more oriented toward the necessity of building a bipartisan basis of support for what they knew was going to be a controversial policy.

The result of the policy review was the adoption of a stated policy of promoting democracy in which the United States would combine military assistance with efforts to foster economic reform and political development. Assistant Secretary of State for Inter-American Affairs Thomas Enders set out the policy in a speech in July 1981 entitled "El Salvador: The Search for Peace," the first full-length address on El Salvador by a Reagan administration official. After stating that "the conflict [in El Salvador] was Salvadoran in origins," but that "Cuba is manipulating and feeding the violence in El Salvador," Enders declared, "We believe that the solution must be democratic because only a genuinely pluralist approach can enable a profoundly divided society to live with itself without violent convulsions, gradually overcoming its differences."[8] To achieve a democratic solution, Enders stated, the economic reforms undertaken in 1980 must be continued, "violence from all sources" must be stopped, and "a serious, reliable electoral process must be developed." A crucial element of this policy, one that moderates and hard-liners agreed firmly on, was that the Salvadoran government must not negotiate with the rebels. According to Enders, elections would obviate the need for negotiations:

> In this regard, we should recognize that El Salvador's leaders will not—and should not—grant the insurgents through negotiations the share of power the rebels have not been able to win on the battlefield. But they should be—and are—willing to compete with the insurgents at the polls.

### Drawing the Line

Although the policy announced by Enders in 1981 appeared to signify that the administration had adopted the moderates' approach, during the early 1980s the hard-liners actually dominated the policy-making process and the bulk of the administration's energies were directed toward the military domain. An ambitious U.S. military assistance effort took shape in the second half of 1981 when a special U.S.-Salvadoran military planning team, led by a U.S. Army general, Frederick Woerner, drew up a long-term strategy and planning paper, known as the Woerner Report, for rebuilding the Salvadoran military and winning the war against the rebels. The United States played a key role in all aspects of the rebuilding effort, funding the dramatic expansion of the Salvadoran military and the modernization of its equipment, sponsoring a major training program for Salvadoran military personnel of all levels, and overseeing the restructuring of the antiquated Salvadoran military command structure.

This military assistance policy proceeded only with great difficulty, encountering serious problems in both El Salvador and the United States. In El Salvador, it rapidly became evident that the war was not going to be a short, decisive campaign but instead a messy, protracted struggle that would require a long-term, steady commitment from the United States. The Reagan administration, or at least the U.S. military advisers in the field and their superiors at the Pentagon, quickly confronted the fact that the Salvadoran military was a poorly trained, badly led force fighting a nine-to-five war against rebels who were dedicated, disciplined, and able to draw on strong support in some areas of the countryside. Furthermore, the Salvadoran military and police were regularly committing atrocities in the countryside, weakening their already tenuous popular legitimacy. After recovering from their defeat in the final offensive, the rebels began to operate actively again in late 1981 and throughout 1982. In 1983 they harassed the Salvadoran military effectively, and succeeded in holding significant portions of eastern and northern El Salvador.

In the United States the policy was dogged by a lack of public and congressional support. The U.S. public was extremely wary of anticommunist crusades in obscure countries where the United States was defending a government of dubious character and flirting with the possibility of an escalating military involvement. The constant reports of brutal political violence by the Salvadoran security forces, in particular the December 1980 murder of four U.S. churchwomen by members of the Salvadoran security forces, ensured an extremely negative image of El Salvador in many Americans' minds. The churchwomen were just four out of thousands of victims of right-wing violence in El Salvador, but the fact that they were American and that they were nuns gave the case a special visibility in the United States. The Reagan administration's initial cavalier attitude toward the case (Secretary of State Haig joked about it in testimony before Congress)[9] and the Salvadoran government's long delay in solving and prosecuting the case galvanized liberal opposition to U.S. policy.

Human rights concerns were the foundation of the U.S. liberal view of El Salvador policy. U.S. liberals emphasized the roots of the Salvadoran conflict in the deeply entrenched repressive structures of Salvadoran society and viewed the Salvadoran military more as the problem than the solution. In their view, the conflict was clearly a civil war; they did not believe external assistance to the Salvadoran rebels was significant in quantity or impact. Liberals also held that the rebels had a genuine base of political support in El Salvador and represented a part of the political spectrum that must be incorporated into any political solution. This liberal view became a steady and fairly powerful oppositional chorus against the Reagan administration's efforts in El Salvador during the early 1980s. Many organizations, including church groups, human rights organizations, and nonprofit political advocacy groups with an interest in Latin America, actively lobbied against U.S. policy.

The U.S. Congress was the main battleground of this clash between the Reagan administration and its liberal critics. The Senate was controlled by the Republicans, but the House of Representatives was in Democratic hands and became the focal point of liberal lobbying efforts. Many Democrats in Congress were sympathetic to the liberal view of El Salvador. They did not want to approve large sums of military assistance for a government involved in political terror. But most Democratic Congressmen were also very reluctant to stand aside and risk the possibility of a leftist takeover in El Salvador. After months of arguing with the Reagan administration and among themselves, congressional Democrats (and some moderate Republicans) settled in 1981 on a middle ground approach. They would permit military assistance to El Salvador but only if the President certified that the Salvadoran government was making "a concerted and significant effort to comply with internationally recognized human rights" and was "achieving substantial control over all elements of its armed forces, so as to bring to an end the indiscriminate torture and murder of Salvadoran citizens by these forces."[10] By accepting the need for military assistance and giving the President the power to decide when human rights conditions for aid were being met, congressional Democrats actually went at least halfway to accepting the administration's policy approach.

The Reagan administration certified El Salvador for military aid twice in 1982 and twice again in 1983. These certifications provoked fierce congressional-Executive Branch debates. The Reagan administration took a hard line on the human rights issue, denying that large numbers of abuses were occurring and blaming the rebels for much of the political violence. To the extent the administration did admit that the Salvadoran right was involved in political terror, it argued that the death squads operated *outside* the security forces and were led by shadowy, unknown figures. U.S. and West European human rights organizations and journalists consistently reported a very different picture: very large numbers of serious human rights violations were continuing to occur in 1982 and 1983; the Salvadoran military and police were the perpetrators of much of the violence against Salvadorans not involved in the war; and the death squads were made up of active duty Salvadoran security personnel and led by well-known right-wing military officers.

The administration's stonewalling on the human rights issue reflected several interrelated attitudes on the part of the Reagan Latin American policy team. Many administration officials, particularly hard-liners, did not believe that the Salvadoran security forces were guilty of extensive political violence. They were convinced that the guerrillas were responsible for much of the violence and whatever civilians were killed by the security forces were persons involved in some way with the rebels. Other officials were aware that a great deal of right-wing political violence was occurring but felt that human rights issues should be dealt with only once the war was over; they did not want to slow down the Salvadoran military by burdening it with human rights concerns. A Defense Department official asked about the human rights issue expressed this attitude as follows: "When your house is on fire you don't call an interior decorator."[11] The Salvadoran house was on fire, and human rights were a kind of decorative concern that would get attention once the important task at hand, quenching the rebel blaze, was accomplished. This attitude exemplified the fatal flaw of the administration's early approach to the war. The administration believed the war could be seen in strictly military terms and that the Salvadoran military's political behavior, such as its relations with the peasants, was separate from its war-fighting capabilities.

The military campaign dominated the Reagan administration's involvement in El Salvador in the early 1980s and U.S. policy generally followed the hard-liners' approach. Nonetheless, the moderates were also engaged and began to build economic and political components into the policy. Assistant Secretary of State Enders and his principal deputy Stephen Bosworth believed strongly that unless the Salvadoran government improved the miserable economic lot of the average Salvadoran, the revolution would continue indefinitely. This view was rooted in the "poverty breeds communism" notion that has informed much U.S. policy toward the developing world since the late 1950s. In the first half of 1981 the administration reprogrammed $63 million of economic assistance for El Salvador, which, when combined with the economic assistance already approved by Congress the year before, resulted in $114 million for El Salvador in 1981, a huge increase over previous aid levels and the largest quantity of aid to any Latin American country that year.

El Salvador was included in the Caribbean Basin Initiative (CBI), an economic aid plan for Central America and the Caribbean that President Reagan announced in February 1982.[12] The CBI was a region-wide extension of the moderates' belief that economic development was a key tool in fighting the spread of communism. It was a high-level initiative that attracted much public attention in the United States and the Caribbean Basin countries. Congress failed to support the program, however, because U.S. business and labor groups had the power to block trade preferences and tax incentives for foreign investment abroad and CBI ended up as only a minor program with little impact on Central America.[13] In his speech announcing the initiative, President Reagan also stated that the administration was making a $350 million supplemental request for economic assistance to Central America and the Caribbean, $128 million of which was for El Salvador. Congress did approve most of this request; economic aid to El Salvador rose to $182 million in 1982 and then $245.6 million in 1983.

The economic component of the Reagan policy included not only increased economic assistance but also support for the land and banking reforms the Salvadoran junta had initiated in 1980 and which had been a major element of the Carter policy. The hard-liners were initially hostile to the reforms, seeing them as socialistic measures that would only increase the sociopolitical chaos in El Salvador. The moderates shared the Carter administration's conviction that the reforms were crucial to lessening the domestic causes of political dissatisfaction in El Salvador, however, and persuaded the hard-liners early on that if only for reasons of pure expediency (that is, pleasing Congress) the administration must back the reforms. The main reform at issue was the controversial land reform program. After some initial hesitation, the administration did support the land reform program and included references to that support in almost every major statement on El Salvador. Most of the real support for the land reform program, however, came from State Department and AID officials in the U.S. embassy in San Salvador. Little real support or interest was given by high-level administration officials in Washington, a lack that was strongly felt at the times when major logjams or problems in the program occurred. After the March 1982 elections, for example, the Salvadoran right suspended indefinitely the crucial second phase of the land reform, the redistribution of medium-sized holdings. This action was a major blow to the program but brought little reaction from high-level officials in Washington.

The political component of the Reagan administration's El Salvador policy also got underway in the early 1980s. The early Reagan administration translated its stated goal of "promoting democracy" into an effort to foster an electoral process that would culminate in presidential elections and a transition to elected civilian rule. The administration, or at least the moderates in the administration, did not want just any elected civilian president, they wanted a moderate. They believed that only a moderate could heal the left-right division in the country. And they knew that if a rightist became president, such as the notorious Roberto D'Aubuisson, a powerful, charismatic former military officer associated with the death squads, Congress would likely remain hostile to military aid.

José Napoleón Duarte, the prominent Christian Democratic leader who led the Salvadoran junta in 1981, announced in the first half of that year that elections for a Constituent Assembly would be held in 1982 with presidential elections to follow a year or two later. The Reagan hard-liners were skeptical of the capability of the Salvadoran junta to carry off elections and of the wisdom of engaging in an electoral process in the midst of a chaotic war effort. The moderates, however, backed the electoral process strongly. The U.S. embassy in San Salvador, led by Deane Hinton, a career diplomat, took up the moderates' approach (although the military and intelligence sections of the embassy tended to subscribe more to the hard-liners' outlook) and threw itself into a vigorous effort to bolster the fledgling electoral process. The embassy spread to all sectors of the Salvadoran political community the message that successful Constituent Assembly elections were important to the United States and crucial to obtaining increased economic and military aid. Embassy officers maneuvered behind the scenes to ensure participation of the three main parties, the Christian Democrats, the Party of National Conciliation (PCN, the traditional conservative party), and the Nationalist Republican Alliance (ARENA, a far-right party formed by Roberto D'Aubuisson in conjunction with elements of the oligarchy and the military in 1981).

The Constituent Assembly elections were held in March 1982 and, to the surprise of most observers, including many administration officials, actually came off despite the ongoing civil war and the general incoherence of the civilian political sector. The administration championed the elections as a major advance for the democratization of El Salvador, capitalizing on the elections as a public relations victory in the struggle for congressional and public support. President Reagan was enthralled by the story of humble Salvadorans standing for hours in the sun to vote and told anecdotes about the elections for months, even years afterwards.[14] The elections were held out as confirmation of the administration's no negotiations policy toward the rebels—the administration argued that the elections demonstrated the rebels' lack of popular support. In fact the elections were inconclusive on this point since the left did not participate owing to its own rejection of the electoral process and the Salvadoran right's unbending opposition to any leftist participation.

Although the fact of the elections was a success for the administration, the actual results were not. The Salvadoran right did better than the administration expected; four rightist parties, including ARENA, together won a majority of seats in the Constituent

Assembly. The U.S. embassy had to act quickly and exert all the influence it could muster to prevent D'Aubuisson from becoming the provisional president. The embassy engineered a compromise in which D'Aubuisson became the president of the Constituent Assembly but a political independent, Alvaro Magaña, was given the post of provisional president, with a mandate to rule until national presidential elections were held.

The next way station on the electoral road was the drafting of a new constitution, a process that took place primarily in 1983. As with the preparations for the Constituent Assembly elections, the U.S. embassy involved itself very actively in the process, brokering compromises between the Christian Democrats and the right, advising on the electoral provisions, and pressing to keep the economic reforms that had been launched in 1980, particularly the land reform, from being completely gutted. The effort was fairly successful; the constitution contained no major disasters for U.S. policy and was successfully promulgated in December 1983.

## *Moderation by Necessity*

By early 1983 the various problems in El Salvador and in Washington with the administration's military assistance policy were becoming inescapably evident. In December 1982, Congress had finally appropriated military aid for El Salvador for fiscal year 1983 but approved only $26 million, less than the amount approved for the previous year. The administration had used its special drawdown authority in February 1982 to send $55 million of military aid to El Salvador but the administration could not avoid the fact that congressional and public support for its policy remained extremely weak. In El Salvador the war was going badly despite the $55 million of U.S. military assistance. President Reagan sent U.S. Ambassador Jeane Kirkpatrick on a fact-finding tour to Central America in early February of 1983. She returned with a very pessimistic account of the war, one that caught President Reagan's attention and spurred him to action.

Reagan and his advisers did not interpret the policy's lack of success as a sign that a different substantive tack should be taken. In particular, the administration continued to reject the idea of some kind of negotiated power sharing agreement that was increasingly being proposed by U.S. liberals as the way to end the war.[15] When Assistant Secretary Enders floated the idea of publicly supporting the possibility of negotiations between the Salvadoran government and rebels (largely as a means of winning congressional support) he was forced out of his job by the hard-liners.[16] Instead the White House decided to redouble the military effort by seeking huge new amounts of military assistance. In March, President Reagan gave a speech on El Salvador, his first full-length address on El Salvador, in which he underlined his strong feelings about the need to strengthen the anticommunist drive. In April he gave a major address on Central America before a joint session of Congress, quoting from President Truman's famous 1947 address to Congress on the rising Soviet threat to the world, declaring that "the national security of all the Americas is at stake in Central America" and calling for Congress to approve a $298 million supplemental aid request for Central America, more than half of which was for El Salvador ($110 million of military aid and $67 million of economic aid).

Although the thrust of the attempted reinvigoration of the El Salvador policy was a renewed military assistance effort, President Reagan pointedly cast the policy in prodemocracy terms. In his March speech he stated:

> Despite all I and others have said, some people still seem to think that our concern for security assistance means that all we care about is a military solution. That's nonsense. Bullets are no answer to economic inequities, social tensions or political disagreements. Democracy is what we want.[17]

And before Congress in April he set out promoting democracy as the first and foremost of the administration's goals in Central America.

Despite the special lobbying efforts by President Reagan, Congress continued to chip away at the administration's military aid requests for El Salvador. Faced with the prospect of endless disagreement with Democrats in Congress over El Salvador policy, in July 1983 President Reagan appointed a blue-ribbon commission, the National Bipartisan Commission on Central America (led by Henry

Kissinger and commonly known as the Kissinger Commission), to study Central America and formulate a bipartisan policy for the region.[18] The Kissinger Commission was dominated by moderate conservatives and conservative Democrats and its final report, issued in January 1984, reproduced the Reagan moderates' policy outlook on El Salvador almost exactly. It stressed the mix of local and external factors in the Salvadoran conflict and recommended a combination of increased military assistance, increased economic assistance, and further support for democratization.[19]

The Kissinger Commission report did not create a new El Salvador policy but it strengthened the moderates' hand within the administration and pointed President Reagan toward the moderate line. The administration's growing acceptance of the need for a more moderate approach was signaled by the decision to have Vice President Bush meet with Salvadoran military leaders in San Salvador in December 1983. Bush lectured the Salvadorans on the importance of curtailing human rights violations and handed them a list of persons (mostly military officers) associated with the death squads that the United States wanted to see removed. The Bush visit was the first (and last) high-level initiative on human rights by the Reagan administration and was precisely the sort of intervention that U.S. liberals had been recommending for almost three years.

Just two months after the Kissinger Commission report came out, the first round of the long-awaited presidential elections in El Salvador were held. The elections were the culmination of the electoral process the administration had been nurturing since 1981 and were a critical juncture for both El Salvador and U.S. policy. The administration approached the elections with two goals: ensuring that technically credible elections were held and that the Christian Democratic candidate, José Napoleón Duarte, won. To increase the probability of technically credible elections, the administration, or more particularly AID and State Department officials in the U.S. embassy in El Salvador, developed a large election assistance program, the first such program carried out by the United States in the 1980s anywhere in the world.

The election assistance program began after the March 1982 elections when the Salvadoran electoral commission requested computers and funds from the United States to develop a new electoral registry. AID hesitated at first, uncertain of the suitability of a relatively high-technology registry system for El Salvador and wary about getting involved in electoral matters. The Salvadorans, however, well on their way by that early point to understanding the two-way nature of dependency relationships, "told us that if they didn't get the assistance for a registry, there would be no more elections."[20] The assistance was duly provided. The AID mission in El Salvador provided several million dollars of local currency assistance for the registry and for electoral supplies such as indelible ink and ballots.[21] AID and State Department officials became increasingly involved in overseeing the mechanics of the electoral process, an involvement that reached extraordinary levels right around the elections. At one point in the first round elections, for example, voter lists were printed on the U.S. embassy's computer after the Salvadoran computer failed.[22]

To assure that Duarte defeated the right, or at least to improve his chances as much as possible, the administration provided Duarte both covert and overt assistance. The CIA reportedly gave a significant amount of funds, possibly between $1 million and $3 million, for Duarte's campaign (Duarte also received considerable support from the Venezuelan and West German Christian Democratic parties).[23] On the overt side, the U.S. embassy lobbied very actively on Duarte's behalf in El Salvador, making sure that all major political sectors understood that the United States government favored a Duarte victory and that a victory by the right would jeopardize the extensive economic and military aid relationship between the two countries. Some administration officials, in particular, some of the hard-liners in Washington, were sympathetic to D'Aubuisson and hoped for his victory. Others favored José Francisco ("Chachi") Guerrero, the PCN candidate, seeing the very conservative Guerrero somehow as a kind of moderate between Duarte and the extreme right.[24] Overall, however, Duarte was the administration's choice, a fact evident to almost all observers in El Salvador and the United States.

## The Duarte Years

Duarte fulfilled U.S. hopes by winning the presidential elections, gaining 53.6 percent of the second round vote against 46.4 percent for D'Aubuisson. Duarte's ascension to the presidency led to a shift in emphasis in U.S. policy. Duarte was popular among many congressional Democrats and U.S. liberals; although some questioned the validity of the elections (because of the intense U.S. involvement in the electoral process and the nonparticipation of the left), they accepted the idea that the new Duarte government must receive strong U.S. economic, political, and military backing. The problem of weak congressional support that had plagued the Reagan policy since 1981 almost disappeared. In May 1984 Congress approved a large military and economic aid package for El Salvador that removed most of the human rights conditionalities imposed on military aid in December 1981. The vote was a turning point; from that time on Congress approved essentially every request for military and economic assistance the Reagan administration made for El Salvador.

Another important change was that in the first year of Duarte's presidency the training, expansion, and rearming of the Salvadoran military finally took effect and the tide of the civil war turned decisively against the rebels. The rebels were driven out of many of their territorial strongholds and reduced to operating sporadic hit-and-run actions. Victory remained out of the military's reach but for the first time in the 1980s, the possibility of a rebel takeover appeared to be foreclosed. This fact, combined with the assurance of large regular quantities of U.S. military assistance, defused the earlier, panic-generating military situation in El Salvador. The hard-liners in the Reagan administration, who had taken an interest in El Salvador because of the leftist threat, largely lost interest in the country and became exclusively preoccupied with Nicaragua. The moderates gained control of the policy. The U.S. embassy in El Salvador became the main policy actor, with the State Department playing a back-up role.

The thrust of the lower-profile, more moderate policy toward El Salvador in the Duarte years was helping Duarte maintain his hold on power against the many pressures he faced, including pressure from the far right, the ongoing civil war, and the disastrous economic situation of the country. The idea was that as the Duarte government gradually consolidated the center, the political extremes would weaken in corresponding fashion, leading to the eventual end of the civil war and the political domestication of the Salvadoran right. This policy was publicly formulated as a policy of consolidating democracy. In the early 1980s the Reagan administration had defined its goal of democracy in El Salvador in terms of a transition to elected civilian rule. Duarte's election was considered the achievement of democracy; the policy in the Duarte years accordingly was conceived as being a policy of consolidating democracy.

The basic operational elements of the policy were the same as before: military, economic, and political assistance. Military assistance continued at high levels, hitting a peak of $196.6 million in 1984 then decreasing year-by-year down to the still very substantial figure of $81.5 million in 1988. Economic assistance increased sharply to range between $300 million and $500 million per year throughout the Duarte years. In 1987, for example, the United States provided $462.9 million of economic assistance, making El Salvador far and away the largest recipient of U.S. aid in Latin America and the second highest per capita recipient in the world after Israel. U.S. economic aid to El Salvador came to constitute over half the Salvadoran national budget.

Political assistance was less easily quantifiable but was also very important. The U.S. embassy, led by two vigorous, experienced diplomats (Thomas Pickering from late 1983 to 1985 and Edwin Corr from 1985 to 1988), appointed itself the guardian of Duarte's government and became deeply involved in helping Duarte govern. U.S. embassy officials met constantly with Salvadoran officials to advise, cajole, and harangue them on the full range of domestic and foreign issues they faced. In very few other countries in the world in those years did a U.S. embassy have the kind of access and influence that the U.S. embassy in El Salvador had. The embassy involved itself closely in the internal politics of the Christian Democratic Party, attempting to prevent the party from splitting irremediably. It also helped mediate and resolve Duarte's clashes with the different sectors of the wider Salvadoran political community, including the right-wing political parties, the private sector, and the labor unions. Furthermore, the embassy advised Duarte and his cabinet on relations with Washington, showing the Salvadorans how to avoid conflicts with the Congress and the White House, how to get what they needed, and generally how to understand the arcane but inevitably crucial (for Duarte) world of Washington politics.

Duarte's first year was unexpectedly positive, giving the administration hope that he might prove to be the kind of strong, successful leader that El Salvador needed. Duarte opened talks with the rebels in October 1984, a move the administration disfavored but

later attempted to take credit for when the talks did not p⟍
a right-wing backlash in El Salvador and strengthened Duar⟍⟍
hand.²⁵ Duarte's party, the Christian Democrats, won an unexpected victory in the March 1985 legislative elections, underlining
his popularity. The military refused to support an ARENA challenge
to those elections, signaling an important weakening of the military's traditional alliance with the oligarchic right. Duarte was also
buoyed by the progress of the war effort and the significant decrease in human rights violations that occurred after he assumed
the presidency.

Before long, however, the situation in El Salvador soured. The
first serious blow was the kidnapping of Duarte's daughter by the
FMLN in September 1985. The paralysis of the government that ensued and Duarte's willingness to bargain with the rebels to get his
daughter back greatly undercut his authority in El Salvador. From
that point on the Duarte presidency underwent a steady downhill
slide, driven by a host of negative developments. Economic problems were one important factor. The debilitating recession of the
early 1980s bottomed out, but the Salvadoran economic situation remained very bad. Per capita GNP languished at pre-1970 levels, despite the enormous quantities of U.S. aid. Duarte's economic leadership was weak and his economic policies often badly conceived.
The administration tried to pressure Duarte to adopt free market
economic reforms, such as reducing public sector spending, devaluing the currency, lowering taxes, and loosening restrictions on
foreign investment, but Duarte was generally unwilling or unable to
carry out serious belt-tightening measures. In addition, the Salvadoran private sector fought bitterly with Duarte and did little to
contribute to a positive economic plan. And of course the civil war
was a constant serious drain on the economy.

The war, like the economy, was going better than in the early
1980s, but was still a terrible burden. The FMLN remained well-
organized and determined, pursuing a sophisticated, ruthless campaign to disrupt the Salvadoran economy (by targeting key infrastructure installations) and sociopolitical order by utilizing tactics
such as assassinating local officials, spreading land mines in the
countryside, and carrying out high-visibility murders in the capital). The war did not simply bleed the economy, it harmed the well-
being of thousands of Salvadorans and imposed a permanent climate of hatred and fear, aggravating the still profound sociopolitical

division of Salvadoran society. U.S. military assistance in the Duarte years became somewhat more attuned to the political character of the war. U.S. military advisers tried to encourage their Salvadoran counterparts to develop counterinsurgency strategies that took into account the needs and concerns of the Salvadoran peasantry. These efforts met with little success, both because the U.S. military was only half-hearted in its commitment to developing alternatives to conventional war tactics and because the Salvadoran military remained an inflexible, reactionary force deeply out-of-touch with the Salvadoran population.[26]

Duarte was also weakened by the continuing autonomy of the military. The military tolerated civilian rule, aware that a civilian government was necessary to ensure a regular flow of military aid from the United States and that in a period of economic and political turmoil it was better for civilian politicians than the military to be in the position to take the blame for the country's problems. The military did not, however, subordinate itself to civilian rule. It remained a sovereign authority within Salvadoran society, with the actual power of decision on most important issues of state. This autonomy actually increased in 1987 and 1988 as a new class of younger officers less sympathetic to the heavy dependence of the military on the United States took up leadership positions in the armed forces. The military not only kept the civilian government on a short leash but maintained violent limits on the political process. Human rights violations by the military and police rose in 1987 and 1988 after their initial decline at the outset of the Duarte government. Military and police death squads continued to strike against persons engaging in populist or leftist political activities of any sort. Hundreds of human rights activists, labor leaders, community organizers, student leaders, and other civilian actors were tortured and murdered in those years.[27]

The United States embassy attempted to improve cooperation between the civilian government and the military as well as to back military officers it saw as more politically flexible and progressive. The embassy's influence over the military was fairly limited, however, despite the high degree of financial dependence of the military on the U.S. government. The Salvadoran military was well aware that the U.S. government was very unlikely to cut off military aid and risk a leftist takeover; the aid lever was thus quite weak. The embassy did not make much effort to stop the rising level of human rights abuses, despite a strong stated commitment to improving the human rights situation. The embassy was convinced that with Duarte in power the human rights situation was essentially solved and stopped paying much attention to it. Also, the embassy was so involved in trying to project a positive image of the Duarte government that it increasingly tried to soft-pedal human rights issues to avoid negative publicity for Duarte.

The State Department and AID did initiate assistance programs aimed at reforming El Salvador's judicial system and improving the investigative skills of the Salvadoran police; both programs were driven by concern over the Salvadoran government's weak response to the political murder cases involving Americans or prominent Salvadorans and a more general desire to strengthen basic civic institutions in El Salvador. As will be discussed in chapter 6, however, the programs were tiny in comparison to the magnitude of the problems they addressed and had few, if any, demonstrable effects on either the independence or efficiency of the judicial system and the police.

A final, very important factor in the decline of the Duarte government was the poor quality of the government itself. Ineptitude, disorganization, infighting, and cronyism were endemic features of Christian Democratic rule in El Salvador. The Christian Democrats had little experience in government and were ill-prepared to run a country with the kinds of problems facing El Salvador. The deluge of U.S. aid funds pouring into the country created almost unlimited opportunities for fraud and cheating—ranging from the padding of project payrolls to outright theft of funds—and the Duarte government became notoriously corrupt.[28] The corruption was strongly resented by the Salvadoran populace and constituted one of the main causes of the loss of respect for the government that occurred in the late 1980s.

There was not much the U.S. embassy could do about the poor quality of people in the Duarte government. With respect to corruption, the fact that much of it involved U.S. aid funds did give the United States a potential corrective role. The embassy, however, did not take it up very actively. The embassy did attempt to curtail some projects clearly identified as being corrupted and Ambassador Corr raised some instances of corruption directly with President Duarte. In general, however, the embassy did not attack the problem very strongly. As with the human rights problem, this shortcoming was connected to the embassy's desire to promote as positive an image of the Duarte government as possible in Washington and the tendency to accept negative elements of the government as a necessary cost of promoting the political center.

By late 1988 the Duarte presidency was in bad shape. The Christian Democrats had lost most of their public support, a fact evidenced by their defeat in the 1988 legislative elections where ARENA captured a majority in the National Assembly and control of 200 out of 244 municipalities. The war was heating up, human rights violations were rising, and the economy was still stagnant. President Duarte had been diagnosed with terminal cancer in midyear and was both physically and politically a greatly diminished man. The Reagan policy was reduced to a stubborn effort to keep the Duarte government afloat, with the hope that Duarte would at least make it to the March 1989 presidential elections. The U.S. embassy and the administration tried to put the best face possible on a very difficult situation in El Salvador, portraying the survival of the elected civilian government as proof of success. In the words of a State Department report on El Salvador issued in November 1988:

> The center has held. Its members are developing self-confidence and trust in the maturing democratic framework. The center's challenging objective is to complete El Salvador's democratic transformation despite the resistance and provocation of the extremes.[29]

## Continuity and Change Under Bush

The incoming Bush administration pledged itself to continuing the Reagan policy in El Salvador and faced the first policy juncture early on when presidential elections were held in March 1989. As expected, ARENA, led by Alfredo Cristiani, a moderate conservative who had replaced Roberto D'Aubuisson as party leader after the 1985 legislative elections, soundly defeated the Christian Democrats. The election did mark a broadening of the political process. Guillermo Ungo and Rubén Zamora of the Democratic Revolutionary Front (the coalition of leftist parties allied with the FMLN) returned to El Salvador and participated in the election in alliance with the Social Democratic Party. This leftist grouping, which participated as the "Democratic Convergence," received less than 4 percent of the votes.[30]

The 1989 elections unquestionably represented the failure of the Christian Democrats' attempt to run El Salvador, an attempt in which the United States had invested several billion dollars and untold quantities of bureaucratic resources. Whether the Christian Democrats' defeat represented the collapse of the political center depended on one's view of ARENA. The Bush administration claimed that ARENA had transformed itself into a genuinely democratic party and that Cristiani was a sincere moderate who had real authority as party leader. Bush officials also argued privately that Cristiani might well be in a better position to make peace with the rebels than the Christian Democrats had been because as a conservative his peace-making efforts would be more trusted by the military. Liberal critics contended that ARENA remained a far right party with antidemocratic convictions and active ties to repressive elements in the security forces. They charged that Cristiani was little more than a figurehead, that Robert D'Aubuisson was still the main power in ARENA.

The Bush administration appealed to Congress to take a wait-and-see approach with the new Salvadoran government and Congress accepted that line, approving in 1989 the continuation of large quantities of military and economic assistance. The test of the Cristiani government was not long in coming. After some preliminary peace talks between the government and the rebels broke down in late 1989, the rebels launched a major offensive. The offensive involved the fiercest fighting in the countryside since the early 1980s and brought the war to San Salvador where the rebels penetrated some of the exclusive areas of the city that had long been isolated from the conflict. Although the offensive led to no lasting territorial gains for the rebels, it demonstrated that they were still a powerful force that could not simply be written off. Four days after the offensive began, six Salvadoran Jesuit priests were murdered by members of the Salvadoran security forces (President Cristiani acknowledged the military's involvement two months after the killings). The priests were only six among many noncombatants killed by both sides during the offensive but the premeditated, cold-blooded nature of the killings and the eminence of the victims made the case a front-page event in the United States.

The Jesuit case reopened the debate in the United States over military aid to El Salvador and as Congress grappled with the issue in 1990 the debate often closely resembled those over the same issue in the early 1980s. The Bush administration argued that Cristiani was truly committed to improving the human rights situation and must not be abandoned by the United States. Liberals asserted that the Cristiani government had shown its true colors and that the United States should not support a tainted government. Congress, as before, was caught between a reluctance to give military aid to a government connected to heinous political crimes and an unwillingness to cut off aid and risk a leftist takeover. Unlike in the 1980s, however, there was the growing perception that significant factions within both the FMLN and the Salvadoran military were exhausted with the war and ready to negotiate seriously toward a peace accord which would entail the political reintegration of the left, a restructuring of the Salvadoran military, and new national elections. Senator Christopher Dodd (D-Conn.) formulated an aid plan which would reduce U.S. military aid to El Salvador by 50 percent and make the remaining 50 percent conditional on the military negotiating in good faith with the rebels. The Bush administration attempted to resist Dodd's plan but moved toward a compromise because it wished to avoid Congress gaining control over the policy and because officials in the Bush administration, such as Assistant Secretary of State for Inter-American Affairs Bernard Aronson, were themselves coming around to the idea that a negotiated solution was desirable and possible. As the U.S. government shifted toward a new consensus on a policy aimed at a negotiated solution, the question became whether the Salvadoran military and the FMLN would be able to get past the hatred and scars of over ten years of brutal civil war and make peace.

## Debate Over Democracy

The Reagan administration's El Salvador policy was enmeshed in constant controversy over its real nature, with liberal critics denouncing it as a militaristic, anticommunist crusade in which democracy concerns were only window dressing and the administration insisting that democracy was its true goal and its triumph. From the analysis of the policy set out above, an answer to this debate can be offered.

The Reagan administration's El Salvador policy was an anticommunist policy. The United States engaged itself in El Salvador in 1979 and stayed intensely engaged throughout the 1980s to prevent a takeover by the FMLN. Promoting democracy, which the Reagan administration interpreted in the very narrow sense of fostering the emergence and maintenance of an elected civilian government, was one operative element of that anticommunist policy, alongside large military and economic assistance programs. Promoting democracy had both demonstrative and substantive functions within the policy framework. Fostering a transition to elected civilian rule was a vital ingredient of the administration's effort to persuade Democrats in the U.S. Congress to approve the funds necessary for the huge military assistance program to the Salvadoran military. Furthermore, fostering an elected government was seen as a way of lessening the economic and political injustices that had given rise to the revolutionary movement in El Salvador and permitting some kind of eventual national reconciliation. The moderates within the administration believed in both these functions. The hard-liners were generally skeptical of the feasibility or utility of the democracy goal but came to accept it when faced with persistent congressional reluctance to approve military aid for El Salvador. The hard-liners and moderates vied for primacy in the policy-making process with the hard-liners usually coming out ahead in the first Reagan administration and the moderates in the second Reagan administration.

A number of aspects of the Reagan administration's use of the democracy theme in its El Salvador policy fed the fierce debate over the true significance of promoting democracy. In response to the wariness of the U.S. Congress and U.S. public for out-and-out anticommunist crusades, the administration did not simply characterize its El Salvador policy as an anticommunist policy with a pro-democracy component, but described it as a prodemocracy policy in which anticommunism had merely been an initial motivating factor. For example, a State Department report of November 1988 on El Salvador policy, entitled "The Battle for Democracy" summarized the policy in these terms:

In the early 1980s, the United States made the historic decision to join in El Salvador's effort to transform itself from a closed oligarchy into a modern democracy. The immediate impetus was the emergence of a Marxist-Leninist insurgency.[31]

This exaggerated characterization of the democracy component of the policy obscured the more limited, but nonetheless genuine, role democracy concerns played in the policy and led many critics to reject the democracy theme altogether as self-serving rhetoric.

The divisions within the administration over El Salvador policy also nurtured the debate over the true significance of the democracy theme. The administration frequently emitted conflicting signals over the role of democracy promotion in the El Salvador policy, particularly in the early 1980s. From the outside (and in fact from the inside as well) it was hard to know what the policy really was. Critics tended to be struck most by the activities and statements of the hard-liners and to assume that they represented the totality of the policy. Yet it was usually the moderates rather than the hard-liners who concerned themselves with responding to criticism from the outside. Thus a pattern occurred in which the Congress and the public assumed the worst about the democracy element in the administration's policy, based on their reading of the hard-liners' actions, while the moderates gave an overly expansive account of the democracy component to placate those critics. The multilayered, ambiguous nature of the policy-making process thus got translated into an overstated, simplistic debate.

Controversy over the administration's conception of democracy and the process of democratization in El Salvador also contributed to the uncertainty over the place of democracy in the policy. Most critics of the administration's policy disagreed strongly with the administration's election-oriented view of democracy. This disagreement led many critics to dismiss the democracy element altogether. They lapsed into the tendency to assume that because the administration was pursuing democracy promotion in a way they did not believe in, the administration was not serious about promoting democracy.

### Anticommunism and Democracy: Mixed Results

As an anticommunist policy, the Reagan administration's efforts in El Salvador were successful in the limited sense that they helped prevent a victory by the leftist rebels. The U.S. military assistance program, which absorbed close to one billion dollars in the 1980s, was the key factor in the transformation of the El Salvadoran armed forces from a poorly trained, badly equipped force of ten thousand men into a relatively well-trained, well-equipped force of fifty thousand that could at least fight the rebels to a stalemate. The fact that the military assistance program achieved its basic goal does not, however, mean that it was well-conceived or well-executed. As detailed in a revealing report by four active duty U.S. military officers, U.S. military policy in El Salvador was plagued by serious shortcomings: the lack of any sophisticated counterinsurgency strategy integrating political, economic, and social programs with military aid; the dearth of genuine interest in El Salvador among high-level U.S. military officials; and the engendering of a counterproductive, costly dependency of the Salvadoran military on inappropriate, grandiose conventional war technology.[32]

The Reagan administration policy was successful on anticommunist terms only on the very narrow grounds of preventing a leftist victory. The policy did not succeed in eliminating the rebels, only keeping them from winning. The fundamental sociopolitical divisions and problems in Salvadoran society that caused the war were not healed. The civil war continued in the 1990s, limited largely by the fatigue of both sides rather than any significant reduction of the causes of the conflict. The policy also entailed high costs for the United States. Over four billion dollars of U.S. economic and military assistance went to El Salvador in the 1980s. The U.S. involvement in the civil war created serious divisions within the U.S. public, absorbed large amounts of the administration's vital political capital in Congress, and drew much criticism in Latin America and Western Europe. These costs were accepted by the Reagan administration as the price of an unpopular but necessary policy, reflecting the U.S. government's traditional willingness to sink extraordinary resources into anticommunist policies, or essentially to eschew normal cost-benefit analyses when anticommunism is at issue.

What then of the Reagan administration's El Salvador policy as a prodemocracy policy? The Reagan administration defined democracy in El Salvador narrowly, as the achievement of elected civilian rule, and declared victory in those terms. Reagan officials habitually pointed to El Salvador as an example of a successful U.S. policy of democracy promotion, heralding El Salvador's "remarkable democratic experiment."[33] The achievement of elected civilian rule fell short, however, of the achievement of democracy. Although from 1984 on El Salvador had an elected government, that government never managed to gain genuine authority over the society. As discussed previously, the Salvadoran military remained a sovereign force, and an increasingly large and powerful one, that exercised de facto authority over most important political issues in the country. The autonomy of the military was demonstrated by the inability of the Duarte government to bring to justice any of the military officers involved in the numerous political murder cases, including not only the prominent cases from the early 1980s but also cases that occurred during Duarte's rule. The military continues to live outside the rule of law, or rather, within the framework of whatever laws it chooses to obey.

The economic elite, the informal sector of landowners and industrialists who traditionally ruled Salvadoran society, did lose some of their power, in particular their automatic partnership with the military, but they maintained many sources of formal or informal influence and remained capable of resisting the government's authority and frustrating the government's economic policies.

Owing to these countervailing power centers and its own corruption and ineptitude, the Duarte government failed to become an effective government that enjoyed the trust and represented the interests of the Salvadoran population. It was just one of at least five major power sectors in El Salvador (the others being the military, the economic elite, the rebels, and the U.S. embassy) and arguably the least cohesive and powerful of the five.

Not only did the elected government in El Salvador fail to achieve genuine authority, the country did not develop an open, participatory political process. Regular presidential and legislative elections were held, but elections are only one part of a full participatory process. Citizens must be able to express their political views and participate in the political process on an ongoing basis, not simply in periodic votes at national elections. There is no simple way to measure the degree of political participation in a society. The level of respect for human rights, particularly political and civil rights, such as free association and free speech, is one reasonable indicator.

The human rights situation in the Duarte years deteriorated

fairly steadily and by 1987 and 1988 had reached the point where even the State Department, whose human rights reporting was always on the low side, acknowledged that eighteen deaths a month were occurring in 1988.[34] Eighteen deaths a month was far less than the hundreds of deaths per month that occurred in the early 1980s but the decrease in number was due more to the diminishment of the war than to any lessening of the military's repressive control over the political process. To conceptualize the degree of repression such deaths constituted, it is useful to think in U.S. per capita equivalents. Imagine, for example, that the police and army in the United States were targeting and assassinating *every day* twenty-seven labor leaders, human rights activists, student leaders, university professors, and other persons involved in political activity of a populist bent. Such a level of repression (the per capita equivalent of eighteen deaths per month in El Salvador) would be considered a horrifying level of repression, not the triumph of democracy.

The transition to elected, civilian rule in El Salvador did not constitute the achievement of democracy, but it was nonetheless an improvement over the decades of military rule that preceded it. The 1980s saw a genuine broadening of the political space in El Salvador to the point in 1989 where a wide variety of political forces from the left to the right participated actively in the electoral process. The transition also brought in a new relationship of accountability between Salvadorans and their government. When the Duarte government disappointed the people, the Christian Democrats were voted out of office; Salvadorans did get to make a choice about their government, even if that government was only one of many power centers in the country.

El Salvador did not become what the Reagan administration claimed, that is, a working democracy. Yet neither did it remain the same archaic political fiefdom as before. El Salvador became a kind of semidemocracy in which the traditional ruling alliance of the military and the economic elite was weakening and being replaced by a new and different sort of alliance between the civilian political sector and the military. The military does not act in concert with the civilian political sector, or subordinate itself to it, but tolerates civilian rule as necessary to ensure the continuation of U.S. military aid that feeds what has become a bloated, economically voracious military establishment. Civilian rule also puts the military out of the direct line of blame for terrible socioeconomic problems of the country and helps El Salvador maintain a certain legitimacy in the international community.

The fact that El Salvador did not become a democracy should not automatically be seen as a consequence of a misconceived U.S. policy. U.S. policy was an important factor in El Salvador's political evolution in the 1980s but by no means a determinant factor that could point the country in any direction it chose with no regard to the historical configuration of forces or the political culture of the society. Nonetheless, it is evident that in terms of promoting democracy, the Reagan administration's policy was seriously flawed.

The most serious problem was the fundamental tension inherent in trying to foster an authoritative civilian government while simultaneously strengthening the military. Both in attitude and practice the Salvadoran military was and is a profoundly antidemocratic institution. Among the military's cardinal values are a refusal to obey any outside authority, an abiding disrespect for civilian politicians and civilian political life, and a reflexive, violent opposition to any political activism outside narrowly defined forms or bounds. Strengthening the military inevitably clashed with the goal of promoting democracy. With U.S. assistance the military grew enormously in size and power, becoming the best financed, most technically modernized sector of Salvadoran society. The increase in the military's strength gave it that much more weight as a force within the Salvadoran political system. And the U.S. assistance led to the military gaining a formidable, highly corrupt economic empire in El Salvador, a fact that only increased the military's domestic political interests and powers, as well as its insistence on remaining a force outside civilian control.[35]

The administration's response to this contradiction was a mix of denial and inadequate measures. Administration officials persistently claimed that the Salvadoran military was prodemocratic, that the antidemocratic right was a shadowy fringe outside the military and that the military's toleration of a civilian government was really acceptance of civilian rule. The Reagan administration, or more particularly the U.S. embassy in El Salvador, did devote much effort to trying to persuade the military to put up with a civilian government. These efforts helped smooth the path for the military-civilian alliance that developed in the Duarte years. They did not, however, go to the issue of the military's fundamental attitudes about its own sovereignty and about the need to accept a genuinely open, participatory political process in which human rights were fully respected. The human rights issue was the key to these more fundamental political questions, but the administration never really pushed hard on human rights (never, for example, reduced military aid in response to human rights violations). The Bush visit to El Salvador in 1983 was the only high-level intervention on human rights in the entire eight years and stood as the exception rather than the rule with respect to the Reagan administration's commitment to human rights.

The political contradictions inherent in strengthening the military were the core element of the overall problem with the Reagan administration's El Salvador policy as a democracy promotion policy. The Reagan administration sought to promote democracy in a country dominated by deeply antidemocratic structures of power without significantly altering those structures. Democratization was to occur by the creation of a functional political center and the steady accretion of power by that center away from the extremes. The problem, however, was that there was nothing in the policy to make the right give up power. The administration helped the civilian center get established, then kept it afloat with several billion dollars of assistance funds, but had no real formula for changing the traditional configuration of forces that had led to the absence of a center and the dominance of the political extremes in the first place. Some hope was initially pinned on the land reform program as a means of changing the economic structures of Salvadoran society but this was a greatly overrated program that in any case weakened only the oligarchy, not the military. And when the oligarchy negated a significant part of the program in 1982, the administration did little about it.

The notion of a step-by-step centrist transition reflected the United States's traditional allegiance to gradualist models of political change in the developing world and strong fear of deep-reaching change as the harbinger of communism. The pressure for leftist revolutionary change in El Salvador alarmed the Reagan administration and made it extremely wary of any kind of populist political activity. The administration's democracy promotion approach thus emphasized working from the top down rather than the bottom up, modifying the institutions of government, not building grassroots political awareness and involvement among the Salvadoran population. For many officials in the U.S. embassy in El Salvador or in Washington, Salvadorans engaged in populist political activities—such as human rights advocacy, labor organizing, or student demonstrations—that are accepted as a normal part of democratic life in the United States, were automatically viewed as sinister agents of radical change who posed a threat to U.S. interests.

A further problem with the Reagan administration's efforts to promote democracy in El Salvador was that they involved a high level of interference in El Salvador's political sovereignty. The clearest example of this was in the various Salvadoran elections. The United States wanted El Salvador to hold elections but also wanted the elections to produce particular results, that is, a centrist government. When the 1982 Constituent Assembly elections failed to produce the outcome the United States wanted, the administration pressured the victorious right to accept a nonrightist figure, Alvaro Magaña, as president. In the 1984 presidential elections, the administration took few chances; it backed Duarte strongly, utilizing covert and overt measures of support. More generally, U.S. officials involved themselves deeply in Salvadoran political life throughout the 1980s with the purpose of producing outcomes deemed favorable to U.S. interests.

The U.S. officials involved, particularly the U.S. ambassadors to El Salvador, were well aware that the level of U.S. involvement in Salvadoran political affairs constituted a significant infringement on Salvadoran sovereignty, but they were convinced that this involvement was in El Salvador's best interest and was necessary as a small, short-term deformation to produce large, long-term gains. Inevitably, however, the extraordinary degree of U.S. involvement weakened the democratic legitimacy of the Duarte government. The Duarte government was trying to establish itself as the sovereign authority of the country and such authority implied freedom from external as well as internal controls. The U.S. role continually undermined this effort at the same time it was supporting it. Duarte was widely seen in El Salvador as being in the U.S. government's pocket, a perception that contributed to his decline. In some sense at least, the more the United States tried to bolster what it saw as a democratic government in El Salvador, the more it undercut the legitimacy of that government.

# 2

# Democracy by Transition (II)

## HONDURAS, GUATEMALA, AND COSTA RICA

### HONDURAS

For much of this century Honduras was an exceptional country relative to its neighbors. Although it was the poorest country in Central America, it was not plagued by the same profound socio-political divisions and conflicts that marked other countries in the region. Honduras did not have a powerful landed oligarchy and its military was not the automatic partner of the upper class against the peasantry. Two large, historical political parties, the National party and the Liberal party, though dominated by elites, constituted a genuine civilian political sector. In the 1960s and 1970s Honduras experienced some of the same pressures for economic and political reform that provoked armed leftist insurgencies in Nicaragua, El Salvador, and Guatemala, but the pressures were much weaker and were contained by a series of military and civil-military governments that were neither democratic nor severely repressive.

Given the absence of any strong leftist threat in Honduras, the United States government paid relatively little attention to it during the 1960s and 1970s. The United States began to take note of Honduras in the late 1970s when the upsurge in leftist revolutionary movements in Central America, in particular the Nicaraguan revolution of 1979, provoked the Carter administration to engage itself more actively in the region. Honduras appeared to be relatively stable compared to its turbulent neighbors but the Carter administration was concerned about keeping it that way and settled on the same sort of centrist-oriented anticommunist policy that it had arrived at in El Salvador. The Carter administration strongly backed the emerging transition to elected civilian rule that the Honduran military was overseeing and increased U.S. military assistance, both to strengthen the Honduran military's capacity to resist any internal or external leftist aggression and to gain political leverage over the military.[1]

## A Military Policy

When the Reagan administration came to power and raised Central America to the top of the U.S. foreign policy agenda, Honduras was one of the countries thrust into the limelight. The early Reagan team saw Honduras as a likely victim of Soviet-Cuban aggression in Central America, another domino that could fall at any time. Assistant Secretary of State Thomas Enders stated in 1981 that "El Salvador and Honduras are the two most threatened countries. The buildup in Nicaragua threatens both."[2] Administration officials played up the specter of a growing guerrilla threat to Honduras, portraying what was a scattering of leftist Honduran guerrillas as a well-organized Cuban-backed striking force. The Reagan administration saw Honduras not only as a potential victim of communist aggression but also a potential base for a U.S. military counterforce in Central America. Given its long border with Nicaragua, its relatively benign political situation (its being less offensive to Democrats in Congress than the situation in Guatemala or El Salvador), and its corrupt, malleable military, Honduras appeared to be the most suitable site in Central America for the various U.S. military undertakings being planned for the emerging anti-Sandinista policy.

In 1981 the basic contours of these undertakings unfolded. The administration opened contacts with the small but growing group of militant anti-Sandinista Nicaraguans in Honduras and worked out a plan in conjunction with Gustavo Alvarez Martínez, the ambitious, fanatically anticommunist Honduran colonel who was on his way to becoming head of the Honduran armed forces, for an anti-Sandinista rebel force that was to be financed by the United States, trained by the Argentine military, and based in Honduras (see chapter 3 for details). It was Alvarez, not the United States, who originated the idea of Honduras serving as the contras' base. Alvarez saw the incipient anti-Sandinista rebel force as a means of attracting U.S. support for the Honduran military as well as a vehicle for his rise to glory. Yet without U.S. support, Alvarez's plans would not likely have gone far. The administration also began preparing the ground for large increases in U.S. military aid to Honduras and a major stepping up of military cooperation between the two countries that would entail a semipermanent U.S. military presence in the country.

On the political front, the administration moved less rapidly and decisively. Constituent Assembly elections had been held in April 1980; presidential elections were expected for late 1981. Some of the hard-liners in the early Reagan team, such as Jeane Kirkpatrick and Vernon Walters (a retired general who was serving as an aide to Secretary of State Haig), were sympathetic to elements in the Honduran National party and the military who wanted to call off the elections, accepting the Honduran right's arguments that the Liberal party (which was expected to win the elections) was infiltrated with leftists and could not be trusted to fight communism. Quiet, informal contacts developed between hard-liners in Washington and the Honduran far right in the first half of 1981.[3] The White House was conspicuously silent on the domestic political situation in Honduras, fueling rumors in Honduras that the new U.S. administration did not support a transition. At the same time however, U.S. Ambassador to Honduras, Jack Binns, a carry-over from the Carter administration, continued backing a civilian transition. Binns spoke out on the importance of the elections, maintained good relations with the prodemocratic sectors of the Honduran political community, and emphasized that U.S. aid was dependent on a successful political transition. Binns clashed with hard-liners in Washington but was generally supported by the State Department.

This division over Honduras paralleled the hard-liner-moderate split over El Salvador that was going on at the same time. As in El Salvador, the hard-liners eventually agreed to at least a public position of support for a civilian transition, in significant part out of recognition that Congress was unlikely to support U.S. military undertakings in Honduras unless an elected civilian government emerged. The moderates in the early Reagan administration backed the civilian transition in Honduras for the same reasons the Carter administration did; it was a way of moderating the political divisions in Honduras, thereby undercutting existing or potential pressures for radical leftist change. Presidential elections were successfully held in November 1981. Roberto Suazo Córdova of the Liberal Party won the elections and Honduras gained its first directly elected civilian President in decades. The Reagan administration greeted the elections with enthusiasm, proclaiming that "Honduras has made what is by any measurement remarkable progress . . . in the establishment of civilian democratic institutions."[4] And once the Suazo Córdova government was in place, the administration's Honduras policy settled into the form it would very consistently maintain all the way through 1988. The core of the policy was an aggressive, multifaceted military program targeted against Nicaragua, consisting of three elements: the controversial program of support for the Nicaraguan contras (who were based primarily in Honduras); the establishment of a semipermanent U.S. military presence in Honduras; and a large U.S.-financed expansion of the Honduran military. A lesser element of the policy was support for the continuation of elected civilian rule in Honduras, publicly characterized as support for democracy.

The contra program began in earnest in 1982 as the CIA developed in Honduras what was to become a massive paramilitary infrastructure of training, material support, and financial assistance for a force of anti-Sandinista rebels who eventually numbered over ten thousand. Although the contra program was directed against Nicaragua, it was the main issue in U.S.-Honduran relations in the 1980s. Neither the Honduran military nor the Honduran political and business sectors (not to mention the Honduran public) was happy about Honduras serving as the main territorial base for the contras. The U.S. embassy in Honduras was kept busy smoothing the Hondurans' feathers through a combination of economic and military aid, political jawboning, and other forms of persuasion. During the second half of the 1980s the Honduran government began to balk openly at the presence of the contras and the Reagan administration had to work hard to keep the issue from derailing the contras during the crucial years of their struggle.

The build-up of a U.S. military presence in Honduras progressed rapidly. Beginning in 1982, the U.S. military carried out a series of increasingly large and sophisticated joint exercises with the Honduran military. These exercises involved thousands of U.S. troops and went beyond the usual one or two week military exercises typical in many other countries and were in some cases months-long programs involving road and bridge building, searching for arms traffickers, developing psychological operation capabilities, and more.[5] Accompanying these exercises was a steady development of infrastructure for the U.S. military to maintain usually more than one thousand U.S. troops in Honduras at all times and to permit rapid, large-scale access of many more U.S. military forces if necessary.

The third element of the Reagan administration's military policy in Honduras, the massive build-up of the Honduran military itself, also developed rapidly. U.S. military assistance to Honduras increased from $8.9 million in 1981 to $31.2 million in 1982 to $77.4 million in 1984 and surpassed $50 million per year from 1984 to 1988. The infusion of large quantities of military supplies and hardware, the extensive training of Honduran officers and soldiers, and the continual support and drive from U.S. military advisers transformed the Honduran army from a constabulary force of less than 15,000 men to a well-armed, heavily trained force of some 50,000 supported by a greatly expanded air force.

In parallel with these large-scale, multifaceted military undertakings, the Reagan administration also sought to "promote democracy" in Honduras, which for the administration meant assuring the continuance of elected civilian rule. One element of this political component was the exertion of U.S. pressure on the Honduran military to refrain from retaking the reins of power. The U.S. embassy in Honduras was able to use the aid lever, telling the Honduran military that the generous flow of military aid would stop almost immediately if a military coup took place. In fact, the military had few incentives to oust the civilian government. Even with a civilian government in place the military was enjoying near-absolute sovereignty as well as significant control over important domestic issues. Furthermore, the country was in a severe economic recession and whoever governed was bound to be blamed for the economic difficulties.

Another element of the political policy was making sure the

electoral process stayed on track. Presidential elections were held in 1985 and the U.S. embassy played a significant role in keeping the process together. The major challenge came from President Suazo Córdova himself who, near the end of his term, began making moves to postpone the elections and extend his stay in office indefinitely. The U.S. embassy, which was widely recognized as a major source of power in the country, worked with the Honduran military to block Suazo Córdova's schemes and assure that the elections were held on schedule.

Support of the electoral process also took financial forms. As planning for the 1985 elections advanced, the U.S. embassy became worried that the Honduran electoral tribunal was so disorganized and inexperienced that it would not carry off technically credible elections. The embassy, with the support of the Agency for International Development in Washington, initiated an electoral aid project under which the electoral tribunal received over $5 million worth of local currency aid and $680,000 of dollar aid from AID in Washington for the voter registry system as well as for the purchase of election-related materials such as ballot paper, ballot boxes, and indelible ink.[6] U.S. embassy officials worked very closely with the electoral tribunal on the planning for and administration of the elections. Embassy officials later bragged in private of having personally insured that the elections came off, taking steps such as assembling ballot boxes in their own offices and making sure the boxes were distributed to the polling sites.[7]

The elections were held as scheduled and were not the administrative nightmare the administration had feared. The complicated results of the election, however, presented a further challenge to the continuation of elected civilian rule and a further opportunity for the United States to weigh in on behalf of the electoral process. Rafael Leonardo Callejas of the National party won 45 percent of the vote while José Azcona Hoyo of the Liberal party won 25 percent. Under the electoral rules, however, Azcona was to become president because the Liberal party field as a whole had won 51 percent of the vote. This result provoked great unhappiness within conservative political and military circles in Honduras (the National Party was the preferred party of most military officers) and some rumblings of a coup. The U.S. embassy, which itself generally preferred the Nationals, subordinated that preference to its desire to see the electoral process upheld and openly acknowledged the Liberals' victory. According to one account:

> This alarmed John Ferch, who had replaced Negroponte [as U.S. ambassador]. To make sure that everyone understood completely that the United States would allow no tampering with the pact, he went immediately to Azcona when the totals were announced, and embraced him warmly as President of Honduras.[8]

Along with its military undertakings in Honduras and its support of the maintenance of elected civilian rule, the Reagan administration also gave large quantities of economic assistance to Honduras. Honduras experienced the same calamitous economic recession as most Latin American countries in the early 1980s and one of the Honduran government's main challenges was to stabilize and if possible improve the economy. The Reagan administration weighed in with significant economic aid, between $80 million and $110 million per year from 1982 to 1984, increasing to $229 million in 1985, making Honduras the second largest Latin American recipient of U.S. aid that year. The economic assistance served both the military and political components of the administration's policy. The assistance was one part of the explicit or implicit quid pro quo that the United States provided in return for Honduras's toleration of the contras (with U.S. military aid being the other main part). It was also a way of bolstering the civilian government and improving the prospects for the continuation of civilian rule.

## The Effects of Militarism

In the 1980s, Honduras, along with El Salvador, became another case of a country led by elected civilian governments that was not a working democracy. Although the Suazo Córdova and Azcona Hoyo governments came to power through reasonably fair elections, they did not uphold democratic values during their tenure and cannot be considered to have been representative governments that gained the trust of the people and served their interests. Both were corrupt, self-serving governments more interested in self-enrichment than in democratic governance. The Suazo Córdova government was particularly bad. Suazo Córdova devoted his considerable political cunning to amassing power and laying the groundwork for a continuation of his rule beyond his constitutional terms:

> Although Suazo governed a full four years and completed his constitutionally mandated term in early 1986, he was almost forcibly ejected from office. Few of his political efforts were designed to strengthen, nurture, and expand the country's nascent democratic interests; on the contrary, they were designed to consolidate his style of personal rule. . . . Suazo's project was power, not democracy.[9]

Moreover, the extended period of civilian rule did not alter the traditional antidemocratic structures of power in Honduras. The military and the economic elite maintained their position as dominant forces beyond the reach of direct governmental control. The civilian governments were obliged to bargain with them over what were essentially power-sharing arrangements. The military in particular dominated the Honduran political system. The armed forces constituted a state within a state and set limits on civilian political life that were enforced by violence. Honduras suffered a regular pattern of human rights abuses carried out by military and police personnel against persons who strayed outside the bounds of what the military considered acceptable political activity. The level of human rights violations was low by comparison to El Salvador or Guatemala but was very significant within the Honduran political context.[10]

The Reagan administration was well aware that the elected governments in Honduras were hardly representative bodies and that a small circle of military officers and business leaders exercised a good deal of control over the society. U.S. officials nonetheless consistently characterized Honduras as a democracy and included it on the administration's oft-repeated list of democratic success stories in Latin America. To some extent this reflected the administration's formal, institution-oriented view of democracy. For the Reagan administration, any country with an elected government was a democracy, no matter how undemocratic the government was in practice, or how much it was curtailed by other power sectors within the society. The overoptimistic labeling was also an expression of the administration's lack of real interest in Honduran domestic politics. The Reagan administration's Honduras policy was not a Honduras policy per se; it was one part of the administration's militant Nicaragua policy. As long as Honduras had an elected government that was tolerant of the contras and did not suffer such serious human rights problems as to excite the attention of Congress or the U.S. public, the administration did not care about the state of Honduran political life.

Through extensive economic assistance and politicking with the Honduran military, the Reagan administration did help preserve elected civilian rule. The main effect of U.S. policy, however, was the heightened militarization of the country. The huge inflow of U.S. military assistance in the Reagan years, a total of $396.8 million, was without precedent in Honduran history. The assistance vastly increased the military's size and strength, yet did not change its traditionally antidemocratic outlook; the military emerged with an even greater capacity to dominate Honduran political life than before. The transformation of the armed forces into a huge, technically modernized sector only heightened its preoccupation with autonomy and its distance from the Honduran people. The assistance funds also tremendously fueled the long-standing corruption of the military. The corruption went beyond graft and fraud into more sordid activities, such as international drug trafficking.[11] Honduras became a transshipment point for drugs going from Colombia to the United States, a fact that was well known among U.S. officials. The heightened corruption of the military increased its tendency to resist all civilian control, a further backward step for democratization.

Perhaps the clearest example of the inherent clash between the U.S. military assistance to Honduras and the stated goal of promoting democracy in Honduras occurred in the early 1980s. An army intelligence unit, Battalion 316, that had received CIA training and was partly supported by U.S. military assistance, carried out a "dirty war" against the scattering of Honduran guerrillas and guerrilla sympathizers. Dozens of Hondurans were tortured and killed in what was the most serious campaign of political repression in recent Honduran history. The CIA (which gave counterinsurgency training to the unit beginning in 1980) apparently did not instruct the Hondurans to torture or kill their prisoners, but was nonetheless closely involved with the unit. Colonel Gustavo Alvarez Martínez, who became commander of the Honduran army in 1982, masterminded the dirty war.[12] Until his ouster in 1984, Alvarez was a favored figure among U.S. military advisers and was the main Honduran force behind both the contra program and the renewing of U.S.-Honduran military relations.

In El Salvador the deleterious political effects of U.S. military assistance reflected a tension built into the policy: although strengthening the military was harmful with respect to the internal political balance, it was necessary to prevent a leftist takeover, at least in the early 1980s. In Honduras no such inherent tension existed: there was no strong need to give the massive assistance to the Honduran military that had such a negative effect on Honduran society. Honduras faced no significant rebel threat. There was a scattering of leftist rebels in the early 1980s, but they did not constitute a large-scale insurgency that required an unprecedented build-up of the armed forces. Neither was there a significant external threat to Hondurans despite the administration's frequent claim that Nicaragua aimed to conquer Honduras.

There is little indication that the Nicaraguan government had any plans to invade Honduras. There were border skirmishes between the two countries, and Nicaraguan troops did in several cases cross the border, but these incidents were directly related to the presence of the contras in Nicaragua. It was not particularly surprising that Nicaragua, faced with a well-financed rebel group operating from Honduras, clashed with those rebels on the border and occasionally sought to disrupt their bases. When the contras' cross-border activities diminished, Nicaragua's forays across the Honduran border stopped. Furthermore, it was obvious to all observers, and to the Sandinistas, that any invasion of Honduras by Nicaragua would have provided the Reagan administration with the excuse it needed to intervene militarily against Nicaragua and oust the Sandinistas. Neither the contras, the expanded Honduran military, nor the U.S. troops in Honduras were necessary for this blanket deterrent to be effective against a Nicaraguan invasion of Honduras.

The U.S. military assistance to Honduras was never measured in terms of its consequences for Honduran political life. It was a way of buying Honduran cooperation with the contra war (as well as keep-ing the Honduran military from getting too resentful about the huge U.S. military support for the Salvadoran military, which is the Honduran military's traditional enemy). Its negative consequences on Honduras were a little-noticed (at least by the Reagan admin-istration) side effect of the relentless U.S. anti-Sandinista campaign.

The militarization of Honduras was one main legacy of the Reagan administration's policy. The other was the diminishment of Honduras to the status of a client state. Even more than in El Salva-dor, the level of U.S. political influence and involvement in Hon-duras, particularly the huge covert war against Nicaragua the United States administered from Honduran territory, made a mockery of Honduran sovereignty. The contras were increasingly unpopular in Honduras and the Honduran government obviously tolerated them only because of the huge quantities of U.S. assistance and the gen-eral weight of the United States in the region. As a result, Honduras was widely seen in the international community as the Reagan ad-ministration's lackey in Central America and the elected Honduran governments gained little credibility despite their elected civilian nature. A particularly striking example of Honduras' impaired sov-ereignty occurred in March 1986 when some Nicaraguan troops crossed into Honduran territory in a skirmish with the contras. The Reagan administration, embroiled in a difficult struggle with Con-gress on contra aid, saw the invasion as a potential public relations boost for the administration's cause and loudly denounced the Nicaraguan "invasion" of Honduras. When the Honduran govern-ment made no statement about the event, U.S. Ambassador Ferch was instructed by Washington to tell President Azcona to make a request for emergency military aid. Azcona was reluctant to blow the event out of proportion; Ferch visited him and told him, "You don't have a choice on this one." Azcona made the request.[13]

This overbearing U.S. policy inevitably created serious strains on the Honduran social fabric. Hondurans grew increasingly re-sentful of the United States using Honduras as a platform for its anti-Sandinista policy and treating it as a vassal. This resentment came to a head in April 1988 when the United States kidnapped in Honduras a Honduran wanted on drug trafficking charges in the United States. In response to the kidnapping, approximately two thousand demonstrators sacked a U.S. embassy annex and set fire to more than twenty embassy vehicles. The Honduran police were slow in coming to the embassy's aid, further signaling Hondurans' resentment. The demonstration was widely recognized as an expression of Hondurans' pent-up anger over U.S. heavy-handedness.[14] When U.S. Attorney General Edwin Meese argued that the demonstration was sponsored by drug traffickers, one Latin American ambassador in Honduras replied, "When he [Meese] says that, he's not just on another planet, he's in another galaxy."[15]

## Guatemala

The history of Guatemala since at least the 1940s is a story of recurrent clashes between forces of societal change and a deeply entrenched, reactionary business elite defended by a violent, repressive military. In the 1950s, a strong reformist movement culminated in the election of a reform-oriented government led by Jacobo Arbenz, who was ousted, however, in a CIA-sponsored coup, after which Guatemala returned to military rule. In the 1960s, Guatemalan security forces, with considerable counterinsurgency assistance from the United States, combatted recently formed guerrilla bands made up of some former Guatemalan military officers who had become disaffected after a failed military rebellion in 1960. Despite its military origins, the rebel movement took on an increasingly leftist character during the 1960s. In the 1970s, a number of more clearly ideologically based guerrilla groups formed and began waging a prolonged "popular" war against the military government. The Guatemalan military fought back viciously, employing terror-based counterinsurgency tactics, torturing and killing thousands of civilians.

The traditionally warm U.S.-Guatemalan relationship, rooted in mutual anticommunist interests, grew chilly in the late 1970s. The Guatemalan military refused to accept the human rights conditions imposed on U.S. military assistance by the United States in 1977, leading to a suspension of U.S.-Guatemalan military cooperation. The Carter administration's vocal criticisms of the Guatemalan government's abysmal human rights record angered the Guatemalan military and business elite, fostering an attitude of defiant independence from the United States and scorn for a government they saw as having gone soft on communism.

## A Difficult Friendship

The Guatemalan right celebrated the 1980 election of Ronald Reagan, anticipating a return to the good old days of close U.S.-Guatemalan relations. The incoming Reagan team was indeed sympathetic to the Guatemalan military government led by General Lucas García. Reagan officials saw Guatemala as another victim of Soviet-Cuban aggression in Central America, and potentially the last domino that would fall after El Salvador, Costa Rica, and Honduras, opening the door to the communist subversion of Mexico. Reagan administration officials portrayed the Guatemalan rebels as being "heavily supported and influenced by our adversaries,"[16] propagating the incorrect notion that Soviet/Cuban interference was an important cause of what was in fact a very Guatemalan civil war.[17]

Administration officials repeatedly ascribed the political violence in Guatemala to "the cycle of provocation from the left and overreaction from the right."[18] Implicit in this misleading formula was the notion that Guatemala had been in a reasonably good political and economic situation until without warning a group of Guatemalans irresponsibly or inexplicably launched a violent leftist rebellion, drawing a predictable, even understandable, "overreaction" from the right. Missing from this view were the twin facts that Guatemala had long been a profoundly unequal and unjust society in desperate need of political and economic reform and that the Guatemalan right had been systematically stamping out all nonviolent civil and political dissent for generations, eliminating any possibility of moderate opposition and fueling or creating the radical tendencies of those who sought reform.

As with El Salvador and Honduras, there was some disagreement between the hard-liners and moderates in the early Reagan administration over the formulation of a new policy toward Guatemala. The hard-liners were sympathetic to what they saw as a pro-United States regime battling Soviet-Cuban aggression. They believed that Carter's human rights criticisms had been inappropriate as well as counterproductive. They wanted to abandon the Carter policy and reestablish U.S. military assistance to help the Guatemalans defeat the rebels. The moderates were somewhat less openly sympathetic to the Guatemalan right but they agreed that U.S. military assistance should be reestablished and that the public human rights criticisms should be abandoned or at least replaced with quiet diplomacy. The moderates differed from the hard-liners with respect to the causes of the conflict in Guatemala. They were not persuaded that the rebels were agents of Soviet-Cuban expansionism and they paid greater attention to the domestic economic and political roots of the conflict. Accordingly, they believed that the United States should encourage political and economic reforms to reduce the economic inequality and political stultification that had long marked Guatemalan life.[19]

After some internal debate in the first half of 1981, the hard-liners and moderates were able to reach at least some agreement on a policy. They agreed that renewing military assistance would be the core element of a general policy of improving relations with the Guatemalan government to support that government in its anti-leftist struggle. As with El Salvador, the hard-liners accepted, at least formally, the need for a political component to the policy, if only to appease congressional Democrats and the general policy community. The liberal view of Guatemala, which had widespread influence among congressional Democrats, policy institutes, universities, and the U.S. public, was extremely negative. Guatemala had the (deserved) reputation of being the most politically savage country in Latin America and there was little sympathy for the idea of assisting Guatemala in its war effort. The administration hoped that by encouraging political reforms in Guatemala, the path for military assistance could be cleared. And the moderates within the administration further believed that political reform was a necessary part of the war against the rebels as a means of alleviating the causes of leftist revolt.

The political reform component of the policy, unlike that in El Salvador and Honduras, was not initially characterized as a policy of promoting democracy. Guatemala was obviously so far from democracy that even the Reagan administration's habitually loose use of the term could not be stretched to apply to its starkly repressive political situation. Instead, the administration focused the political component of its policy on the need to reduce political violence. The way for the United States to encourage a reduction of violence, according to the administration, was not to censure the Guatemalan government but to engage it in dialogue on human rights issues:

We are convinced that dialog is the only approach which can be effective in diminishing overreaction by government forces and toleration of illicit rightist activity.[20]

This new policy soon got underway. In May, John Bushnell, acting assistant secretary of state for inter-American affairs, declared that "given the extent of the insurgency and the strong communist support worldwide for it, the administration is disposed to support Guatemala."[21] In June, the Department of Commerce granted an export license for the sale to the Guatemalan military of $3.1 million of jeeps and trucks. Administration officials tried raising the human rights issues with the Guatemalan government but were rebuffed by an unrepentant government that condemned any external human rights pressure, no matter how oblique, as intervention in its internal affairs. The administration also began what was to prove a long, relatively fruitless campaign to put a good face on Guatemala's human rights violations. In July 1981, for example, Deputy Assistant Secretary of State Stephen Bosworth told a congressional committee that the Guatemalan left was responsible for most of the political violence in Guatemala and claimed that the Guatemalan military was "taking care to protect innocent bystanders."[22]

Congressional Democrats were angry at the decision to sell military vehicles to the Guatemalan military. They were not impressed by the administration's public relations efforts in the human rights domain and while they were willing to move on military assistance to El Salvador and Honduras, they remained adamantly opposed to any renewal of military assistance to Guatemala. Guatemalan military leaders in turn were surprised and disappointed that the Reagan administration was not coming through with military assistance and complained about the fact that the Salvadoran military had gotten a large grant of assistance and they had not.[23] Presidential elections were scheduled for March 1982. The administration hoped to encourage Guatemala to join its neighbors in moving toward civilian rule and lobbied the military at least to run a civilian candidate. The Guatemalans ignored the administration, however, and ran Lucas García's Defense Minister, General Aníbal Guevera, who was elected on March 7, 1982, in what were widely recognized as fraudulent elections.

Just two weeks after Guevara's election, a group of junior military officers overthrew the outgoing government and installed a military junta headed by General Efrían Ríos Montt, who himself had been elected President in 1974 but had been ousted before taking office. The coup was the work of a group of junior officers who were concerned that the Guatemalan military leadership was blind to the lessons for Central American militaries in the fall of Somoza in Nicaragua. The junior officers were dissatisfied with the terror-based tactics and the absence of a positive political program in Lucas García's war-fighting strategy. With Ríos Montt in power the military devised and began implementing a multiyear plan to defeat the rebels based on a forceful counterinsurgency strategy aimed at destroying the rebels' rural bases of support and establishing control of the rural population through forcible relocation of large numbers of peasants in strategic hamlets and the creation of numerous civil defense patrols.[24] This counterinsurgency effort was better planned than the indiscriminate terror campaign of the preceding years but still entailed horrendous levels of violence against the civilian population. It also initiated a process of militarization of the countryside in which the military achieved a level of repressive control over the rural population unmatched anywhere in Latin America.

The Reagan administration seized on the March 1982 coup and the emergence of Ríos Montt as a decisive political turnaround in Guatemala. Administration officials began a new campaign to gain congressional approval for military assistance by trying to sell Ríos Montt to a skeptical U.S. Congress as a reformist committed to reducing human rights abuses and initiating a transition to democracy. In April 1982, U.S. Ambassador Frederick Chapin declared, "The killings have stopped. . . . The Guatemalan government has come out of the darkness and into the light."[25]

The administration's exaggerated position on the human rights situation provoked a bitter debate throughout much of 1982 between the administration on the one hand and the U.S. human rights community and congressional Democrats on the other. The debate coincided with and paralleled the debate over human rights in El Salvador. President Reagan himself weighed in during December 1982 when he met briefly with Ríos Montt in Guatemala and afterward described the Guatemalan leader to be "totally dedicated to democracy" and said the Guatemalan government had been getting "a bum rap" on human rights.[26]

Despite these efforts, the administration was unable to convince Congress to approve any military assistance. In addition to not getting U.S. military assistance reestablished, the administration was also not able to have any noticeable influence on the Ríos Montt government in terms of convincing it to move ahead on a transition to civilian rule, despite lobbying efforts on that point by the U.S. embassy. The administration did reward Ríos Montt on its own, announcing in January 1983 that "in light of human rights improvements which have taken place in Guatemala since the Ríos Montt government came into power" it was approving the sale of $6.3 million worth of military parts and equipment, primarily helicopter parts and radio equipment, that the Lucas García regime had requested.[27] The administration did succeed in getting congressional approval for increased economic aid, which almost doubled from $15.5 million in 1982 to $29.7 million in 1983.

Ríos Montt's somewhat peculiar, even messianic evangelism alienated many Guatemalan military officers and his rigid imposition of military control over the entire political system offended some of the oligarchic political elites. He was ousted by his defense minister, General Oscar Mejía Víctores, in August 1983. Mejía Víctores continued the harsh counterinsurgency campaign. In 1984 the war finally began to turn decisively in the military's favor. The rebels were driven out of many of their traditional strongholds and isolated in limited areas of the country. With the decrease in the number of active military battles came a decline in human rights violations, although the actual level of military control of the rural population remained as high or higher than before.[28] The progress in the war permitted the Guatemalan right to move ahead with the second major phase of its overall counterinsurgency campaign, putting the political process in the hands of civilians and pursuing international political legitimacy. Constitutional Assembly elections were held in July 1984, a new constitution drafted thereafter, and presidential elections were scheduled for late 1985.

The Reagan administration was very pleased to see the human rights situation improve and the civilian transition begin. Although the Reagan administration had been engaging in cheerleading for the Guatemalan government in Washington, the U.S. embassy in Guatemala, led by Ambassador Frederick Chapin, had for some time been pushing quite firmly behind the scenes on the human rights issue. These efforts were little appreciated by the Guatemalans. When Chapin left Guatemala in 1984 the Guatemalan government did not award him the civilian medal normally given to outgoing U.S. ambassadors. Mejía Víctores explained the decision brusquely, stating of Chapin: "He did nothing for Guatemala."[29] Chapin's successor, Alberto Piedra, a conservative political appointee, was more sympathetic to the Guatemalan right and got along with it better. He also, however, stressed the importance of human rights and civilian rule, arguing to the Guatemalans that civilian rule was a precondition for a substantial U.S. military assistance relationship and increased economic aid.

In 1984 and 1985 the Reagan administration touted the decline in the number of political killings in Guatemala as proof of a lessening of political repression and heralded the process of civilian control as the start of the long-delayed democratic transition. The administration successfully persuaded Congress to approve very large increases in economic aid, which rose from $20.3 million in 1984 to $106.9 million in 1985. The administration also managed to secure congressional approval for $500,000 of military training assistance, finally breaking the barrier to military aid (although only nonlethal aid). In 1985 the administration requested $10.3 million of military aid, a request it had made before without success. Congress went along in part and Guatemala ended up receiving $5.4 million of nonlethal aid in 1986.

## The Cerezo Years

Presidential elections were held in late 1985, with the first round in November and the runoff in December. Vinicio Cerezo Arévalo, the Christian Democratic candidate, decisively defeated his main challenger, Jorge Carpio Nicolle of the National Union for the Center, and a variety of candidates from the right. Cerezo's victory was favorably received in Washington. The new Guatemalan president appeared to be vigorous and competent; he enjoyed credibility as a genuine civilian politician, not a puppet of the military. At Cerezo's inauguration in January 1986, Vice President Bush hailed "this historic step Guatemala has taken" and declared that the United States would be "hand-in-hand with Guatemala as they [sic] go down the democratic path."[30] The administration hoped that the election of

Cerezo, like the election of Duarte in El Salvador, would dampen liberal criticism of the administration's efforts to normalize relations with Guatemala and would remove congressional objections to military assistance.

The policy context in early 1986 was of course very different from what it had been in 1981. Guatemala was no longer in the midst of an active war against leftist insurgents. The war had largely been brought under control and the main issue facing Guatemala was whether Cerezo could establish credible civilian rule. In this new context the Reagan administration recast its Guatemala policy away from the earlier emphasis on trying to help the Guatemalan military defeat the rebels to a policy of helping Cerezo consolidate civilian rule. This was conceived of and presented as a policy of democracy promotion. In the words of Assistant Secretary Abrams, for example, "The primary U.S. objective in Guatemala is the promoting of a democratic government."[31] As with El Salvador after Duarte's election, Guatemala in the Cerezo years was no longer of much interest to the hard-liners in the Reagan administration (because the leftist threat was no longer pressing) and the policy fell largely into the moderates' hands (although Alberto Piedra remained U.S. ambassador to Guatemala until 1987).

Military assistance remained a priority of U.S. policy in the Cerezo years but it was viewed as one of several coequal components along with economic assistance and political assistance, all of which were aimed at helping bolster Cerezo. Military assistance was no longer seen as necessary to keep Guatemala from succumbing to communism (the Guatemalan military had managed to defeat the rebels with no U.S. aid) but to reward the military for accepting a civilian government and to keep it happy during Cerezo's tenure. Congressional Democrats and the U.S. policy community were still very hesitant about U.S. aid to the Guatemalan military, however, and Congress agreed only to relatively small amounts of nonlethal military assistance, between five and ten million dollars per year. In 1988 the administration granted an export license for the sale of 20,000 M-16 rifles to the Guatemalan military. Despite some protests in Congress and the policy community, the sale went ahead and 16,000 M-16s were delivered in 1989.[32]

Economic assistance was a large feature of U.S. support for the Cerezo government. U.S. aid increased to $116.7 million in 1986 and then grew to $187.8 million in 1987. Much of the assistance was balance of payments support to keep the economy afloat. Guatemala in the latter half of the 1980s, like all of Central America, was still mired in the economic recession of the early 1980s and improving the economic situation was one of the crucial challenges Cerezo faced. The administration encouraged Cerezo to implement economic reform programs, an effort that proved difficult as Cerezo was hindered by the political difficulties of imposing austerity measures on an already impoverished population and resistance from the reactionary economic elite to any kind of governmental assertion of economic control.

In the political realm, the U.S. embassy played an active supporting role, giving advice to Cerezo and his advisers on the many internal problems he faced, attempting to mediate disputes between the government, the economic elite, and the military. The embassy backed the Cerezo government's attempts to reform the deeply compromised judicial system and to establish civilian control over a reorganized national police force. As in El Salvador, the U.S. embassy carried out most of these efforts on its own, with little specific direction from Washington other than the general goal of maintaining Cerezo in power through his term. Unlike Salvadorans, however, Guatemalans tolerated a much lower degree of U.S. involvement and the United States had much less leverage to draw upon. The administration combined its political support with efforts to induce Cerezo to embrace the administration's hard-line anti-Sandinista policy. Cerezo held stubbornly to an official position of neutrality on Nicaragua, a source of great irritation to the White House which led to periods of diplomatic coolness toward Cerezo but did not have much concrete effect on the day-to-day policy of economic, political, and military assistance being implemented in Guatemala itself.

A significant element of the political support for Cerezo came in the form of efforts by the U.S. embassy in Guatemala to fend off or dampen down the continual rumblings of dissatisfaction and rebellion from the Guatemalan military. Much of the army's leadership supported the existence of a civilian government. They considered the transition to civilian rule their project and believed it brought tangible benefits to Guatemala without infringing greatly on the military's autonomy. A number of army officers, however, balked at this policy. They saw Cerezo as an out-and-out leftist trying to impose socialism on Guatemala and were skeptical of the value of closer ties with the United States. In conjunction with members of the economic oligarchy these dissatisfied officers were constantly plotting against Cerezo. Coup rumors and attempted coups became frequent occurrences in 1987 and 1988. The U.S. embassy, led in those years by a skillful career diplomat, James Michel, labored hard to head off any possible coup, politicking within the military ranks and marshaling whatever sources of leverage it could plausibly draw upon, primarily the threat of an aid cutoff, to counteract pressures for a military takeover.

Cerezo did manage to survive in power but his presidency was a great disappointment. Cerezo came into office on a great wave of local and international expectation that Guatemala was at last headed away from the decades of terrible repression and conflict. Little positive change actually occurred, however, during the Cerezo years. The military tolerated a civilian government but ceded it very little authority, remaining by far the most powerful institution in Guatemala and a resolutely antidemocratic one. Human rights abuses initially declined after Cerezo came to power but from 1987 on they returned to very high levels and Guatemala was once again one of the worst human rights violators in the Western Hemisphere. A certain civilian political space was permitted but was narrowly bounded by a steady level of political terror that resulted in the deaths of hundreds of labor leaders, student activists, political organizers, and other persons involved in politics in any way.[33] Even this very circumscribed civilian rule hardly extended outside Guatemala City. In the countryside, military control of economic, political, and social life remained almost absolute.[34]

Not only were the traditional structures of repression unchanged by the advent of civilian rule, but Cerezo himself proved to be a weak, ineffective leader. The Guatemalan Christian Democrats, like the Salvadoran Christian Democrats, were an inexperienced party that proved feckless once in power. Cerezo only exacerbated this institutional weakness. He was inconsistent, and seemingly lacked willpower and real political skills. He was unable to mobilize his initial public support into a base for bold initiatives and quickly settled for an obvious dependency on the military. Guatemala in the late 1980s remained a deeply troubled country, buffeted by a continuing economic crisis fraught with social tensions, and still plagued both by a guerrilla insurgency that the military could control but not end and serious human rights problems. Cerezo limped through the final year of his five-year term a widely discredited and unpopular president.

## *Sharp Limits*

At least in conception, the Reagan administration's Guatemala policy resembled its El Salvador policy. It was an attempt to support a traditionally pro-U.S. neighbor against a leftist insurgency that the administration saw as part of a Soviet-Cuban campaign to subvert Central America. The policy contained military, economic, and political components. The military component was the core element, but the policy was presented publicly in terms of its prodemocratic political component to lessen congressional and public opposition. As with El Salvador, the transition to elected civilian rule in Guatemala coincided with the insurgency being brought under control, leading to a shift in U.S. policy away from a hard-line, military-oriented approach to a more multifaceted, moderate policy focused on the consolidation of civilian rule.

Although similar in conception to the El Salvador policy, the administration's Guatemala policy was very different in execution. Despite repeated efforts by the administration, U.S. military assistance to Guatemala was not renewed in the early 1980s. The United States provided no military assistance to Guatemala between 1981 and 1985 (other than the half million dollars of training assistance in 1985) and only small amounts in the Cerezo years. In contrast to its extensive military role in El Salvador, the United States had almost no part in the Guatemalan conflict; the Guatemalan military's successes, and its many atrocities, were almost entirely its own making. The administration's policy thus had little relevance with respect to its main goal—preventing a leftist takeover of Guatemala.

The United States also had little role in the transition to elected civilian rule. The Reagan administration encouraged the transition, but it had nothing like the influence or involvement it had in the Salvadoran transition. The transition was the Guatemalan military's doing. As mentioned above, a civilian transition was the latter phase of the Guatemalan military's counterinsurgency campaign, to be carried out once the insurgents had been brought under control. There were several motivations for permitting a return to civilian rule.[35] The military saw that with the severe economic downturn in the early 1980s, a civilian government would be useful both because it would help Guatemala attract economic assistance from the United States and it would put civilians in the position of absorbing the criticism and blame from Guatemalans about the bad economic situation. More generally, a civilian transition was a route to regaining international legitimacy. The Guatemalan military was proud of its independence and scornful of the Western governments that snubbed Guatemala, but nonetheless aimed to regain a normalized status in the international community once the civil war was brought under control. The trend toward civilian rule in Central America was also a factor in this regard; after 1984 Guatemala was the only Central American country with a nonelected military government. The civilian transitions in El Salvador and Honduras also had underlined how easy it was for a military to permit a civilian transition yet give up very little in terms of authority and autonomy. Finally, a desire for U.S. military aid may have motivated the Guatemalan military although it was unlikely to have been a major factor. The civilian transition came when the war was winding down substantially and the urgency of the Guatemalan military's material needs were diminishing. There was also a great skepticism in the Guatemalan military about the value of a close assistance relationship with the United States. Many Guatemalan military officers looked with contempt at the Salvadoran army and believed that it was soft because of overreliance on the United States.

The second phase of the Reagan administration's Guatemala policy, the support for Cerezo, was somewhat similar in execution to the second phase of the El Salvador policy, although the levels of U.S. economic and military assistance and the degree of U.S. political influence was much lower. The U.S. support did significantly contribute to Cerezo surviving his term. Even more than in El Salvador and Honduras, however, the achievement of civilian rule in Guatemala was only an extremely limited advance, a far cry from the democratic transformation the administration attempted to claim. The administration policy was not to blame for the lack of a genuine democratic transition in Guatemala. The political situation in Guatemala in the late 1980s was the result of generations of domination by Latin America's most reactionary and cruel military and economic elites.

The Reagan administration policy was nonetheless seriously flawed. As in El Salvador, the notion of democracy by centrist transition was problematic. The formal transition from military to civilian rule was not a means of breaking up the Guatemalan right's traditional stranglehold on power. The transition was, if anything, part of an effort by the military to consolidate and stabilize its own power. The Reagan administration believed in a political center that did not really exist and clung to the idea that the right would somehow give up power voluntarily to the center. The policy was thus based both on a denial of the true configuration of political forces in Guatemala and of the usual laws of political power and political change in Central America.

The most glaring operational flaw of the policy was its human rights component. Human rights violations were the symptom of the Guatemalan right's antidemocratic attitudes and the handle by which the administration could call attention to its commitment to bringing about a change in those attitudes. Yet the administration's human rights policy was extremely weak. During the first half of the 1980s the administration consistently played the role of apologist for the Guatemalan government. Administration officials struggled to minimize the political violence that was occurring or to blame it on the rebels. Most of the administration's time and energy on human rights was devoted to fighting with U.S. human rights groups rather than investigating human rights problems in Guatemala and trying to do something about them. During the Cerezo years, the administration's human rights policy was still substantially defensive. The U.S. embassy and administration officials in Washington habitually defended the human rights situation in Guatemala, attempting to deny the increasingly grim reality there. The U.S. embassy did try behind the scenes to persuade the Guatemalan military to improve its human rights performance but its efforts were inevitably weakened by its persistent tendency to defend the human rights situation publicly and to fight with U.S. human rights groups.

## COSTA RICA

When the Reagan administration took office in 1981 it had little interest in Costa Rica. Although Reagan officials saw Costa Rica as one of the potential "dominoes" in Central America that might fall to Soviet-Cuban aggression, Costa Rica was not under active siege by leftist rebels as were El Salvador and Guatemala. Furthermore, although Costa Rica was plagued by the worst economic crisis of its modern history—resulting from external factors such as the fall of coffee prices and the rising interest rates on foreign debt as well as internal factors such as high governmental spending and the proliferation of inefficient state-dependent enterprises—it was Central America's only democracy and appeared far more politically stable than any other Central American country. To the extent that the early Reagan administration had a view of Costa Rica, it was likely to be a vaguely unfavorable one, both because Costa Rica had given substantial aid to the Sandinistas in the latter years of their struggle against Somoza and because Costa Rica had long pursued a social democratic model of economic development.

Within its first year, however, the Reagan administration gained an interest in Costa Rica and incorporated Costa Rica into its emerging Central American policy. Throughout 1981 the U.S. ambassador to Costa Rica, Frank McNeil (a career diplomat appointed in the Carter years), sent strongly worded messages to the new Latin America policy team in the State Department on the calamitous economic situation in Costa Rica and the importance of preserving the only working democratic system in Central America. The economic element of these messages found a receptive audience with Assistant Secretary Enders and his principal deputy Stephen Bosworth who believed strongly that economic problems were the root of much of Central America's political problems. The political component of McNeil's messages also fit into the State Department's emerging emphasis on promoting democracy as the central theme of its policy of bolstering the various besieged Central American governments. Costa Rica was proof that democracy could work in Central America; ensuring the survival of Costa Rican democracy became a necessary component of the overall policy.

Impetus for attention to Costa Rica came from the U.S. Congress as well. Some Democrats in Congress were determined that the United States should not ignore Costa Rica in the rush to fight communism in Central America. They pushed the administration to include Costa Rica in its expanding assistance program to Central America. In its first request for economic aid to Latin America, presented to Congress in March 1981, the administration requested only $8.5 million for Costa Rica, little more than half of what Costa Rica was then receiving. When the Foreign Affairs Committee of the House of Representatives reviewed the administration's foreign aid requests for 1982, it recommended that $25 million of economic support funds be added for Costa Rica.[36] The administration discovered that raising aid levels for El Salvador and Honduras would be easier if aid to Costa Rica was also increased.

The Reagan administration committed itself to insuring the survival of Costa Rican democracy and developed a two-part military-economic policy to serve that goal. As with the policies in other Central American countries, the hard-liners and moderates within the administration differed in their level of interest in the two components, with the hard-liners concerned more about the externally oriented military component and the moderates pushing the internally oriented economic program.

With respect to the economic realm, the Reagan administration worked closely with the Costa Rican government and the International Monetary Fund to develop an economic recovery plan for Costa Rica and then funded that plan very heavily. U.S. economic aid to Costa Rica increased from $15.3 million in 1981 to $51.7 million in 1982, $214.1 million in 1983, reaching a high of $220 million in 1985. During the Reagan years, Costa Rica received a total of $1.135 billion of U.S. economic aid, putting it ahead of Honduras as the second largest recipient of such aid in Latin America (after El Salvador).

The Costa Rican economic recovery program reflected the views of the IMF and the Reagan administration; it was an austerity program which consisted of large reductions in government spending, revised foreign exchange rules, the elimination of various tax subsidies, and the raising of fuel and utility prices. The program created powerful social tensions, particularly in the labor sector, but did succeed in pulling Costa Rica out of its economic crisis. The economy was stabilized in 1982 and 1983 and by the second half of the 1980s the per capita gross domestic product in Costa Rica was growing, unemployment was decreasing, and inflation was at manageable levels. Costa Rica's economic problems were by no means solved—the country was still burdened with a very large external debt—but compared to the persistent economic stagnation afflicting most other Latin American countries, Costa Rica of the late 1980s was in relatively good shape.

In the military realm, the Reagan administration encouraged Costa Rica to strengthen its modest security forces, the small, lightly equipped Civil Guard, as a trip wire against potential Sandinista aggression. In June 1982 President Luis Alberto Monge, who had gained office in the elections of February 1982, announced that he was requesting security assistance from the United States and several other countries in response to a wave of leftist terrorist incidents in Costa Rica. The United States responded with a $2 million assistance program later that year.

From the beginning, the new U.S.-Costa Rican security assistance relationship was marked by ambiguity about how much it reflected true desire on the Costa Rican government's part for U.S. military assistance and how much the Reagan administration was pressuring the Costa Ricans to take it. Costa Rica was very proud of its demilitarized nature and hesitant about expanding its Civil Guard (which is a police force rather than an army). Nonetheless, many Costa Ricans were concerned about the growing regional turmoil and felt that the Civil Guard should at least be capable of routing terrorist actions.

As the administration's anti-Sandinista policy intensified, and when U.S. Ambassador Frank McNeil was replaced by a very hardline political appointee, Curtin Winsor, in 1983, U.S. encouragement of Costa Rica to strengthen its security forces clearly evolved into pressure. Winsor and other Reagan hard-liners were convinced that Nicaragua posed a serious, imminent threat to Costa Rica and that Costa Rica should take immediate action to build up its security forces. They were unsympathetic to Costa Rica's demilitarized posture and believed that Costa Rica had its head in the sand with respect to the Nicaraguan threat. Winsor became notorious in Costa Rica for his rabid anti-Sandinista views and his tendency to involve himself loudly and bluntly in Costa Rica's internal affairs. U.S. military assistance to Costa Rica increased steadily to a peak of $11.2 million in 1985. From 1982 to 1985 the United States provided almost four times as much military assistance to Costa Rica than it had in the past forty years combined.[37]

At the same time that the Reagan administration's anti-Sandinista policy was spilling over into Costa Rica through the issue of military assistance, it was also beginning to involve Costa Rica as a base for contra operations against Nicaragua. In 1982, Eden Pastora, the former Sandinista commandante who had become disaffected and left Nicaragua in 1981, set himself up in Costa Rica and began to gather his Nicaraguan followers into an armed anti-Sandinista force, known as the Democratic Revolutionary Alliance (ARDE). Pastora received some U.S. backing although the massive U.S. contra assistance program remained focused on the main contra forces based in Honduras. Pastora's forces operated out of Costa Rica through 1985, resulting in regular skirmishes with the Sandinista army on the Nicaraguan-Costa Rican border. These skirmishes provoked a great deal of tension between the Costa Rican and Nicaraguan governments and the fear in Costa Rica that it was being inextricably drawn into the Nicaraguan war. Furthermore, the clandestine U.S. contra resupply operation run by NSC staff member Oliver North (see chapter 3) built an airstrip in northern Nicaragua in 1985 (with President Monge's permission) and used that facility regularly during 1986 for resupply missions to Nicaragua.

As pressure from the Reagan administration for greater Costa Rican participation in the U.S. anti-Sandinista policy intensified, President Monge attempted an increasingly difficult balancing act. On the one hand, Monge did not want to risk losing the substantial economic aid that was flowing to Costa Rica by not going along with the Reagan administration's anti-Sandinista policy. On the other hand, he had to respond to his core base of public support in Costa Rica, the center-left and center, which was opposed to the growing U.S.-Costa Rican military ties and the contra war. His approach was publicly to commit Costa Rica to neutrality in the U.S.-Nicaraguan conflict but simultaneously to accept increasing quantities of U.S. military assistance, to make only a minor fuss about the contras operating in northern Costa Rica, and to agree quietly on the building of the contra airstrip.

By late 1985 this balancing act was becoming untenable. The contra activity in northern Costa Rica was producing heightened border tensions with Nicaragua. The U.S. military assistance had grown to the point where in May 1985 the United States began sending Green Berets to Costa Rica to give counterinsurgency training to

Costa Rican security forces. A significant part of the Costa Rican public was angry about the situation and believed that Monge was letting the United States drag Costa Rica into open conflict with Nicaragua and was overturning the Costa Rican antimilitarist tradition.

This tense situation was relieved by the departure of Monge and the arrival of Oscar Arias after the February 1986 presidential elections. Although Arias was from the same party as Monge, he charted a very different foreign policy course. He steered Costa Rica away from its growing military ties with the United States. U.S. military assistance declined rapidly; by 1988, for example, it was down to $200,000. Arias also insisted that the contras stop using Costa Rican territory for military operations. North's network used the secret airstrip in 1986 after Arias ordered that it be shut down; with the eruption of the Iran-contra scandal in late 1986 the whole secret contra resupply operation stopped. Additionally, immediately upon taking office Arias began to pursue a skillful, high-profile campaign to negotiate a peace accord among the five Central American countries. This campaign, known as the Arias Plan (see chapter 3 for details), converted Costa Rica from a reluctant, passive partner in the Reagan policy to a truly independent and internationally respected policy actor in the region.

In the mid-1980s some U.S. commentators argued that the Reagan administration's Costa Rica policy was having serious deleterious effects on Costa Rican democracy, including forcing a remilitarization of a traditionally nonmilitarized society, pushing Costa Rica into open war with Nicaragua, and provoking a dangerous polarization of Costa Rican political life.[38] From the perspective of the end of the 1980s, however, the balance sheet of the policy is not so negative. The Reagan administration's attempt to involve Costa Rica in its anti-Sandinista campaign clearly had noxious political effects on Costa Rica and led to a heightening of tensions between Costa Rica and Nicaragua. The Reagan administration treated Costa Rica as a tool of U.S. foreign policy, disregarding Costa Rican sovereignty and giving little regard to the features of Costa Rican society that have made it a uniquely successful Central American country. In the end, however, the Reagan policy did not do lasting harm to Costa Rican democracy. Costa Rica was not remilitarized, dragged into war with Nicaragua, or profoundly polarized.

At the same time, the Reagan policy did have major, lasting

positive effects on Costa Rica in the economic domain. The massive U.S. aid to Costa Rica in the 1980s, together with aid from the multilateral development banks, played a significant role in helping the Costa Rican economy begin to grow again after the recession of the early 1980s. Costa Rican democracy would undoubtedly have survived without the U.S. aid, but the country would almost certainly have been much worse off. The positive economic component of the Reagan policy in Costa Rica was less visible than the negative political component but in the end was probably more important. The irony, one that Costa Ricans were well aware of, was that without the Reagan administration's obsession with Nicaragua, which was so widely criticized in Costa Rica and had objectionable political effects there, the U.S. would never have given the massive amounts of economic assistance that were so beneficial to Costa Rica.

# 3

# DEMOCRACY BY FORCE

## NICARAGUA AND GRENADA

For the first time since the invasion of the Dominican Republic in 1965, the United States under the Reagan administration used military force in Latin America and the Caribbean. The United States financed and directed a covert war against the Sandinista government of Nicaragua and invaded the Caribbean island of Grenada. The war against the Sandinistas spanned all eight years of the Reagan presidency and was a policy of extraordinary controversy that absorbed incalculable amounts of the administration's energy and had only ambiguous effects. The invasion of Grenada was a three-day military campaign which gained wide popular support in the United States and clearly achieved the administration's goal. Both were anticommunist policies aimed at ousting leftist governments and both were publicly cast as efforts to promote democracy. The Reagan administration repeatedly asserted that its goal in Nicaragua was getting the Sandinistas to accept democracy and that the Nicaraguan contras were a group of freedom fighters committed to bringing democracy to Nicaragua. Similarly, the administration emphasized from the first day of the invasion of Grenada that the United States was intervening to restore democracy.

It is tempting to dismiss the administration's democracy rationales for these policies as transparently hypocritical efforts to cloak militaristic anticommunist campaigns in the garb of democratic principles. Yet such a dismissal is premature. To start with, the democracy rationales, sincere or not, had a significant impact on the way the policies were conceived within the government and debated in the United States. Furthermore, almost by dint of repetition, the democracy rationales gained some real currency in the government and led to the growing conviction on the part of some U.S. officials and members of the policy community that the United States can and should use military force to promote democracy abroad. This chapter examines the Reagan administration's controversial policies in Nicaragua and Grenada, with a focus on the role promoting democracy occupied in the formulation and execution of those policies.

## NICARAGUA

*Competing Conceptions*

The Reagan administration's policy toward Nicaragua was a byzantine affair peopled by a bewildering cast of characters, torn by continual struggles between rival factions in the government, and marked by constant controversy and scandal. If one looks beneath the welter of secretive and often contradictory policy measures and the turbulent debate over policy, however, what is striking is that the Reagan administration's approach to Nicaragua was not especially complex and was almost constant throughout the Reagan years. The policy can be understood as a blend of three competing conceptions of the Nicaragua situation, one maintained by the hard-liners in the administration, one by the moderates in the administration, and one by U.S. liberals (as well as many Latin Americans and West Europeans).

The hard-liners' conception, distilled to its essence, was the following. The Sandinistas are hard-core communists intent on establishing and maintaining totalitarian control over Nicaragua. Sandinista Nicaragua is an expansionist state committed to working with Cuba and the Soviet Union to foment leftist revolutions throughout Central America. The Sandinistas' internal and external policies are inextricably linked. Nicaragua exports revolution because of its domestic political ideology and will continue to do so as long as it has a communist government. Although the Sandinistas might agree on paper to change their external policies, as communists they cannot be trusted to honor their pledges; a regional or bilateral security agreement is useless. The United States's security concerns about the spread of leftism in Central America, therefore, can only be answered by ousting the Sandinistas. The U.S. public will not support U.S. military intervention in Nicaragua; the only way to get rid of the Sandinistas is indirect military pressure combined with direct economic and political pressure. The contras are the best available means of exerting military pressure. U.S. policy therefore will concentrate on supporting the contras. Although a negotiated agreement is worthless, engaging in negotiations with Nicaragua may be useful to convince Congress and the U.S. public to support the contra policy.

The moderates' conception can be summarized as follows. The Sandinista government is a repressive, Marxist-Leninist government but permits a limited political opposition and a beleaguered but extant private sector. The Sandinistas do aid the Salvadoran rebels but do not represent a serious threat to Latin America as a whole. Although the Sandinistas pursue objectionable domestic political practices, the United States's main concern with Nicaragua is the Sandinistas' role in El Salvador. The Sandinistas' internal and external policies are separable—the Sandinistas can be induced to stop exporting revolution in return for a U.S. "hands-off" pledge. A negotiated security accord based on that inducement should be the goal of U.S. policy in Nicaragua. The contras are useful to pressure the Sandinistas to sign a security accord but are not an end in themselves.

The U.S. liberals' conception varied somewhat over time and was subject to many small variations but was essentially the following. The Sandinistas are romantic leftists more than hardened Marxist-Leninists. Although the Sandinista government has some absolutist tendencies, it exerts less harsh repression than neighboring governments, such as those in El Salvador and Guatemala, even after the electoral transitions in those countries. It is unclear if the Sandinistas are aiding the Salvadoran rebels; even if they are, such aid is not a major feature of the Salvadoran conflict. The United States can live with a Sandinista government in Nicaragua. A policy of pressure will drive the Sandinistas further to the left domestically and further into Cuba's and the Soviet Union's arms. The contras are a squalid force dominated by ex-Somocista military officers that has little support in Nicaragua. U.S. aid to the contras only prolongs a pointless civil war that is wreaking serious harm on Nicaragua.

Each of these three conceptions had a role in the administration's policy. The hard-liners' conception formed the core. The moderates' conception competed for priority with the hard-liners' conception. The moderates were almost always overruled by the hard-liners, however, and the primary role of their conception was serving as the basis of the administration's public presentation of its policy. In other words, the administration followed the hard-liners' approach but described its policy to the outside world as though it were based on the moderates' conception. The liberals' conception was an oppositional force that the administration continually attempted to defuse through anticipation, to negate by public persuasion, or simply to denounce.

The U.S. anti-Sandinista policy evolved in numerous phases: the Carter administration's efforts to find a *modus vivendi*, the formulation of the hard-line Reagan policy in 1981, the early implementation of the Reagan policy in 1982 and 1983, the brief rise of the moderates in 1984, the reassertion and solidification of the hard-line policy in 1985 and 1986, the disintegration of the policy in 1987 and 1988, and the Bush administration's wrap-up in 1989 and 1990.

## Background to Conflict

The beginning of the end of the generations-old rule of the Somoza family in Nicaragua occurred in 1967 when Anastasio Somoza Debayle, the younger son of the father of the dynasty, Anastasio Somoza García, became president. Anastasio Somoza Debayle's corruption and repressiveness exceeded the already generous bounds set out by his elder brother and father, and he steadily alienated the once supportive middle class and set a number of other prominent elite families against him. He also faced opposition from the Sandinista National Liberation Front (FSLN), a group of leftist rebels that had formed in 1961 and were supported by Fidél Castro. The FSLN was not very strong throughout the 1960s and most of the 1970s, but represented the increasing political polarization of Nicaragua. In 1977 and 1978 the Sandinistas gained strength, surprising Somoza's vaunted National Guard with several daring, showy raids, and broadening its base of international support to include two influential Latin American democracies, Costa Rica and Venezuela. The civic opposition to Somoza also crescendoed and Nicaragua was clearly headed toward civil war.

Faced with the growing crisis in Nicaragua, the Carter administration attempted to shift away from the U.S. government's longtime loyalty to the Somozas. The Carter administration was caught between three somewhat conflicting imperatives or perceptions: it recognized that Somoza was bad for Nicaragua and did not wish to support him; it saw the Sandinistas as leftists likely to be unfavorable to U.S. interests, and wanted to preclude their attaining a military victory; and it wished to avoid acting as a hegemonic power by intervening in Nicaragua's internal affairs. The result was a complex, confused, and ultimately unsuccessful attempt to mediate Somoza's departure, the preservation of a reorganized National Guard, and the coming to power of some kind of democratically oriented transitional government. The Sandinistas forced Somoza out of power in July 1979. Somoza's National Guard collapsed and a political coalition with a dominant Sandinista component took power.[1]

After the Sandinista revolution, U.S.-Nicaraguan relations proceeded uneasily. The Carter administration sought to keep the United States constructively engaged in Nicaragua, believing that a rejectionist approach would only push the Sandinistas further into the arms of Cuba and the Soviet Union. To this end, Carter proposed a $75 million aid package for Nicaragua in November 1979. The aid proposal became the subject of a fierce congressional debate, however, with conservatives arguing that Nicaragua was already communist and should therefore not receive U.S. aid and liberals generally supporting the aid proposal.[2] The aid was not approved until July 1980 and Congress added a requirement that no aid could be disbursed until the president certified that the Nicaraguan government was not "aiding, abetting, or supporting acts of violence or terrorism in other countries." After some internal debate over the question of Sandinista support for the Salvadoran rebels, the Carter administration issued the necessary certification in September 1980. In the closing months of that year, however, the Sandinista government's assistance to the Salvadoran rebels in their preparations for the January 1981 "final offensive" caused a distinct cooling of relations with the outgoing Carter administration, including a suspension of U.S. aid in January 1981.

### The Reagan Administration Against the Sandinistas [3]

U.S.-Nicaraguan relations quickly went from bad to worse when President Reagan took office. Reagan and his top foreign policy advisers believed the Sandinistas were devout Marxist-Leninists and saw a Sandinista Nicaragua as a second Cuba working as a proxy for the Soviet Union and Cuba to spread revolution throughout Central America. For the early Reagan team, the Carter administration's attempt to mediate the Nicaraguan conflict had been a policy of weakness and stupidity that was directly responsible for the fall of Somoza. They thought the Carter administration's attempt at constructive engagement with the post-July 1979 Nicaraguan government had been a dangerous waste of time. In their view, Sandinista moderation could not be bought by the United States; it was a contradiction in terms. President Reagan moved rapidly toward a policy of open hostility with Nicaragua. The Nicaraguan support of the Salvadoran rebels was singled out by administration officials in the early months of 1981 as a key factor in the Salvadoran civil war and Nicaragua was featured heavily in the administration's barrage of alarmist calls about the communist threat to Latin America.

The linchpin of the Carter policy of constructive engagement had been the economic aid relationship. Although U.S. aid had been suspended in 1981, the suspension was an informal one that did not necessarily signify the end of an aid relationship. On April 1, 1981 the Reagan administration signaled the end of constructive engagement by formally terminating economic aid. The termination was made despite strenuous arguments by U.S. ambassador to Nicaragua Lawrence Pezzulo (a Carter administration holdover) that the aid relationship was a key lever of influence as well as evidence that the flow of arms from Nicaragua to the Salvadoran rebels had diminished significantly or even stopped since January. The official U.S. statement explaining the aid termination reflected the ambiguity of the issue of Nicaraguan assistance to the Salvadoran rebels and the administration's determination to take a hard-line approach no matter what the evidence of Nicaraguan external interventionism:

This Administration has made strong representations to the Nicaraguans to cease military support to the Salvadoran guerrillas. Their response has been positive. We have no hard evidence of arms movements through Nicaragua during the past few weeks, and propaganda and some other support activities have been curtailed. We remain concerned however that some arms traffic may be continuing and that other support very probably continues.[4]

While the early Reagan administration was taking a hostile public stance toward the Nicaraguan government, it was also working behind the scenes to develop what would become the main element of its policy, the Nicaraguan contras. Since 1980, Colonel Gustavo Alvarez Martínez, who was head of the Honduran national police, had been providing training facilities and encouragement to small groups of Nicaraguan ex-National Guardsmen who had survived the Sandinista revolution and were beginning to form paramilitary units in Honduras. In 1981 the CIA joined forces with Alvarez, agreeing to a three-way plan to build up the contras whereby the CIA would provide financial support, Honduras the territorial base, and Argentina the military training. The CIA, as well as the hard-liners at the White House and elsewhere, talked up the contra plan within the inner circle of the Reagan Latin America policy team and rapidly transformed the initiative into established policy. On November 17, 1981 President Reagan approved a $19 million program of covert assistance to the nascent contras.

It is not clear what President Reagan and his advisers thought the contras would accomplish at the time the program was started. The contras were much too small for anyone to believe that they might be able to topple the Sandinistas. Most U.S. officials behind the program probably believed the contras would at least shake the Sandinistas up and that it was the only feasible way of hurting the Sandinistas seriously. The administration sold the contra aid program to the congressional intelligence committees as a means of interdicting arms passing from Nicaragua to El Salvador. Some U.S.

officials in Washington may even have believed the interdiction rationale; those officials involved with the contras on the ground, however, knew it was irrelevant, that the contras aimed to strike directly at the Sandinistas.

The administration, or more specifically, Assistant Secretary Thomas Enders, did make a stab at a negotiated agreement between the United States and Nicaragua in 1981. Enders saw the contra initiative gaining momentum and decided to give negotiations a try before accepting what he saw was going to be a policy of armed confrontation. He flew to Managua in August and in a series of high-temperature meetings with the Sandinista commandantes, outlined a proposal for a bilateral security accord in which Nicaragua would agree to limit the size of its military, terminate military ties with Soviet bloc countries, and cease aiding the Salvadoran rebels. In return, the United States would offer a commitment not to use force against Nicaragua, consider doing something to limit Nicaraguan exiles undergoing paramilitary training in Florida and elsewhere, and consider resuming economic aid. Enders's initiative failed because of uncertainties on both sides about the value of such an agreement.

In 1982 and 1983 the administration's Nicaragua policy passed from formulation to implementation. The main contra group, the Nicaraguan Democratic Forces (FDN) led primarily by ex-National Guardsmen, grew rapidly in size and became militarily active in Nicaragua. The CIA also supported some other, smaller contra forces including Miskito Indian groups and the Democratic Revolutionary Alliance (ARDE), led by the ex-Sandinista hero Eden Pastora. Nicaragua was transformed into a battleground as these different groups engaged in sporadic but bloody attacks on a wide range of military and nonmilitary targets. The administration complemented the contras' military efforts with a series of joint U.S.-Honduran military exercises near the Nicaraguan-Honduran border to project a strong U.S. military presence in the region and intimidate the Sandinistas. Additionally, the administration developed economic and political measures to complement the military policy. The administration began to exert economic pressure against Nicaragua by lobbying the multilateral development banks and West European governments to stop giving loans and aid to Nicaragua. And in the political sphere, the administration stepped up its verbal attacks on the Sandinistas and its efforts to isolate Nicaragua diplomatically from other Central American countries.

As the contra war heated up, Democrats in Congress became concerned about the contra aid program (which was still being justified merely as an interdiction effort) and began raising questions about its true goals. In late 1982, Congress enacted the first of a series of restrictions on contra aid (sponsored by Rep. Edward Boland, D-Mass., chairman of the House Intelligence Committee) prohibiting covert actions for the purpose of overthrowing the Nicaraguan government and stipulating that contra aid be used solely to interdict arms shipments from Nicaragua to the Salvadoran rebels. Congress did not, however, set up any mechanism for ensuring that this restriction be obeyed, and the contra program went ahead along the same lines as before—building the contras up as a force that could penetrate into Nicaragua to destroy selected targets and harass the Sandinista army.

A second abortive round of negotiations between the United States and Nicaragua (more accurately, an exchange of communications) toward a security accord took place in 1982. Already by this time the hard-liners had wrested control of the U.S. negotiating effort away from Enders and insisted that the United States would sign an accord only if Nicaragua agreed to accept democracy in addition to limiting its external policies. Adding democracy to the list of U.S. conditions was a qualitative hardening of the U.S. position and as discussed later in this chapter, proved to be a powerful obstacle to achieving a bilateral accord.

In the first half of 1983, reports of the growing scale of the contras' military ventures began to appear in the United States, prompting a major congressional debate about whether the administration was complying with the 1982 Boland amendment and more generally, whether the United States should be supporting the contras. In July, and again in November 1983, the Democratic-controlled House of Representatives voted to end all covert operations in Nicaragua. The Republican-controlled Senate, however, refused to go along with the House measure. In late November 1983, a compromise favorable to the administration was reached. Congress approved the use of up to $24 million of military assistance for the contras for 1984 but prohibited the use of CIA contingency funds or reprogrammings. This $24 million was the first openly approved

U.S. aid to the contras, transforming the program from a covertly funded covert operation to an openly funded one.

A Latin American peace initiative was launched in early 1983 by Mexico, Costa Rica, Venezuela, and Panama. The Contadora initiative, as it came to be known, aimed at a Central American regional accord rather than a bilateral U.S.-Nicaraguan accord. The Contadora initiative was popular with U.S. liberals, West Europeans, and Latin Americans. It was never genuinely supported by the administration, however, despite many protestations to the contrary. The hard-liners in the administration wanted a multilateral peace accord even less than a bilateral one and used the administration's influence with Honduras and El Salvador to head off any possibility of success. The moderates were also not favorable toward the Contadora initiative because they believed that only a bilateral U.S.-Nicaraguan accord would solve U.S. security concerns.

The U.S. invasion of Grenada in October 1983 scared the Nicaraguan government. The Sandinista commandantes wondered if they were the next target on President Reagan's list and were disposed to consider seriously a bilateral security accord with the United States. The administration, however, saw the post-Grenada period as a time to press Nicaragua harder, not to work toward a peace agreement. The core U.S. interagency policy group on Nicaragua devised a plan for the CIA to mine Nicaragua's harbors, with the intention of stepping up economic pressure, and boosting the contras' profile. President Reagan approved the plan in December 1983 and the mines were laid in several stages in early 1984. A number of ships entering Nicaragua's harbors were damaged but international shipping to Nicaragua did not come to a halt or even slow down significantly. The main effect of the mining program was its harm to the contra cause. The administration did not adequately brief the Senate and House Intelligence Committees on the CIA mining operation. When the U.S. press reported in April 1984 that the CIA, and not the contras (as Congressmen had believed), was responsible for the mining,[5] both Republican and Democratic congressmen were outraged at the secret expansion of the U.S. role. The Senate and House passed resolutions condemning the mining and in October 1984 Congress cut off assistance to the contras altogether with an amendment that seemed absolutely clear:

No funds available to the Central Intelligence Agency, the Department of Defense, or any other agency or entity of the United States involved in intelligence activities may be obligated or expended for the purpose or which would have the effect of supporting, directly or indirectly, military or paramilitary operations in Nicaragua by any nation, group, organization, movement, or individual.[6]

After the harbor mining fiasco, the administration's policy passed through a brief period, roughly the second half of 1984, when the moderates asserted themselves strongly. The context of this interlude was not only the congressional cutoff of contra aid but the broader framework of impending presidential elections in both Nicaragua and the United States. The elections in Nicaragua were a political opening that the moderates believed the United States could exploit to bolster civic opposition in Nicaragua. The elections in the United States created pressure on the administration to tone down its policy and give at least the appearance of moderation. Despite frenetic lobbying efforts by the administration, the contra policy remained unpopular with the U.S. public, which was deeply skeptical of murky, drawn-out conflicts in areas of uncertain importance to the United States and between contestants who were not clearly identifiable as good and evil. Reagan's political managers, particularly James Baker and Michael Deaver, were worried that the Democrats might score points by tagging Reagan as a warmonger and in early 1984 instructed the State Department to pursue negotiations to ensure that the administration was seen as interested in a peaceful solution.[7]

The State Department, led on this issue by Assistant Secretary Langhorne Motley (who had replaced Thomas Enders) and his deputy Craig Johnstone, utilized this opportunity to open new negotiations with Nicaragua on a bilateral security accord. The negotiations were launched by Secretary of State Shultz himself when Shultz met with the Nicaraguan leader Daniel Ortega on June 30, 1984 and agreed to a series of talks between U.S. Special Negotiator Harry Shlaudeman and Nicaraguan Deputy Foreign Minister Victor Tinoco in Manzanillo, Mexico. The State Department's goal was a security accord in which the Sandinistas would agree to cease supporting the Salvadoran rebels, limit the size of their army, and cut ties with the Soviet bloc. At the hard-liners' insistence, however, internal democratization of Nicaragua remained on the list of U.S. demands. Shlaudeman and the State Department looked hard for a way to finesse the democracy issue, knowing that if faced directly it would be an insurmountable obstacle. The hard-liners watched the moderates with an eagle eye, repeatedly vetoing concessions on the democracy condition, in effect putting the moderates in the position of having to negotiate with both the Sandinistas and the hard-liners themselves.[8] The negotiations did not progress well, because the Sandinistas were not willing to negotiate about their internal political system and because it became apparent that the hard-liners were not going to permit the moderates to make any significant concessions. In September, the bilateral negotiations got tangled up with apparent movement on the Contadora front. The administration grew frustrated with the bilateral negotiations and essentially lost interest in them, although they continued until January 1985. The Contadora process turned out not to be bearing fruit either and by the end of 1984 the prospects of either a bilateral or multilateral agreement had again faded away.

At the same time they were pushing the Manzanillo negotiations, the moderates were also trying to ensure that the major Nicaraguan opposition parties would participate in the November 1984 elections. The administration was divided over the elections. The hard-liners believed that the Sandinistas, as communists, would never permit free elections and that participation by the opposition risked legitimating a fraudulent process. The moderates doubted that the Sandinistas would permit fair elections but thought the elections were an opportunity for the opposition to make its views known in Nicaragua and to force the Sandinistas to compete seriously in an electoral campaign. While the hard-liners were sending signals to the opposition that the White House did not favor their participating in the elections, the moderates were playing a supporting role in a grueling set of negotiations between Arturo Cruz, the leading potential opposition candidate, and the Sandinistas over electoral procedures and conditions. Cruz and the Sandinistas were unable to reach an agreement and the main opposition parties boycotted the election.

Whether the hard-liners were directly responsible for the opposition's decision not to participate is unclear; unquestionably, however, they were a negative influence counteracting the moderates' positive push. The elections were held as scheduled. The Sandinistas won 67 percent of the vote, a surprisingly weak showing given the nonparticipation of the major opposition groups. Although there was no evidence of outright or systematic vote fraud, the Reagan administration denounced the elections as "a Soviet-style sham," and a "farce."[9]

The failure of the 1984 negotiations and of the attempted accord between Cruz and the Sandinistas ended the moderates' attempt to redirect U.S. policy. The hard-liners reasserted complete control over the policy in late 1984 and maintained it for the rest of the Reagan presidency. The hard-liners kept the policy focused on one objective—building up the contras into a force capable of seriously threatening the Sandinistas. After the setback on contra funding in 1984, the administration mounted a massive campaign to secure congressional approval for new contra aid in 1985 and 1986. The campaign was plagued by the continued lack of public support for a hard-line policy. Despite intensive lobbying by President Reagan, the effort netted only $27 million of nonlethal or "humanitarian" aid in 1985. In 1986 the administration mounted the single largest congressional lobbying effort of the entire Reagan presidency. After a tortuous, see-saw struggle, Congress approved $100 million of aid ($70 million military, $30 million nonlethal) for fiscal year 1987.

Frustrated by the inconsistent support of the contras in Congress, the administration created a vast secret supply network run by the National Security Council staff, particularly Lt. Col. Oliver North, with the assistance of the CIA.[10] This alternative assistance effort began in early 1984, in the wake of the bitter congressional battles over contra aid of 1983 and in response to the administration's realization that the $24 million of military aid approved in late 1983 was going to run out in mid-1984 and was unlikely to be replenished by Congress. National Security Adviser Robert McFarlane and CIA Director William Casey approached or directed other administration officials to obtain funds from South Africa, Israel, and Saudi Arabia. Saudi Arabia came through with $1 million a month for the contras beginning in mid-1984, enough to keep the contras at least operational. With the backing of his bosses at the NSC (first

McFarlane and then McFarlane's successor, Admiral John Poindexter) and with the active assistance of the CIA, Oliver North used this funding as a base on which he built up a major military resupply program for the contras.

The resupply program, which operated from mid-1984 to late 1986, grew into an extremely large, complex operation, funded not only by Saudi and other third country donations, but also the proceeds of secret U.S. arms sales to Iran and the cash generated by a large private fundraising operation North masterminded with the assistance of various private individuals including Carl "Spitz" Channell and Richard Miller. The resupply operation to the contras consisted of frequent, sometimes daily air drops of lethal materials (guns, munitions, grenades, mortars, etc.) as well as the direct furnishing of cash, military intelligence, and logistical advice by North or by his associates whom he brought into the operation (private citizens such as retired Air Force General Richard Secord and Robert W. Owen). North and Poindexter were well aware of the 1984 Boland amendment prohibiting U.S. government assistance to the contras but believed that it did not apply to the National Security Council because it specified only "the Central Intelligence Agency, the Department of Defense, or any other agency or entity of the United States involved in intelligence activities." The NSC's contra resupply program provided the contras with the assistance necessary to keep the contras fighting between the time Congress-approved aid ran out in 1984 and the resumption of official military assistance in late 1986.

Despite the contra resupply operation and the imposition of a total U.S. trade embargo against Nicaragua in 1985, the contras fared poorly against the Nicaraguan army in 1985 and 1986. The contras had grown in the early 1980s into a substantial force, around 10,000 persons, and in 1984 had penetrated major portions of northern Nicaragua and inflicted considerable damage to military and civilian installations. Faced with the growing contra threat, the Nicaraguan military undertook a serious reorganization and retraining effort and by 1985 was operating much more effectively against the contras. The contras were also hurt by the decreased quantity and regularity of supplies from the United States that resulted from the cutoff of official aid and their dependency on North's smaller resupply program. Although the contra war caused great damage to

Nicaragua in these years and resulted in the loss of many Nicaraguan lives, it did not threaten the existence of the Nicaraguan government.

In late 1986, the Reagan administration's Nicaragua policy began to unravel. The secret arms sales to Iran and then the underground contra resupply program came to light in November, creating the biggest public scandal, and the greatest crisis, of the Reagan presidency. Oliver North and John Poindexter were fired and the resupply operation was shut down, although the $70 million of military aid that Congress had approved earlier that year was just becoming available then and so the contras were actually as well or better off than before. Special House and Senate committees and an independent prosecutor, Lawrence Walsh, initiated lengthy, detailed investigations of the Iran-contra affair and the Reagan administration's entire foreign policy machinery was thrown into a cautious, even static mode. The revelations about the sordid and clandestine NSC-led contra resupply operation confirmed the doubts many Americans had about the U.S. procontra policy. The Iran-contra affair also made clear the administration's contempt for Congress and shattered the fragile congressional consensus on contra aid that the administration had managed to build. The retaking of the Senate by the Democrats in November 1986 further dimmed the prospects for future U.S. military assistance to the contras.

In the wake of these events, many observers believed the contras were finished in Washington and consequently finished in the field as well. The Reagan administration refused to give up, however, particularly since with the infusion of the new U.S. military assistance in late 1986 and early 1987 the contras were fighting more effectively than ever before. Aware that a frontal assault on Congress for more military aid was unlikely to succeed, the administration looked for more creative solutions and settled on the idea of a peace gambit. In July 1987 the administration approached House Speaker James Wright with the idea of Wright participating in the development of a peace plan with Nicaragua under which a cease-fire would be negotiated, all outside military aid to both Nicaragua and the contras would be terminated, and Nicaragua would hold elections and institute a reintegration of the contras into Nicaraguan society. The administration's idea was that Nicaragua would reject the proposal (the administration was certain that the Nicaraguan government would never agree to elections) and that Nicaragua's rejection of a plan that Wright had helped shape would enlist Wright's crucial assistance in securing congressional approval for further military aid to the contras.

The Reagan-Wright plan was formally proposed on August 5, the day before the five Central American presidents met in Guatemala to continue negotiations on a regional security accord that President Oscar Arias of Costa Rica had proposed in early 1987. The administration also did not expect Nicaragua to agree to the regional accord, but contrary to those expectations, the five presidents announced on August 7 that they had signed a regional peace accord. Unlike the administration, Wright had believed in the possibility of both the bilateral and multilateral accords and viewed them as complementary. To the great distress of the administration, he used the initial progress made with Nicaragua on the bilateral accord as a tool to help Arias forge an agreement on the regional accord. The regional accord, known as Esquipulas II, called for all the countries of Central America "suffering from the activity of irregular or insurgent groups" to arrange cease-fires, to establish processes of national reconciliation, and "to promote an authentic, democratic, pluralist and participatory process" including national elections in the first half of 1988.[11] The accord also called for an end to military assistance to insurgent groups by any regional or extraregional government.

The Esquipulas II agreement provoked one last, bitter struggle between the hard-liners and moderates in the administration. The moderates liked the plan and wanted the administration to support it by opening direct negotiations with the Sandinistas. The hard-liners opposed it on the grounds that it did not prohibit Soviet military assistance to Nicaragua and that its provisions regarding democratization had no real "teeth" to ensure compliance. As they had on every previous major battle over Nicaragua policy, the hard-liners prevailed; the administration cold-shouldered the plan, despite its extraordinary international popularity (Arias was awarded the Nobel Peace Prize later in 1987). Secretary Shultz announced in September that the administration would seek $270 million for the contras, a clear rejection of the plan. The administration rapidly saw that congressional support for such aid was lacking, however, and presented a pared-down request for $36.2 million (only $3.6 million of which was for military assistance) in January 1988. Congress rejected all further military aid, however, and approved only limited amounts of nonlethal aid to keep the contras together while the regional peace negotiations progressed. The regional negotiations advanced slowly but did not break down. The Sandinistas signed a cease-fire with the contras in February 1988, an accord which again caught the administration by surprise and displeased it. At the end of 1988 the contras were languishing in their base camps, seemingly finished as a fighting force, the administration had lost almost all influence in the ongoing regional peace process, and the Sandinistas remained in power.

## The Unexpected Victory

The Reagan administration's moribund Nicaragua policy fell ungracefully into the lap of the incoming Bush administration. President Bush's instincts toward Nicaragua were very different from President Reagan's. The Reagan policy toward Nicaragua was rooted in the resurgent Cold War paradigm of the early 1980s, in particular the idea that Central America was the hottest flashpoint of an unremitting U.S.-Soviet struggle for global supremacy. The Bush administration, in contrast, came into power at a time of declining U.S.-Soviet tensions. Nicaragua appeared as a distraction from the newly emerging U.S.-Soviet rapprochement, a problem of declining relevance that the Bush administration did not wish to devote much time or energy to. President Bush and his pragmatic Secretary of State, James Baker, were particularly intent on not wasting valuable political capital with the Congress on battles over contra aid. Given this context, their initial approach to Nicaragua was simply to put it on the back burner without actually backing away from the contras to such an extent as to ignite the passions of the right-wing of the Republican party, which remained adamantly committed to a procontra, anti-Sandinista policy.

In February 1989 the five Central American presidents met in Tesoro Beach, Honduras to reinvigorate the Esquipulas II peace process. They surprised the U.S. government by finalizing another bold peace agreement, one focused only on Nicaragua. According to this agreement, known as the Tesoro Beach accord, the Nicaraguan government agreed to institute an open electoral process culminating in national elections no later than February 25, 1990, in return for the joint formulation (between the Central American presidents) of a plan for the demobilization and relocation of the contras. The Bush administration expressed reservations about the accord, particularly the fact that the contra demobilization plan was to be formulated during the electoral process rather than after. But the Bush administration did not react as the Reagan administration had to the Esquipulas II agreement by seeking further military aid for the contras. Instead the administration skillfully negotiated a bipartisan accord with Congress on contra aid whereby the contras would get approximately $4.5 million of nonlethal aid per month through February 1990. The accord was aimed both at putting to rest the troublesome issue of contra funding for at least a year and providing the contras enough funding at least to stay in place until the elections were held. The Bush administration's insistence that the contras not be demobilized until after the elections put the United States partially in conflict with the Tesoro Beach accord. But the Bush administration's implicit willingness to give elections a try in Nicaragua, something the Reagan administration had never been willing to do, moved the United States into a much more positive position with respect to the regional peace process.

The Bush administration, however, was not inclined simply to stand aside and watch the election process unfold. Bush officials scrutinized the early planning for the elections, concluded that the electoral "playing field" was tilted in favor of the Sandinistas, and decided it was up to the United States to do something about it. Covert aid to the opposition was considered but eventually rejected in favor of overt aid. The administration and Congress worked together on an aid package and in October 1989 Congress passed a bill that appropriated up to $9 million to assist opposition political groups. The National Endowment for Democracy was to administer most of the aid and divide it between direct assistance to the National Opposition Union (UNO) and civic education projects by nonpartisan groups (which were in fact generally dominated by UNO supporters). Owing to bureaucratic delays in the U.S. government and to obstacles put up by the Nicaraguan government, very little aid was actually disbursed to UNO until the closing weeks of the campaign.

The contra issue rocked the electoral process. In mid-1989 the contras said they would ignore the Tesoro Beach accord and began reinfiltrating Nicaragua and resuming military actions. President Daniel Ortega suspended the nineteen-month-old Sapao cease-fire agreement in November and the fighting surged. The electoral process held together, however, and on February 25, 1990, the elections were successfully held. They were among the most extensively observed elections in history, with over 2,000 persons from the United Nations, the Organization of the American States, the United States, Western Europe, and Latin America observing every aspect of the process. Contrary to the predictions of most pollsters, UNO decisively defeated the Sandinistas. And contrary to the expectations of many U.S. conservatives, President Ortega accepted the results and peacefully handed over the reins of power to Violeta Barrios de Chamorro, the leader of UNO, on April 25, 1990. President Chamorro took office and immediately faced monumental challenges, including reconstructing the nearly defunct Nicaraguan economy, forging a process of political reconciliation in a society riven by ten years of civil war, and dismantling the Sandinistas' control of the military and of most civil institutions. The early months of Chamorro's rule were marked by civil tensions and conflict, highlighting the magnitude of the past conflict and the present challenge. Chamorro demonstrated some strong political skills, however, and Nicaraguans held to the hope that their country might at last be moving toward an era of peace and democracy.

## The Rhetorical Web

The Reagan administration's Nicaragua policy was haunted from start to finish by the inescapable fact that it was not widely supported by the U.S. public. A majority of Americans did not believe that the United States should be in the business of trying to overthrow a sovereign government. They were also not persuaded that the Sandinista government presented a grave security threat to the United States. Nor did they accept that the contras were "freedom fighters." The Reagan administration labored mightily to sway the U.S. public on Nicaragua, spinning a rhetorical web around its policy so tangled that the truth was often indiscernible. The publicity campaign grew with each congressional vote on contra aid and became a massive, well-orchestrated effort directed by the Office of Public Diplomacy for Latin America in the State Department, an office created especially for that purpose.

One part of the rhetorical web was the administration's effort to portray the Sandinistas as evil incarnate and the Sandinista threat to the United States as a dire security concern. Perhaps no government in the world was described in such negative terms by the Reagan administration as was Nicaragua. What was a moderately repressive government that permitted a limited political opposition and a beleaguered private sector was denounced as "a communist reign of terror" that had transformed Nicaragua into a "totalitarian dungeon." [12] Administration officials tore into the Sandinista government at every opportunity, straining to outdo each other in the harshness and colorfulness of the attacks. The administration's breathless hyperbole about the Nicaraguan government was the inverse of its overstated declarations about the democratic achievements of El Salvador, Honduras, and Guatemala.

The administration combined its condemnations of the Nicaraguan government with a stream of doomsday messages about the threat Nicaragua posed to the United States. Nicaragua was cast as the agent of the Soviet Union and Cuba, spearheading "a campaign to subvert and topple its democratic neighbors." [13] A sporadic flow of arms and supplies from Nicaragua to El Salvador was not a limited security issue of primary relevance to El Salvador but the first step of an advancing red tide that threatened to wash across Central America into Panama on the south and Mexico on the north. Reagan administration officials punctuated speeches on Latin America with references to the number of miles between Nicaragua and various cities in the United States, ranging from Harlingen, Texas to Baltimore, Maryland, as proof of the gravity of the Nicaraguan threat to the United States's own territorial security. Not since the Vietnam War did U.S. officials articulate such classic Cold War statements of the domino theory and the red threat to America. In case the threat of a Soviet-sponsored, Cuban-Nicaraguan takeover of the United States was not enough to persuade Americans to support contra aid, the administration worked up a variety of other threats posed by Nicaragua, including an outpouring of Nicaraguan refugees, Sandinista collusion in international drug trafficking, and the persecution of the Nicaraguan Jewish population.

The administration also struggled to create a publicly acceptable characterization of its policy toward Nicaragua. In the early 1980s, the administration portrayed U.S. policy as an effort to stop Nicaragua from aiding the Salvadoran rebels, in other words, justifying its own interventionism as a means of fighting interventionism by Nicaragua. In August 1983, for example, President Reagan declared, "And anything that we're doing in that area [Nicaragua] is simply trying to interdict the supply lines which are supplying the guerrillas in El Salvador." [14] Gradually the administration began deemphasizing the interdiction rationale and replacing it with a democracy rationale. The abandonment of the interdiction rationale reflected the administration's inability to make a convincing public case that any significant quantity of arms was flowing to the Salvadoran rebels from Nicaragua. It also stemmed from the fact that as the contras became militarily active it was increasingly obvious their mission had nothing to do with interdicting arms.

Promoting democracy became the primary stated goal of the administration's Nicaragua policy from 1984 on, for reasons discussed below. Administration officials constantly declared that what the administration sought in Nicaragua was democracy. In 1984, for example, President Reagan said, "And we've made it plain to Nicaragua—made it very plain that this [U.S. aid to the contras] will stop when they keep their promise and restore a democratic rule and have elections." [15] This notion of *restoring* democracy, a staple of administration statements on Nicaragua, was somewhat curious in that democratic rule had never existed in Nicaragua and thus could not simply be restored. In 1987, President Reagan formulated the demand in simple terms, "All we're asking for is true democracy." [16] This too was a puzzling phrase; it implied that developing a "true democracy" in a country that has never been democratic is a minor concession that a government can make overnight rather than a gradual, profound process that has taken most countries generations or even centuries to achieve.

Throughout the 1980s, President Reagan and his advisers were often asked whether the administration was aiming to overthrow the Nicaraguan government. In the early 1980s, Reagan repeatedly denied that the United States sought overthrow. In 1983, for example, he said, "We are not doing anything to try and overthrow the Nicaraguan government."[17] After he was reelected, however, and the hard-line policy on Nicaragua moved into high gear, the categorical denials turned into coy affirmations. In 1985, he remarked that the United States wanted to remove the Nicaraguan government and when asked to explain what he meant, replied, "Well remove in the sense of its present structure, in which it is a Communist totalitarian state."[18] He declared that the administration was willing to stop funding the contras "if the present government would turn around and say, all right, if they'd say, Uncle."[19]

The administration insisted that it was interested in a negotiated solution, despite the hard-liners' relentless attempts to torpedo any proposed negotiated agreement. Reagan stated in 1986 that "the United States will support any negotiated settlement or Contadora treaty that will bring real democracy to Nicaragua."[20] "Real democracy" was of course the catch. The administration did not believe that Sandinista rule could ever be democratic and by "real democracy" meant non-Sandinista rule. The administration thus could not stomach the prospect of any negotiated agreement unless it clearly pointed to an end to Sandinista rule. And the Sandinistas were not about to sign any such agreement. For all intents and purposes, therefore, the administration was not interested in a negotiated solution.

A crucial section of the rhetorical web was the portrayal of the contras as the sole means to a democratic outcome in Nicaragua. This entailed selling the contras as a democratic force to a skeptical Congress and U.S. public. The administration approached this challenging task by developing the notion that the contras were not a group of ex-National Guardsmen but people who had fought against Somoza only to have their revolution stolen by the Sandinistas. In 1984 Reagan asserted, "Many of the people now fighting as contras are elements of this revolution."[21] Later that year he carried that remarkable proposition further: "No, actually, what those people are, those so-called guerrillas, or contras, as they're called in Nicaragua, are actually—and for the most part, people who were participants in the original revolution and then had that revolution stolen from them by the Communist Sandinistas."[22] By 1985 it was no longer "many" or "most," Reagan declared flat out, "The contras are made up and led by revolutionaries who fought against Somoza."[23]

These statements were serious distortions of the facts. Many of the contra rank-and-file, particularly after the early 1980s, were Nicaraguans not associated with the National Guard. But they were not, in the main, revolutionaries who had fought against Somoza. Moreover, the military leadership of the core fighting force of the contras, the FDN, was dominated by former officers in Somoza's National Guard. Some former high-level Sandinistas and anti-Somocista figures left Nicaragua and associated themselves with the contra leadership in the early and mid-1980s. To combat the problem of the contras' Somocista public image in the United States, the administration engineered the creation of a political directorate for the contras made up of some of these persons and attempted to graft it onto the FDN to give the contras some democratic credibility. The political directorate never gained real authority over the FDN and remained largely a public relations effort.

The administration was not content simply to distort the political origins and character of the contras, it portrayed them as a heroic democratic force, a group of "freedom fighters" struggling to light the lamp of liberty in Nicaragua. President Reagan pulled out all rhetorical stops in praising the contras, declaring that they were the "moral equal" of the U.S. Founding Fathers and that he was in fact "a Contra, too."[24] The contras were analogized not only to the Founding Fathers but to whichever other famous rebel groups the administration thought might strike a responsive chord with the U.S. public, including the French Resistance and the Hungarian Freedom Fighters. Aside from the obviously great differences with respect to political character between the contras and these historic groups, these overwrought comparisons shared a common conceptual error: each of the historic groups to which the contras were compared had struggled against a foreign occupying army for political independence whereas the contras were fighting a civil war. The administration used these skewed analogies, not simply to glorify the contras, but implicitly to portray the Sandinistas as an illegitimate outside force occupying Nicaragua.

## The Uses of Prodemocracy Rhetoric

Promoting democracy was the defining strand of the rhetorical web the Reagan administration spun around its Nicaragua policy. To understand the utility of making democracy the primary stated goal of the policy, it is useful to look at the incorporation of democracy into the public policy formulation. When Enders negotiated with the Sandinista commandantes in August 1981 he emphasized security issues and made little or no reference to Nicaragua's internal political practices. Upon his return to Washington he was harshly criticized by the hard-liners for this approach. The hard-liners contended that the "internal democratization" of Nicaragua must be one of the elements of any bilateral accord. Their insistence on democracy was a crucial point. The hard-liners, like the moderates, were focused in 1981 on Nicaragua's aid to the Salvadoran rebels. Unlike the moderates, however, they saw Nicaragua's external policies as a symptom of a problem and considered treatment of the symptom alone to be futile. They believed that the problem was the presence of a leftist regime in Managua and that U.S. policy should be aimed at getting rid of that regime. Openly advocating the ouster of the Sandinistas was not a publicly acceptable course. Advocating the internal democratization of Nicaragua became their fallback. The hard-liners were convinced that the Sandinista regime was communist and as such was incompatible with democracy. Pressing for democracy in Nicaragua thus was a way of expressing their aim of ousting the Sandinista regime in a principled and publicly acceptable manner.

The moderates understood the hard-liners' reasoning and saw that making democracy in Nicaragua a condition for a negotiated agreement was likely to foreclose any possibility of reaching one. They resisted including democracy in the list of U.S. negotiating points, resulting in an internal tug-of-war over the issue in late 1981 and early 1982. The hard-liners won out. In April 1982, democracy in Nicaragua appeared on the list of negotiating points the United States gave to Nicaragua.[25] And in a major speech on Nicaragua policy in September 1982, Thomas Enders declared that "the development of democracy, or at least, "pluralist institutions" in Nicaragua was obligatory for regional peace.[26]

It is interesting to note that whereas in El Salvador the inclusion of democracy as a stated goal of U.S. policy represented a victory of the moderates over the hard-liners; in Nicaragua the reverse was true. The incorporation of democracy as a condition of a negotiated agreement and later as the primary stated goal of the overall policy represented the consolidation of the hard-liners' hold on the Nicaragua policy. In El Salvador the hard-liners were unenthusiastic about promoting democracy because it appeared to them to be a distraction from fighting communism. In Nicaragua, promoting democracy was a way of articulating their anticommunist aims.

Once settled upon, promoting democracy served at least two important functions as a stated goal of the Nicaragua policy. In the first place it was a useful line of attack for the hard-liners' assaults on various proposed bilateral and multilateral negotiated agreements. In the successive rounds of U.S.-Nicaragua negotiations, the administration's insistence that the democratization of Nicaragua be one element of an agreement consistently constituted the primary stumbling block. In the early 1980s, the Sandinistas were simply unwilling to negotiate over internal political issues. In the mid and late-1980s the Sandinistas became willing to consider an agreement that included democratization provisions provided that U.S. aid to the contras would be terminated before political liberalization measures were implemented. The Sandinistas believed that reducing their military and opening up their political system while the contras were still receiving military funding from the United States was potentially suicidal. The administration (at least the hard-liners) refused to agree to deactivate the contras before the Sandinistas carried out their end of the deal. The result was a stand-off, and no negotiated agreement.

Similarly, the administration objected to the proposed or completed multilateral accords, arising from both the Contadora and Central American regional peace processes, on the basis that their democracy provisions for Nicaragua lacked enforcement "teeth." Given the considerable pressure in Latin America and the United States for the administration to support these multilateral processes, the democracy issue was very useful as a way of putting the administration's fundamental rejection of any negotiated accord in principled terms.

In the second place, the democracy theme was useful in the administration's endless struggle to persuade Congress to approve contra aid. When the contra program first came under congressional and U.S. public scrutiny in the early 1980s, it was heavily criticized as illegitimate interference in Nicaragua's affairs. The administration developed the democracy rationale for the policy and used it ceaselessly in the innumerable rounds of contra aid votes from 1984 on. In so doing, the administration was able to shift the focus and to some extent the terms of the debate over Nicaragua. The focus of attention changed from the Sandinistas' external behavior, especially the much-debated issue of whether Nicaragua was aiding the Salvadoran rebels, to the Sandinistas' internal policies, in particular the degree of political freedom in Nicaragua. And the terms of the debate over contra aid gradually shifted from the early formulation of the issue as "Should the United States be interfering in Nicaragua's internal affairs?" to "How should the United States pressure the Nicaraguan government to accept democracy?"

The key element of that shift was the implicit acceptance of the need and the right of the United States to concern itself with Nicaragua's internal affairs. By hammering away at the issue of the need for democracy in Nicaragua, the administration provoked or obliged opponents of U.S. policy to engage the administration on the issue of Nicaragua's internal political practices. The opponents of the policy tended to be proponents of making human rights and democracy an emphasis of U.S. policy in Latin America (and the world) generally. If they criticized the administration's Nicaragua policy on the grounds of noninterventionism, administration officials would respond, "So you don't care about democracy in Nicaragua?" raising the suspicion of liberals' double standards. In the congressional debates over contra aid the policy's opponents found themselves having to argue, "I support promoting democracy in Nicaragua but I don't think the contras are the right tool" rather than simply, "I oppose the contras as illegitimate interference in Nicaragua's affairs." The appeal of the democracy rationale was enough to break loose a small group of moderate Democrats who had opposed contra aid earlier but in 1985 and 1986 became the administration's key swing votes. They bought into the idea of promoting democracy in Nicaragua and the notion that the contras were a means of pressing the Sandinistas to negotiate seriously on the democracy issue rather than a force aimed at overthrowing the Sandinistas.[27]

Most critics of the Reagan administration's Nicaragua policy dismissed the stated democracy rationale as a cynical, rhetorical cover for a militant anticommunist crusade. In the early 1980s this view was probably correct. The U.S. officials working to build up the contras were concerned with hurting or if possible ousting the Sandinista government and gave little time to the question of what sort of government might replace the Sandinistas. To the extent they did consider the shape of a post-Sandinista Nicaragua, they held to the vague notion of some sort of nonleftist, pro-U.S. regime. From the mid-1980s on the situation was somewhat more complex. The pro-democracy rhetoric associated with the policy grew more intense and began to take on some real meaning. The spread of democracy or at least of elected civilian rule in Latin America in the early 1980s weakened the hard-liners' conviction that the choice facing the United States was between authoritarians and totalitarians and moved them toward an acceptance of the idea that supporting democracy (however narrowly defined) was compatible with an anticommunist policy. In the rest of Central America, as described in chapters 1 and 2, the administration began to combine its initial militant anticommunist policies with a flawed but genuine prodemocracy concern. This interest in democracy spread to the Nicaragua policy as well.

The administration also shifted to some real concern about democracy in Nicaragua because the incessant repetition of the democracy rationale inevitably had some effect on the policymakers' beliefs. It was difficult constantly to say that the United States was trying to promote democracy in Nicaragua without actually starting to believe it. In order to improve the credibility of the democracy rationale the administration had to take actions, such as coaching the contras to adopt a prodemocracy program, which ended up persuading administration officials that they really were promoting democracy.

This is all not to say that the policy was a well-designed prodemocracy policy. The Reagan administration gave only the crudest thought to the question of how democracy might one day come about in Nicaragua, a country with no tradition of democracy, and maintained only superficial, formalistic notions of what Nicaraguan democracy might look like. It is also not to say that the policy was something other than an anticommunist policy in which promoting democracy was entirely a derivative concern. The only reason the Reagan administration expended so much time and energy on Nicaragua was because of the presence of a leftist government there; without the presence of such a government or some other leftist threat, the Reagan administration would not have paid more attention to Nicaragua than it did to Ecuador or Uruguay.

But this analysis of the administration's motivations in Nicaragua is intended to say that many of the U.S. officials involved in the Nicaragua policy from roughly 1984 on sincerely believed that the policy was increasing the chances of democracy. They were misguided in their understanding of how to promote democracy and were motivated primarily by anticommunism, but they believed the policy was prodemocratic.

### *"Who Won Nicaragua?"*

The unexpected victory of UNO in the 1990 elections suddenly framed the ongoing debate in the United States over the validity of the contra policy into the simplistic but convenient formulation, "Who won Nicaragua?" Predictably enough, two contrasting answers, one favorable to U.S. policy and one not, soon dominated the field. Proponents of the U.S. anti-Sandinista policy credited U.S. pressure against Nicaragua as having been the key to the end of Sandinista rule. They held that the contras and the U.S. economic sanctions kept the Sandinistas from consolidating their hold on power and forced the Sandinistas to agree to the elections that proved to be their downfall. Opponents of the U.S. policy rejected this line and argued that Costa Rican President Oscar Arias was the architect of peace in Nicaragua. In their view the 1990 Nicaraguan elections were the fulfillment of Arias's diplomatic crusade, a crusade the Reagan administration had done next to nothing to support.

Neither of these positions is wholly correct; as usual with the many partisan debates over U.S. policy toward Latin America in the 1980s, the answer lies somewhere in between. Oscar Arias certainly deserves credit for forging the regional peace process. Without his determination, persistence, and diplomatic skills, that process would almost certainly not have held together. The two key contributions of the Arias plan, at least with respect to peacemaking in Nicaragua, were its insistence on the idea that Central Americans could solve their problems themselves, independently of the United States, and its emphasis on elections as a viable means of dispute resolution. Moreover, it was precisely those two elements that irritated the Reagan administration most. Reagan administration officials hated to see the initiative and control of the peace process flow out of U.S. hands and into Central American hands. Although the Reagan administration constantly said it was acting in the interests of the Central American countries themselves, it did not trust them to judge their own interests or protect them. The Reagan administration also did not believe in elections as a solution to the Nicaraguan conflict. Reagan officials were certain that the Sandinistas would lose if fair elections were held and were therefore convinced that the Sandinistas would never permit such elections or not respect the results if fair elections were held.

Although Arias's efforts were of great value, they were at most a necessary rather than sufficient condition for the transition away from Sandinista rule. The Arias plan did not exist independently of the U.S. anti-Sandinista policy; it was a response to it. The Nicaraguan government entered into the regional peace negotiations with other Central American governments, and ultimately agreed to hold elections, primarily as a way of ending U.S. pressure against Nicaragua. This point bears careful scrutiny because the relation between U.S. policy and the Nicaraguan government's actions in the peace process was quite complex.

The Nicaraguan government appears to have signed the Esquipulas II accord in August 1987 primarily as a way of heading off any possible further U.S. military aid to the contras. The Sandinistas knew the Reagan administration was gearing up for a last big push with Congress for contra aid. They correctly surmised that support in the United States for military aid was weak enough that if they were engaged in an active regional peace process, Congress would opt to give that process a chance to run its own course and would reject further military aid. The decision to sign reflected a perception of strength more than weakness on the Sandinistas' part. The contras were very weak in terms of their Washington base and the Sandinistas felt secure enough of their own hold on power to take the very limited risk of committing to the democratization provisions of an accord that had no enforcement provisions and was certain to go through a long negotiating phase before being implemented.

Similarly, the Sandinistas signed the 1989 Tesoro Beach accord, the other major agreement concerning elections in Nicaragua, out of the belief that by doing so they could get rid of the contras once and for all and pave the way for a normalization of relations with their Central American neighbors, Western Europe, and even the United States, without putting their own hold on power seriously at risk. The democratization provisions of the accord were fairly definite but at that time (with President Reagan having left office and the contras having run out of external military funding) the Sandinistas did not fear an electoral process. They strongly believed they would win a fair election, having fallen into the familiar trap of authoritarian leaders grossly overestimating their popularity. If they had thought that there was any significant chance they would lose elections, they would almost certainly not have agreed to them. As with Esquipulas II, they signed the accord out of a sense of strength more than weakness.

Thus one can say that the Sandinistas signed the accords that led to the end of their rule because of U.S. pressure, but also because the U.S. policy of pressure never succeeded in seriously threatening the Sandinistas' existence and had only a shaky foundation in the minds of the U.S. Congress and public. The Sandinistas signed the accords precisely because the contras' base of support in Washington was weak and because the Sandinistas saw a way of negating the possibility of further military aid to the contras without putting their hold on power at risk. In fact they misjudged their domestic support and did put their power at risk, but this was a miscalculation, not a major concession resulting from U.S. pressure. Throughout the 1980s the Sandinistas never signed peace agreements out of a sense of weakness or to get rid of powerful U.S. pressure by jeopardizing their hold on power. It is very likely that if the contras had had a strong base of support in Washington the Sandinistas would have signed no peace accords and continued to fight the contras indefinitely.

The Reagan administration's anti-Sandinista policy must not, of course, be judged merely on the basis of its ambiguous political effects on Nicaragua. By far the most important effect of the Reagan policy was the tremendous destruction it wreaked on Nicaragua. The contra war was an off-again, on-again affair but was nonetheless long and bloody. Approximately 30,000 Nicaraguans were killed and tens of thousands others were wounded, a death total higher in per capita terms than that suffered by the United States in the Civil War, World War One, World War Two, the Korean War, and the Vietnam War *combined.*[28] A generation of young Nicaraguans was devastated.

The contra war and U.S. economic sanctions also caused considerable economic destruction. The contras targeted all kinds of infrastructural facilities including power lines, bridges, oil installations, communications equipment, and municipal buildings, resulting in a frequent bleeding of Nicaragua's already scarce capital resources. Fighting the war absorbed huge amounts of government resources (although Soviet military aid went a long way to financing the military effort) and just as importantly, diverted the energies of tens of thousands of young Nicaraguans away from productive economic activity. The war also wreaked havoc on the country's agricultural system, disrupting the production and distribution of food in many areas of the country. By the end of the 1980s Nicaragua was an economic disaster area and had sunk to being the poorest country in the Western Hemisphere except for Haiti. Some of the economic decline was clearly attributable to the statist economic policies of the Nicaraguan government. Unquestionably, however, the contra war and the U.S. economic sanctions had a major effect.

The policy of pressure against Nicaragua also entailed significant costs outside Nicaragua. As mentioned in chapter 2, the policy created serious tensions in Central America, particularly in Honduras and Costa Rica. It also hurt the United States. Despite the Reagan administration's attempts to justify the war on various principled grounds, the inescapable fact was that the U.S. campaign to oust the Sandinistas violated the basic principle of noninterventionism in the international system. The prodemocracy rationale did not hold water; the Reagan administration's root goal was getting rid of a foreign government it did not like, not promoting democracy. And in any case, under international law one country may not impose a particular political system on another country—be it democracy or anything else—by force. The self defense rationale (the argument that the United States was defending El Salvador against Nicaraguan aggression) also lacked substance. Even if Nicaragua's assistance to the Salvadoran rebels was consistent and substantial (an issue that remains under debate) El Salvador's right of self-defense extended only to stopping the flow of assistance. The contra war never had any significant Salvadoran participation and was aimed at ousting the Sandinistas, not interdicting arms passing from Nicaragua to El Salvador.[29]

The U.S. government's flagrant, persistent flaunting of the basic principle of nonintervention badly hurt the international reputation of the United States, particularly in Western Europe. In simple terms, the Reagan administration's crude attempt to bully, harass, and topple the leftist government of a small Latin American neighbor, and the administration's stubborn resistance to any negotiated agreement, made a mockery of President Reagan's attempt to claim the high moral ground for the United States in international affairs and provided a natural focal point for unfriendly countries to score points against the United States in international forums. The Nicaragua policy also hurt the United States internally. The Reagan administration's insistence over eight years in carrying out a policy that was consistently unpopular with a majority of Americans undermined the popular basis for U.S. foreign policy. When the administration veered off into the illicit and clandestine contra resupply program it ended up damaging the tenor of American democracy itself. And the administration's obsessive pursuit of contra aid from the Congress had debilitating effects on Executive Branch-congressional relations.

These many costs, particularly the human and economic costs to Nicaragua, outweighed whatever political benefits to Nicaragua one might attribute to the policy. For the most part, the Reagan administration simply avoided all mention of costs. The countless speeches, publications, and statements on the contra campaign, almost never contained references to the casualty figures in Nicaragua or detailed descriptions of the destruction wrought by the contras. The ardent supporters of the war within the U.S. government were almost completely isolated from the costs imposed on Nicaraguans but felt no hesitation in making judgments about what was good for Nicaragua. With respect to the costs for the United States, administration officials largely just talked them away. They had little respect for international opinion or traditional principles of the international system and were not bothered by the fact that the United States was almost completely isolated in its Nicaragua policy. They had similarly low respect for U.S. public opinion and when confronted with the force of that opinion responded by trying to hide the true policy (that is, the clandestine resupply effort) and devising a massive campaign to manipulate public opinion into conformity with the administration's views.

The Reagan administration attempted to justify its anti-Sandinista policy not only by exaggerating the gains and discounting the costs, but by denying the possibility of any alternatives. A cardinal element of the justificatory structure around the policy was that the United States must use force to try to get the Sandinistas to accept democracy because the Sandinistas, as Marxist-Leninists, would never evolve toward democracy on their own. At every policy juncture between the hard-line approach and the possibility of a more conciliatory line, the hard-liners would shake their heads grimly and say that the Sandinistas, as Marxist-Leninists, would never change unless forced to at gunpoint.

This notion that Marxist-Leninist governments never evolve toward democracy was a hallowed tenet of the Kirkpatrickian dogma that was embraced by the early Reagan administration and that provided the intellectual framework for the Nicaragua policy. The notion was, however, sharply belied by the facts. In the second half of the 1980s, many Marxist-Leninist governments, including the Soviet Union and almost all the countries of Eastern Europe, began acknowledging the need for economic and political liberalization and taking steps, in some cases dramatic ones, in that direction. The Reagan administration hailed this trend and declared loudly that totalitarianism was giving way in the face of the irresistible attractions of democracy and capitalism. Yet when it came to Nicaragua, the administration held to the line that as Marxist-Leninists, the Sandinistas would never accept political or economic liberalization. Thus the odd spectacle occurred of President Reagan emerging from meetings with Soviet President Mikhail Gorbachev, trumpeting the Soviet leader's commitment to change, and then turning around and insisting that the war in Nicaragua must be continued because the Sandinistas, as Marxist-Leninists, would never change. It was as though the subject of Nicaragua was stuck in a time warp;

the administration applied to it a set of ideas that the administration itself was busy abandoning in the rest of the world.

## GRENADA [30]

The path leading to the 1983 U.S. invasion of Grenada began in 1979 when Maurice Bishop and his supporters in the leftist New Jewel Movement ousted Grenadan Prime Minister Eric Gairy and established the People's Revolutionary Government of Grenada. Relations between the Carter administration and the new Grenadan government quickly turned chilly as Bishop aligned Grenada with the Soviet bloc on many foreign policy issues and developed warm relations with Cuba.

When the Reagan administration came into power, U.S.-Grenadan relations turned outright hostile. The Reagan team saw Grenada not as a minor annoyance but an ominous advance of the perceived Soviet-Cuban conspiracy to spread communism through Central America and the Caribbean. Reagan officials warned that Grenada could serve as a transit point for Cuban military forces going to Africa and a staging ground for Cuban subversion of the Eastern Caribbean and even South America. In April 1982, President Reagan charged that Grenada had joined the Soviet Union and Cuba "to spread the virus" of Marxism-Leninism in the region.[31] Grenada was excluded from the Caribbean Basin Initiative. The U.S. military staged a series of provocative military exercises in the Caribbean in the early 1980s. In October 1981, for example, U.S. military forces carried out an exercise code-named, "Amber and the Amberdines" (an obvious reference to Grenada and the nearby Grenadines), which simulated the invasion and temporary occupation of a small Caribbean island. Bishop reacted defiantly to U.S. pressure, repeatedly accusing President Reagan of planning to invade Grenada and citing invasion fears as the reason for the expansion of the Grenadan army.[32]

In 1983, Bishop's hold on power began to weaken in the face of persistent dissension from hard-liners in the New Jewel Movement, who were associated with Deputy Prime Minister Bernard Coard.[33] Possibly with the goal of improving economic relations with the United States, Bishop attempted a rapprochement of sorts with the Reagan administration in mid-1983, traveling to Washington in the hope of meeting President Reagan or Vice President Bush. Reagan and Bush refused to see him, however, and Bishop returned home empty-handed.[34] His initiative provoked even greater divisions within the Central Committee of the New Jewel Movement, leading to his fall.[35] Members of the armed forces placed Bishop under house arrest on October 13 and then murdered him, along with a number of his close associates, on October 19. A Revolutionary Military Council, representing the hard-liners in the New Jewel Movement, proclaimed itself in charge on October 20, and imposed a strict curfew.

Grenada's Eastern Caribbean neighbors were deeply troubled by the brutal political violence in Grenada and, at the prompting of Barbadan Prime Minister Tom Adams, began planning some kind of joint military action against the Revolutionary Military Council. Similar thinking was going on in the White House. The Reagan administration saw the ouster of Bishop as a dangerous turn to the extreme left in Grenada. Reagan officials, uncertain as to who killed Bishop or why, speculated that Cuba, working with Coard, had masterminded the ouster and that Grenada would be opened fully to Cuban influence. The Reagan administration also began wondering about the safety of the approximately 1,000 U.S. medical students on the island and worrying about the possibility of an Iran-style hostage crisis.

In the days after Bishop's murder, the Reagan administration went into a crisis mode, setting up emergency task forces and monitoring the confusing political events in Grenada hour by hour. Plans for a U.S. invasion were suddenly taken out of contingency files and put on the front burner.[36] When the member states of the Organization of Eastern Caribbean States (OECS) decided on October 21 that military action against Grenada should be taken and made an oral request to the White House for U.S. assistance, the momentum toward an invasion became almost irresistible. The following day, Reagan and his top advisers consulted on the situation and arrived at a consensus on the need for a U.S. invasion.[37] And on the day after that, October 23, the OECS sent a written request for U.S. assistance with an intervention against Grenada and President Reagan signed the formal directive for U.S. military action.

The invasion was launched in the early hours of October 25. Several thousand U.S. troops landed on the island (several hundred Caribbean troops participated in a secondary role) encountering unexpectedly strong resistance from Grenadan forces and from the contingent of 500–1,000 Cubans who had been working on the new airport but were armed and willing to fight. It took three days to secure the island, eliminate most of the armed resistance, and evacuate the American students. Exact casualty figures remain elusive; approximately 100 to 200 Grenadans, 50 to 100 Cubans, and 20 to 30 Americans were killed. The military action, although successful, was beset with many serious operational errors, a fact that emerged only much later owing to the restrictions the Pentagon imposed on U.S. journalists trying to cover the invasion.[38]

With the military victory complete, the U.S. government quickly set up a large, active diplomatic and military presence in Grenada to direct a political transition away from the New Jewel Movement and to a constitutional, elected, and pro-U.S. government. The U.S. military and CIA rooted out all visible traces of the People's Revolutionary Army, expelled all Soviet bloc personnel, and established an anticommunist education campaign. An interim government was formed and in conjunction with the United States' presence on the island oversaw the restoration of a constitutional process. Elections were soon scheduled and the electoral campaign got going in 1984, culminating in elections in December of that year. The CIA spent $675,000 on covert political action related to the election (the per capital equivalent of $1.5 billion of campaign spending in the United States) to ensure that a pro-United States leader won.[39] The elections brought Herbert Blaize, a suitably moderate, pro-U.S. politician to the Prime Ministership.

The United States matched its intensive involvement in the political reconstruction of Grenada with a heavy dose of U.S. aid. Grenada received $48.4 million in 1984, an extraordinary amount of aid in per capita terms, equaled that year only by U.S. aid to Israel. The money went to shore up the new government's finances and for large infrastructure projects. Once an elected government was in place the U.S. political and economic involvement was sharply reduced. The U.S. embassy steadily abandoned its proconsul role. The last of the U.S. troops left the island in mid-1985. And the massive U.S. economic assistance fell to $11.3 million in 1985 and zero in 1986.

## *Restoring Order and Democracy*

President Reagan and his advisers initially justified the invasion on two grounds—as a rescue mission for the U.S. students on the island and as a response to the OECS's request to assist in "a joint effort to restore order and democracy on the island of Grenada."[40] Little mention was made in the early statements by President Reagan and Secretary of State Shultz about the Soviet-Cuban issue, as they attempted to cast the invasion in the most nonideological terms possible. This approach generated only mixed support for the invasion within the United States (the invasion was strongly condemned internationally, even British Prime Minister Margaret Thatcher was critical of it).[41]

The Reagan administration quickly shifted gears and began emphasizing the anticommunist basis of the action. In an address to the nation on October 27, President Reagan linked Grenada to the October 23 bombing of the U.S. marine barracks in Lebanon: "The events in Lebanon and Grenada, though oceans apart, are closely related. Not only has Moscow assisted and encouraged the violence in both countries, but it provides direct support through a network of surrogates and terrorists."[42] He stressed that before the U.S. invasion, Grenada "was a Soviet-Cuban colony being readied as a major military bastion to export terror and undermine democracy. We got there just in time."[43] The administration bolstered this argument with documents recovered in Grenada that detailed the numerous contacts and agreements the Grenadan government had been developing with the Soviet bloc.[44] Many Americans were swayed by these arguments, even prominent Democrats such as Representative Tip O'Neill who were initially critical of the invasion, and the invasion gained widespread popular support in the United States.

Of the three public justifications for the invasion—ensuring the safety of the U.S. students, helping the OECS restore order and democracy, and stopping the spread of communism in the region— only the latter reflected the administration's core motivations. The invasion of Grenada was an expression of the Reagan administration's desire to mount a policy of "rollback" against the Soviet Union by toppling communist governments at the periphery of "the Soviet empire" and then working toward the center. As the smallest and most far-flung of the Soviet Union's perceived client states, Grenada was the natural first target for a rollback policy.

The safety of the U.S. students was a real concern, but of much less importance. Although the Reagan administration had no concrete indication that the students were in danger, the situation in Grenada after Bishop's murder was genuinely confusing and was troubling to an administration hypersensitive about avoiding another Iran-style hostage situation. The Iran experience had left such deep scars in the U.S. psyche that it was enough for the vague possibility of another hostage-taking situation to arise for alarm bells to go off in the U.S. government. In any case, the fear of harm to the students was at most the straw that broke the camel's back, not the root motivation of the invasion. The invasion was a military conquest of an unfriendly government; its function as a "rescue mission" was secondary.[45]

The administration's oft-proclaimed interest in promoting democracy in Grenada was at most a very peripheral concern. The administration officials who had long contemplated a military strike against Bishop and then pushed hard for an invasion in October 1983, were motivated by the goal of hitting at the Soviet Union and Cuba and thwarting communism generally. Although they probably believed that ousting the leftists in Grenada would lead to some sort of democratic or at least less repressive government in the country, they were scarcely driven to use military force out of concern over Grenadans' domestic political welfare. And once the United States had conquered the island and undertaken the political reconstruction process, the administration demonstrated a formalistic, or even cynical approach to the establishment of democracy. For the Reagan administration, democracy in Grenada consisted of little more than elections, and the electoral process was closely monitored and even covertly influenced to ensure it produced an appropriately moderate, pro-U.S. government.

*Force and Principle*

The Reagan administration's militaristic efforts in Grenada, unlike those in Nicaragua, were unquestionably responsible for the demise of leftist rule. Also unlike Nicaragua, the costs of the Grenada policy were relatively low. The death toll of several hundred Grenadans, Cubans, and Americans was a large figure for an operation that was intended as an instantaneous knockout, but was far less than the approximately 30,000 people killed in the Nicaraguan war. Not being a protracted guerrilla war, the Grenada invasion also entailed much less economic devastation and sociopolitical disruption. For the Reagan administration, and almost all U.S. conservatives, the invasion of Grenada was inordinately praiseworthy, in fact, one of the greatest U.S. foreign policy successes of the 1980s. And even for many U.S. liberals and moderates, who generally condemned the policy of force in Nicaragua, the clear-cut results, the relatively low costs, and the popularity of the action among Grenadans, persuaded them that the United States had done right.

Within the United States at least, the only persons who rejected the legitimacy of the invasion were that limited minority, which includes the present author, who believe that the United States should adhere to the principle of nonintervention, which is perhaps the most important principle of the postwar international order.[46] It is true that the invasion of Grenada was a sympathetic case for intervention, but at least two points should be noted. First, the U.S. invasion of Grenada was not a humanitarian intervention. The invasion was a geostrategic move to reduce the Soviet-Cuban sphere of influence in the Western Hemisphere. The invasion had positive effects on the Grenadan political system but the U.S. government was not driven to invade Grenada out of a concern for Grenadans. Life in Grenada was troubled in the early 1980s but it was far better than in dozens of countries that the United States showed not the least inclination to invade. Thus, although the invasion may have had positive effects on Grenada, Americans should not indulge in the notion that it was carried out for the Grenadans' sake. The invasion must be defended for what it was, a use of force to advance U.S. geostrategic interests.

Second, even if a strong case can be made in a particular instance that a principle should be bent or ignored, concern for the long-term health of the principle should override short-term considerations. If the United States wants other countries, particularly its adversaries, to obey the principle of nonintervention, its best course is to strengthen that principle by obeying it, not weaken it by violating it and explaining away that violation as a special case. Special cases, even genuinely sympathetic ones, such as Grenada, are the downfall of valuable principles, such as nonintervention. It is for this reason that almost every other major government in the world, including our closest allies, disapproved or openly denounced the invasion, a fact that cannot or at least should not be ignored.

# 4

# DEMOCRACY BY APPLAUSE

## SOUTH AMERICA

The resurgence of democracy was a dominant fact of South American political life in the 1980s. Between 1979 and 1985, Ecuador, Peru, Bolivia, Uruguay, Argentina, and Brazil underwent transitions from military rule to elected civilian governments.[1] And in the late 1980s, Chile and Paraguay joined this group. Every one of the new democratic governments elected in the late 1970s or early 1980s was itself succeeded by an elected civilian government, a notable achievement for a region that has known little democratic continuity. Furthermore, unlike Central America, the political transitions in South America represented unquestionable movement toward democratic rule; they were not simply the construction of weak civilian forms around military-dominated structures of power.

Preoccupied with fighting leftism in Central America, the Reagan administration devoted little time or attention to South America. Next to Nicaragua and El Salvador, South America was little more than a smudge on the Reagan administration's map of Latin America. Whereas the phrase "the Reagan administration's Central America policy" became redolent with meaning and debate, the phrase "the Reagan administration's South America policy" remained an empty concept. What policies the administration did pursue in South America were cast in prodemocracy terms. Throughout the 1980s, administration officials repeatedly affirmed U.S. support for the remarkable democratic trend in South America. Behind this consistent rhetorical line, however, highly varied policies of uncertain prodemocratic content were actually carried out. In the early

**117**

1980s the administration tried to rebuild relations with the military governments of the region on the basis of common anticommunist interests. After this policy failed, the administration shifted to a low-profile, low-energy policy toward South America whose primary characteristic was verbal support, but little else, for the democratic trend.

Despite its low level of interest in and attention to South America, the Reagan administration claimed substantial credit for the return of democracy there. This chapter evaluates that claim, through an analysis of the various policies as well as the rhetorical themes the administration developed in South America. Economic issues, in particular the debt crisis, are an area of focus, more so than in other chapters of this book, owing to South America's persistent economic crisis of the 1980s and the crucial importance of solving that crisis for the continuation of democracy in the region.

## THE POLICY OF RAPPROCHEMENT

During the 1970s, most of South America was under military rule. In many South American countries leftist guerilla movements arising in the late 1960s had been defeated through brutal force in the early and mid-1970s, scarring societies with a legacy of deep political divisions and harsh repression. In the first half of the 1970s, U.S. relations with South America were generally positive, resting on common anticommunist sympathies and a tradition of close U.S. relations with the military elites of the region. During the Carter years, however, relations with a number of South American countries soured. Carter was unsympathetic to the South American military governments and made human rights an important issue in U.S. policy toward the entire region, most notably toward Brazil, Argentina, and Chile. The South American military leaders, accustomed to uncritical friendship from the United States, were greatly annoyed by the criticisms of their domestic behavior emanating from the State Department and White House. Trade issues also produced conflicts. The United States and Brazil, for example, fought over Brazil's nuclear energy program. The United States and

Argentina clashed over Argentina's grain sales to the Soviet Union in the period after the Soviet invasion of Afghanistan. As political and economic relations deteriorated, military cooperation diminished as well. Formal and informal military ties, including training, assistance, and reciprocal visits, declined in the 1970s. The United States fell from being the largest supplier of arms to South America in 1974 to the fifth largest in 1980.[2]

### The Impetus Toward Rapprochement

The incoming Reagan administration was determined to rebuild relations with South America, particularly with Brazil, Argentina, and Chile, three of the most important countries of the region and three countries with which U.S. relations had distinctly worsened in the Carter years. The impetus for rapprochement was rooted in the administration's fervent anticommunist outlook, in particular its acceptance of Jeane Kirkpatrick's arguments regarding the necessity of supporting anticommunist, authoritarian governments in developing countries as alternatives to leftist totalitarian rule. For the early Reagan team, the military leaders of Argentina, Brazil, Chile, Uruguay, and other South American countries were prime examples of the sort of moderate authoritarians who merited United States backing.

Underlying this view of a necessary choice between authoritarians and totalitarians was the notion of a worldwide communist or totalitarian threat. Kirkpatrick and the early Reagan team believed that the entire Third World was a target of Soviet expansionism. Although the Reagan administration saw Central America as the immediate target of Soviet-Cuban expansionism, it also believed that South America (and in fact the whole world) was in danger. A 1981 report by the State Department on "Cuba's Renewed Support for Violence in Latin America," for example, emphasized that Cuba was working in collusion with the Soviet Union to destabilize governments not just in Central America but also in South America, particularly in Argentina, Colombia, and Uruguay.[3]

Related to this central anticommunist orientation in South America were at least two other security considerations that also impelled the early Reagan administration to seek improved relations with the military governments of South America. One was the administration's desire to enlist those governments as allies in its struggle against communism in Central America. The administration hoped that the South American military leaders would lend diplomatic support to U.S. policy and military assistance to forces in Central America fighting against leftist rebels or leftist governments, particularly the Nicaraguan contras. Such assistance would strengthen those Central American forces as well as add a useful Latin American dimension to the United States campaign.[4]

Another motive for rebuilding relations with the South American military governments was a desire to increase U.S.-South American cooperation in protecting the South Atlantic sea lanes. The Reagan administration declared the South Atlantic to be a zone of "growing strategic importance,"[5] a zone the United States had been neglecting. Administration officials warned of possible Soviet plans to block the sea lanes as part of a Soviet global plan to cripple the mineral and energy resources of the West. As the Defense Department stated in May 1981:

> [Soviet] policy is to pinch off the oil of the Middle East from the economic systems of the West and to disrupt and deny the mineral resources of Africa on which the Western industrial nations depend. The Soviet naval presence in the South Atlantic could play a role in their efforts to achieve these goals in the event of a war or major contingency.[6]

Such references by administration officials to the South Atlantic sea lanes became a standard element of statements on South America in 1981 and early 1982. They were a mix of rhetorical overstatement and real concern. Many U.S. military planners were genuinely worried about Soviet threats to the West's mideast oil supply and saw the South Atlantic as one domain, albeit a remote one, of that general threat.[7]

## The Rapprochement Effort

The Reagan administration's rapprochement with the military governments of South America got underway in early 1981 and quickly took shape as a multifaceted effort involving the upgrading of diplomatic contacts, the adoption of "quiet diplomacy" on human rights, and an attempt to reinvigorate U.S.-South American military assistance and cooperation. The upgrading of diplomatic contacts was marked by the reinstitution of regular high-level visits between the United States and South America. Assistant Secretary Enders went to Brazil in July 1981, followed three months later by Vice President Bush.

The Brazilian president, João Figueiredo, came to Washington in May 1982 and President Reagan visited Brazil during his first and only trip to South America in December 1982. Similarly, Argentine President-designate General Roberto Viola was warmly received in Washington in March 1981; Enders went to Argentina soon thereafter. Chilean Foreign Minister René Rojas came to Washington in June 1981, and U.N. Ambassador Jeane Kirkpatrick visited Chile in August 1981.

During the many visits of this sort, administration officials took a friendly tone, stressing the administration's desire to improve relations and emphasizing areas of U.S.-South American accord. The administration made concessions on issues that had hurt relations during the Carter administration. For example, in October 1981 Vice President Bush announced in Brazil that the United States was dropping its earlier opposition to Brazil's purchasing of enriched uranium for its nuclear energy program. In April 1981 the administration reversed the long-standing ban on Export-Import Bank credits to Chile. In July the administration announced that the United States would no longer oppose loans from the multilateral development banks to Argentina, Chile, Paraguay, and Uruguay.[8]

The Reagan administration's abandonment of Carter's high-profile human rights policy and the adoption of a policy of quiet diplomacy on human rights eased the path of rapprochement. President Reagan and his foreign policy advisers strongly disliked Carter's human rights policy; they were convinced that high-visibility human rights criticism of friendly anticommunist governments was counterproductive to U.S. security interests and of minimal utility in obtaining improvements in human rights.[9] The administration quickly substituted what it called a policy of "quiet diplomacy" on human rights. In principle this policy was to consist of low-key, behind-the-scenes advocacy on human rights issues. In practice, at least in the early 1980s, it meant that human rights issues were essentially dropped from the agenda of U.S. relations with Brazil, Argentina, Chile, and other countries led by right-wing military governments.

To the extent administration officials raised the issue of human rights in their visits with officials from the South American military governments, they usually praised the military governments for recent improvements in human rights practices. The State Department actually declared in 1981 that "the Argentine Government has usually facilitated the efforts of various groups and individuals seeking to investigate allegations of human rights abuses," a remarkable statement given the reality of the Argentine military government's stonewalling on human rights.[10] The level of human rights violations in most of the military dictatorships of South America improved in the late 1970s and early 1980s (relative to the high levels of abuses in the early and mid-1970s) because those governments had largely completed their dirty wars against the leftist guerilla movements that had arisen in the 1960s or early 1970s. Reagan administration officials emphasized the decrease in levels of human rights abuses rather than the fact of continuing violations.

Another part of the new human rights policy was trying to ameliorate the treatment of the South American military governments by various international organizations. The administration's decision to stop opposing multilateral development bank loans to various South American countries was formally based on the administration's positive reassessment of the human rights situation in those countries. The administration opposed a 1981 United Nations General Assembly resolution and a 1982 United Nations Human Rights Commission resolution condemning Chile for human rights abuses. In general, the administration attempted to turn the critical attention paid by international human rights organizations, such as the U.N. Human Rights Commission, away from the South American military governments to left-wing governments, particularly Cuba.

Although the early Reagan administration did manage to downgrade the place of human rights in U.S. relations with South America, it quickly discovered that the issue would not simply go away. In early 1981 Jacobo Timerman, an Argentine publisher and journalist, published in the United States a harrowing account of his imprisonment and torture by the Argentine military.[11] Timerman accused the Argentine military of virulent anti-Semitism and described in detail the special punishment inflicted on him because of his Jewishness. The book received much attention in the United States and was a major blow to the administration's attempt to shelve the human rights issue.[12] The furor over Timerman's account came just as the administration's nominee for the post of Assistant Secretary for Human Rights and Humanitarian Affairs was coming up for congressional approval. The nominee, Ernest Lefever, was criticized by liberals as a known opponent of an activist human rights policy. Timerman, a sort of instant symbol in the United States of the value of a strong human rights policy, attended Lefever's hearings before the Senate Foreign Relations Committee. Lefever came under harsh questioning during the hearings and withdrew his name from consideration shortly thereafter. The collapse of the Lefever nomination marked the failure of the early Reagan administration to eliminate human rights as an element of U.S. policy.[13]

An additional element of the policy of rapprochement was an attempt to revitalize U.S. military relations with South America, particularly with Brazil, Argentina, and Chile. In a congressional hearing in 1981, Assistant Secretary Thomas Enders expressed the administration's dissatisfaction with the decline of U.S.-South American military relations under Carter:

> I submit to you that it was not in the U.S. interest. It is not in the U.S. interest for the military services of our closest neighbors and hemispheric allies to be predominantly equipped by other countries. It is not in the U.S. interest to have Latin America's military advice and training come from other countries; and yet, advisers, technicians, and trainers are most likely to come from the major suppliers of military equipment.[14]

The administration wasted no time in reopening lines of personal contact between senior U.S. military officials and their South American counterparts. In the first two months of the Reagan presidency a group of Chilean air force officers, the chairman of Brazil's joint chiefs of staff, and a Bolivian general came to the United States on official visits. In April 1981 U.S. Army General Edward Meyer went to Argentina as the two-way flow of military visits—a mainstay of U.S.-South American relations in the 1960s and early 1970s—got underway again.

The administration also worked to reestablish or increase military assistance to South America. In early 1981 the administration lobbied Congress to lift the ban on military aid to Argentina, a ban imposed during the Carter years on human rights grounds. After considerable debate between congressional liberals and conservatives, the Democratic-controlled House and Republican-controlled Senate reached a compromise. The ban was lifted but the administration could resume military assistance only if it certified that the Argentine government was making significant improvement on human rights.[15] The administration also petitioned Congress in support of a removal of restrictions on military sales and assistance to Chile. The restrictions were removed in December 1981 but with the proviso that any resumption of military assistance required a presidential certification that the Chilean government had, among other things, made significant progress in complying with international human rights.[16] Also in 1981 the administration proposed to establish new International Military Education and Training (IMET) programs for Venezuela and Brazil and to increase the Foreign Military Sales (FMS) programs to Peru and Ecuador. In 1982 the administration requested start-up military training programs of $50,000 each for Argentina, Chile, Paraguay, Uruguay, and Brazil.

The administration's efforts to increase military assistance to South America bore little fruit. In general, Congress was unwilling to approve substantial military assistance to South America. The administration did not dare to provoke Congress's ire (and risk losing congressional support for military assistance to Central America) by certifying the military governments of Argentina or Chile for a resumption of military aid. U.S. military assistance to South America did increase from almost $9 million in 1981 to $43 million in 1984. Almost all of that increase, however, was to Colombia, Ecuador, and Peru, not to Brazil, Argentina, or Chile, the countries the administration was especially interested in. Very minor amounts of training assistance (less than $100,000 per year) went to

Bolivia, Paraguay, Uruguay, and Venezuela, while Brazil, Argentina, and Chile continued to receive no U.S. military assistance.

## Results of Rapprochement

The policy of rapprochement, which as discussed below lasted scarcely beyond 1982, did produce a superficial warming of U.S. relations with the military governments of South America but no substantial reconfiguring of what were basically distant relationships. Brazil, for example, was pleased by the demoting of U.S. human rights policy and the administration's concession on the nuclear issue. But Brazil was little interested in the security issues the Reagan administration hoped to use as the backbone of a new U.S.-Brazil relationship.[17] When Enders and Bush visited Brazil in 1981, they highlighted common U.S.-Brazilian concerns about Soviet-Cuban intervention in Central America, the Soviet threat to the South Atlantic, and Soviet actions in other parts of the world such as Afghanistan and Poland.[18] This security-oriented approach did not take. Brazil was not interested in helping the United States fight communism in Central America. Brazil believed that the conflicts in Central America resulted from local economic and social problems not external intervention. Brazil also had no interest in associating itself with the U.S. efforts to maintain political control over the United States's own "backyard." As to the South Atlantic, Brazil was simply not seriously concerned about a Soviet threat. And with respect to the Reagan administration's general concern with Soviet global expansionism, Brazil had its own foreign policy agenda, oriented toward North-South issues and the efforts of developing countries to get outside the superpower conflict rather than to take sides in it.

What Brazil was interested in vis-à-vis the United States was economics, particularly issues such as trade and debt, where it believed the United States could be of help. Administration officials, such as Enders and Bush on their visits to Brazil, did refer to Brazil and the United States sharing "the common challenge to foster world prosperity"[19] but the administration's policy of rapprochement had no significant economic component. As a result of this mismatch between the administration's and the Brazilian government's interests, the revitalization of the U.S.-Brazil relationship was superficial.

Similarly, the policy of rapprochement led to friendlier relations with Argentina but no deeply rooted change.[20] The Argentine generals were relieved to see the Carter administration depart and happy to receive the enthusiastic embrace of the Reagan team. In 1981 and early 1982 the Argentine military government was struggling to maintain credibility in the face of a teetering economy and growing popular demands for political liberalization. The Reagan administration's friendship was welcome as an extra source of support and legitimation. Unlike the Brazilians, the Argentines were willing to work with the United States in Central America. In cooperation with the CIA and the Honduran military, the Argentine military gave technical and financial assistance to the Nicaraguan contras in the early 1980s. Although this assistance accorded with the fiercely anticommunist outlook of the Argentine military, it was more a kind of political dabbling than a serious commitment to the defeat of leftism in Central America. For the Argentines it was a relatively cheap way to win the favor of the United States and perhaps to develop a kind of secret special relationship with the new Reagan administration.

The superficiality of the revitalized U.S.-Argentine relationship was revealed when the Argentines invaded the Falkland Islands in 1982. The Argentine military leaders, swayed by their friendly relations with the Reagan administration, calculated that the United States might stay neutral in the conflict. To their bitter disappointment, however, the United States sided with Great Britain. The lack of any deeply rooted convergence of interests was laid bare and the friendship between the Reagan administration and the Argentine military government was shattered beyond repair.

The early policy of rapprochement did not get far in Chile. Pinochet, who had ruled Chile since the military's overthrow of Salvador Allende in 1973, was certainly glad to see Carter replaced by Reagan and human rights removed from the top of the U.S.-Chilean bilateral agenda. When Jeane Kirkpatrick went to Chile in August 1981, she was warmly received by Pinochet and her statement that the Reagan administration sought "to fully normalize our relations with Chile" seemed to augur a new era in U.S.-Chilean relations.[21]

In fact, however, no such era was immediately forthcoming. The Reagan administration was unable to overcome the suspicions and objections that Democrats in Congress maintained about Pinochet. Thus, military assistance, the most important element of the normalization process that the Reagan administration envisioned, did not get restarted. And Pinochet, for his part, was unwilling to change his intransigent domestic policies for the sake of achieving concrete improvements in his relationship with the United States (see chapter 5).

## An Exception—Bolivia

An interesting exception to the policy of rapprochement was the administration's policy toward Bolivia. As with other South American military governments, U.S. relations with Bolivia were at a low ebb when the Reagan administration took power. From 1978 to 1980 Bolivia had been attempting to make a transition from military to civilian rule. The process was a difficult one. Bolivia went through three coups, three presidential elections, and six governments between July 1978 and July 1980. After the military intervened in the wake of the June 29, 1980, elections (in which Hernán Siles Zuazo of a center-left coalition won a plurality of votes) and installed a junta led by General Luis García Meza, the Carter administration recalled the U.S. Ambassador to Bolivia and established four conditions for a normalization of relations: improved human rights, a return to democratic rule, effective handling of the economy, and a reduction of drug production and trafficking originating in Bolivia. None of these conditions was met and relations remained distant through the end of the Carter administration.

President García Meza and the Bolivian right anticipated that the Reagan administration would be friendlier and would reestablish normal relations. Yet though some of the hard-liners in the early Reagan team were sympathetic to García Meza, no policy of rapprochement was pursued. In late 1981, Edwin Corr, a career diplomat, was sent down to La Paz as U.S. Ambassador. Corr pursued what was essentially a continuation of the Carter policy—trying to persuade the Bolivian military leaders (García Meza had been ousted in August 1981, General Celso Torrelio had become President in September) to effect a transition to civilian rule, to improve human rights, and reduce drug production and trafficking.[22] Corr worked very actively on behalf of this policy. He saw President Torrelio frequently and pressed him on these issues. He also developed good relations with several close friends of Torrelio and used them as additional channels of influence. As momentum toward a civilian transition grew in 1982, Corr worked behind the scenes to facilitate the transition, arranging meetings between the various political groups who were at loggerheads about the process of transition. In October 1982 the Bolivian Congress (which had been elected in 1980 but had not been convened since the García Meza coup) was convened and named Hernán Siles Zuazo as president.

The United States government was not especially pleased to see Siles Zuazo become President. Siles Zuazo was a leftist whom the administration believed had been supported in exile by various left-wing groups and governments including the PLO and the North Koreans. Nonetheless, the United States supported the return to civilian rule and the U.S. embassy's primary goal became keeping Siles Zuazo in office. Corr worked quietly but actively in conjunction with the AID mission and the U.S. military liaison officers in Bolivia to bolster Siles Zuazo's precarious hold on power. Corr used the U.S. government's extensive contacts with the Bolivian military to ward off coup attempts and tried to secure an increase in U.S. economic assistance to Bolivia. When Siles Zuazo was abducted by military men on June 30, 1984, his wife called Corr in the middle of the night to tell him of the abduction and get his help in preventing the assassination. Corr immediately called several key Bolivian generals, told them to release Siles Zuazo and warned them that "if there's a coup, you'll have problems with the United States."[23] Siles Zuazo was released the next day. He managed to serve until 1985 when the deteriorating economic situation weakened his position so much that national elections were held a year early and Victor Paz Estenssoro of the Historic National Revolutionary Movement became President, in the first peaceful presidential transition in Bolivia in twenty-five years.

Although the U.S. government was not the main factor in the return to civilian rule in Bolivia, it was an important actor whose positive role is widely recognized in Bolivia and by political scientists who have studied this transition.[24] And although the Bolivian transition did not represent the achievement of a working democracy, it was a genuine step in that direction and an improvement over the preceding years of military rule. The contrast between the early Reagan administration's activist support of democracy in Bolivia and the policy of rapprochement with military governments in other South American countries is striking. What were the reasons for this difference in policy?

Probably the principal reason was the drug issue. The Bolivian military was known to be heavily involved in drug trade from Bolivia, rendering a reembrace of the Bolivian military politically taboo in the United States. For the early Reagan team, drug trafficking was a more irreversible stain than human rights abuses and so the Bolivian military could not be courted like the Brazilian, Argentine, and Chilean militaries. Another reason for the different policy was that, compared with Brazil, Argentina, or Chile, Bolivia was a small, unimportant country in Washington's eyes. Neither the early team of Reagan hard-liners nor Congress paid much attention to Bolivia in the early 1980s. As a result, Ambassador Corr was able to carry out pretty much whatever policy he wanted, as long as it fell within certain basic boundaries. Corr gravitated toward a continuation of the Carter approach and found that "although we were working at the margins [in Bolivia], the margins were very big."[25]

### The Shift Away From Rapprochement

The policy of rapprochement toward the military governments of South America generated considerable controversy in the United States. It was one focus of the heated debate in Washington in 1981 over whether the Reagan administration was abandoning the Carter administration's commitment to human rights in Latin America; the other focus of that debate being of course the administration's emerging hard-line, military-oriented policy in Central America. Ultimately, however, the policy of rapprochement was quite short-lived, though the attention and controversy it provoked lasted beyond its actual life. The policy was launched in early 1981; yet already by late 1982 it was in obvious decline. The shift away from the policy was triggered by two decisive events in 1982 and then carried along over the next several years by more general political changes in South America itself.

The first decisive event was the Falklands War of spring 1982. The war not only shattered the newly rejuvenated U.S.-Argentine relationship but seriously damaged the administration's overall policy in South America. The Argentine military was the keystone of the administration's attempt to persuade the U.S. Congress and public that the military leaders of South America were responsible, moderate professionals deserving of U.S. support. The Argentine military's reckless and unexpected attack on territory belonging to the United States's closest ally completely undermined that effort. Conversely, the war hurt the administration's image in South America. A crucial element of the administration's South America policy was eradicating the notion of the United States as an unreliable ally. The administration's decision to side with Great Britain in the war severely damaged that effort. The South American governments, who had almost unanimously gathered (at least formally) behind Argentina, saw that despite the soothing words of flattery and praise that had been coming out from the Reagan administration for over a year, when the chips were down, the United States's loyalties were elsewhere.

The second decisive event, also in 1982, was the onset of the debt crisis. South America had experienced strong economic growth in the 1970s. In a number of countries, including Argentina, Brazil, Venezuela, Uruguay, Peru, and Ecuador, much of this growth was financed by borrowing from abroad. This debt-financed approach to growth worked as long as the world economy was expanding and interest rates were stable. In 1979, however, a major oil price rise triggered a severe recession in industrialized countries. Over the next several years this recession began to have serious negative consequences for South America and other parts of the developing world as export markets in the United States and Europe shrunk, interest rates skyrocketed, and commodity prices plummeted. In 1981 the economies of many South American countries stopped growing or even began to contract, producing liquidity problems. In 1982 the growing liquidity crunch came to a head. Mexico, the second most-indebted developing nation (after Brazil), announced in August that it was nearly out of exchange reserves and could not make payments on its foreign debt. Although the United States moved rapidly to negotiate a rescue package, the Mexican announcement sent a shock wave through the international financial world and provoked a further reduction in lending to Latin America. This caused acute liquidity problems among many Latin American debtor nations. In November, Brazil found itself on the verge of default and had to seek a rescheduling of its enormous debt. Suddenly a debt crisis had emerged in Latin America and loomed as a grave threat not only to the debtor nations of the region but to the entire international financial system.

The relatively unexpected (at least for the U.S. government) debt crisis caused the Reagan administration to modify its initial "hands-off," private-sector approach to the issue. The administration moved fairly quickly to arrange emergency loan or credit packages for Brazil, Argentina, and other countries. And the administration revised its initial opposition to a broad role for the multilateral lending institutions and in late 1982 agreed to a greatly expanded role for the IMF. More broadly, the onset of the debt crisis obliged the Reagan administration to confront the fact that economic issues, particularly ones involving the United States, such as debt and trade, were going to be of high or even dominant importance to South America in the 1980s. This realization countered the administration's initial notion that political issues, in particular the threat of communism, were the principal issues facing the region and the basis for a rebuilding of U.S.-South American relations.

After the Falklands War and the onset of the debt crisis had taken the wind out of the sails of the policy of rapprochement, two more general political trends assured its abandonment. The first was the unexpected trend toward democracy in South America, which although present in the final years of the Carter administration, advanced most rapidly and broadly in the early 1980s. Brazil progressed through national legislative elections in 1982 and headed toward a transition to a civilian presidency in 1985. Argentina's military government bowed out quickly after the Falklands War; presidential elections were successfully held in October 1983. Uruguay moved steadily toward democracy after the military's attempt to promulgate a new constitution was defeated in a public referendum in 1980. And as mentioned above, Bolivia returned to civilian rule in 1982.

With each democratic transition it became increasingly clear that military dictatorships were on their way out in South America, at least for the time being, and that the most striking political fact of the 1980s was the unexpected success of the moderate democratic center against the extremes of the right and left. This democratic trend rendered increasingly invalid the foundational assumption of the policy of rapprochement—the notion that the United States must make a choice between authoritarians or totalitarians. The trend rapidly made the administration's early expressions of friendship and praise for the South American military governments look anachronistic. And in simple terms, the policy of rapprochement became untenable because the military governments with which the Reagan administration was initially determined to rebuild relations were rapidly disappearing altogether.

## DEMOCRACY BY APPLAUSE

As the Reagan administration gave up on the policy of rapprochement toward the South American military governments, it adopted what can be called a policy of democracy by applause or, in less colorful terms, a policy of verbal support for democracy in South America. The policy shift was by no means a clear break, rather it was a gradual change of emphasis and attitude that took place from 1982 on. The emerging new policy was scarcely articulated as a policy per se. As the administration dropped its early effort to rebuild relations with the military governments it strongly began pursuing regular, friendly relations with the new democratic governments of the region. To the extent there was a theme or conception behind this set of new relations, it was that of supporting democracy. Administration officials reiterated their support for the democratic trend in South America in nearly every policy statement regarding the region. And as discussed below, the administration ended up trying to claim credit for the democratic trend in South America.

## Verbal Support

Although the Reagan administration presented its policy toward the newly emerging democratic governments of South America as a policy of democracy promotion, the only identifiable prodemocracy element of the policy was verbal support. The administration limited itself to expressions of support and encouragement for the process of democratization in the various South American countries. Unlike in Central America, the administration did not attempt to get closely involved in the transition processes, both because of the greater independence of most South American countries vis-à-vis the United States and because the threat of communist takeovers that preoccupied the administration in Central America was almost absent in South America. Langhorne Motley, who was U.S. Ambassador to Brazil before becoming Assistant Secretary of State for Inter-American Affairs, has pithily described this hands-off policy of verbal support for the democratization process in Brazil:

> The U.S. played no role in *abertura*. In the period of time that I was in Brazil, 1981 through 1984, I always counseled Washington, and for once they took my advice, that *abertura* was made in Brazil, and both from a public and private posture the U.S. was better off staying out of it. The Brazilians defined what *abertura* was and what the timetable was to be. All we did was applaud the process.[26]

Once democratic governments emerged in countries such as Brazil, Argentina, and Uruguay, the earlier goal of fully normalized relations (that had not been achieved with the military governments) finally became a reality. The administration took a number of modest but genuine steps to put relations on a warm footing. High-level administration officials repeatedly affirmed the administration's view that the democratic trend in South America was a political trend of major significance. The administration praised the new leaders of South America and accorded them a higher level of diplomatic courtesy than had been commonly given to Latin American leaders in the past. Presidents Raúl Alfonsín of Argentina, José Sarney of Brazil, and Julio María Sanguinetti of Uruguay were all invited to Washington on state visits. And the administration sent high-level officials down to South America with some regularity.

This full normalization of relations was scarcely a weighty form of support for democracy in South America. Nonetheless it was seen by the career officials within the administration and by some South American officials as a genuine step forward. As one State Department official put it, "We began to treat them [the South American governments] like real governments, and that was a real change."[27] Or as one commentator wrote at the time:

> Despite persistent frictions, however, bilateral [U.S.-South American] relations are more or less normal, even satisfactory in most cases. Perhaps that represents a certain maturation of the United States-Latin American relationship and the establishment of relations with the major South American countries on a sound bilateral basis not altogether different from relations the United States had long maintained with the European countries.[28]

Raúl Alfonsín, who gained the Argentine presidency in 1983 and took on the formidable task of consolidating democratic rule in Argentina, was a leading recipient of this favorable political attention from the United States. The administration spoke of Alfonsín in unusually positive terms; Congress accorded him the rare honor (rare for a foreign leader) of being asked to address a joint session. Alfonsín became a symbol in the United States of the appealing face of the reemergence of democracy in South America, just as Duarte had become the symbol of the possibility of centrism in Central America. (And like Duarte, Alfonsín remained an untarnished symbol in the United States even as his own domestic reputation deteriorated steadily and his party was defeated at the next elections.)

The policy of verbal support also included a clear stand by the administration against military coups or any kind of overt military interference with the newly elected governments in South America. High-level administration officials repeatedly declared that the United States would not condone military coups. In 1985, for example, Assistant Secretary Abrams stated that "the Reagan Administration . . . is 100 percent in favor of electoral democracy in Latin America, and wants nothing to do with the overthrow of demo-

cratic governments by the military."[29] When military rebellions occurred in Argentina in 1987 and 1988, the administration rapidly
issued statements of support for Alfonsín. In addition to these public declarations, administration officials at the Department of Defense, the CIA, and elsewhere, privately communicated to South
American military officials the administration's opposition to
coups. In Peru for example, when coup rumbles arose in late 1988,
the United States made quiet demarches to the Peruvian military
expressing opposition to a coup. The Peruvian military sent some
emissaries to Washington to ask what the administration really
wanted. They were surprised to discover that the administration
genuinely opposed a coup, despite its well-known dislike of Peru's
populist president, Alan García.[30] It is unlikely that the administration's opposition to a coup in Peru was anything more than a sub-
sidiary factor in the Peruvian military's decision not to oust García,
but it was at least a positive measure.

A further element of the policy was the initiation of some democracy assistance projects. During the second Reagan administration, USIA carried out various projects oriented toward democratization in South America, such as conferences on democratic
transitions, workshops on press freedom, and exchange visits
focusing on civic institution building. AID included South Americans in some of its Central America democracy projects, such as its
Costa Rica-based regional administration of justice project (see
chapter 6) and initiated judicial assistance projects in Peru, Colombia, and Uruguay. The National Endowment for Democracy carried
out a variety of projects in South America, aimed at party-building,
legislative training, and constitutional reform. The sum total of
these programs was not great; they represented little more than
symbolic support for democracy (with the exception of Chile, see
chapter 5). Nonetheless they reinforced the direction of the administration's policy and reached more diverse sectors of South American societies.

## An Incomplete Policy

The Reagan administration's later policy of support for democracy
in South America was notable more for what it lacked than what it

contained. The main challenge facing emerging democratic governments of South America in the 1980s was improving their stagnant
economies. The recession that hit South America in the early 1980s
proved to be not only of unprecedented severity but also unexpected persistence. Although the recession in the industrialized
countries that had begun in 1979 eventually lifted, almost all of the
South American countries remained plagued by low to nonexistent
growth, high inflation, rising unemployment, and a steady decapitalization resulting from elevated levels of debt service payments and a decline in foreign investment. The calamitous economic situation created strong pressures on the newly democratic
governments of the region. Although these governments generally
had much initial domestic support, their ability to consolidate and
keep that support depended on their economic achievements. Just
as economic problems had been instrumental in the downfall of
many of the military governments of the region, so economic performance would be one of the principal criteria by which the new
governments were judged.

The Reagan administration's response to the economic crisis in
South America was minimal. To start with, the United States gave
little direct economic assistance to South America. Most of AID's
programs in South America has been phased out in the 1970s as
Venezuela, Brazil, Argentina, Uruguay, and other countries experienced enough economic growth to put them above AID's threshold
for direct economic assistance. In the 1980s, the United States had
significant economic aid programs only in Ecuador, Peru, Bolivia,
and Colombia. U.S. aid to these countries (except Peru) did increase
significantly across the 1980s but was still very small by comparison
with aid to Central America. In 1985, for example, total economic
aid to South America was $187.5 million, compared to $728.6 million
for Central America. In per capita terms the difference was dramatic: United States assistance to Central America was approximately fifty times greater per person than that to South America.

Concerning the debt crisis, which for many South American
countries was a key element of the unremitting economic recession, the Reagan administration maintained a largely noninterventionist approach. The administration's debt policy was based on
the view that undisciplined fiscal policies by South American countries, primarily overspending and overborrowing, were the primary
causes of the debt problem. Accordingly, the remedy prescribed

was economic "adjustment" by the debtor countries, meaning the adoption of free market macroeconomic policies, including the encouragement of foreign investment and the adoption of export-oriented production strategies, and the imposition of strict austerity measures (primarily sharp reductions in government spending). New lending from the commercial banks, the administration believed, would be forthcoming once the austerity measures were taken. And economic growth in the debtor countries would revive as the recession lifted in industrialized countries and as South American governments adopted free market policies. The administration firmly rejected a debt reduction approach to the debt crisis, believing that any write-off schemes would irretrievably damage the long-term creditworthiness of the debtors (as well as entail heavy costs to either U.S. lender banks or the U.S. government). To the extent that the administration directly intervened, it was to arrange bail-out emergency loan or credit packages to various debtor countries in order to avoid any acute crisis in the international financial system.[31]

By 1985 it was obvious that the debt crisis was not on the mend. Neither lending from commercial banks nor economic growth in the debtor nations had revived. Even though interest rates had come down and at least some austerity measures had been taken, most South American debtor nations were still facing serious liquidity problems. The U.S. Treasury Department, which was now under the direction of former White House chief of staff James Baker (who switched positions with Donald Regan in January 1985), launched a new debt policy in October 1985. The new policy, which came to be known as the Baker Plan, called for a $20 billion increase in commercial bank lending to debtor nations and a $3 billion increase in lending from the multilateral development banks over the next three years in return for stepped-up economic reform in the debtor nations (the Baker Plan applied to fifteen of the most heavily indebted countries in the world, ten of which were in Latin America). The main new element in the plan was an emphasis on growth-oriented policies rather than austerity policies for the debtor countries. This emphasis reflected a recognition both that economic growth was not occurring and that without substantial growth the debtor countries would remain locked in a punishing cycle of austerity and recession.

The Baker Plan proved to be a failure. The new lending from

commercial banks did not materialize. The banks wanted to see significant structural reforms and at least some sign of economic rejuvenation before lending more money. The debtor governments were waiting for new lending before undertaking any major structural reforms in the knowledge that reforms would cause hardships and tensions that would only be alleviated with an influx of new funds. The result was a damaging standoff that the Reagan administration was unwilling or unable to solve. Secretary Baker's call for large amounts of new lending from commercial banks was really only a hortatory gesture. The administration had no tools to compel private banks to increase their lending. Economic stagnation and illiquidity continued to plague the debtor countries as what had begun as an apparently short-term recession stretched into the worst decade in modern Latin American economic history.

The negative political effects of this economic stagnation mounted steadily. The problems of unemployment, inflation, and chronic shortages of government funds eroded public confidence in the new democratic governments of the region and sowed the seeds of heightened civil tension and conflict. Many South Americans, particularly the younger generation, many of whom had never lived under democratic rule before, began to associate democracy with economic chaos and decline. In Brazil, for example, public confidence in President Sarney fell steadily as he was unable to check the repeated bouts of high inflation and restart the "economic miracle" of the 1970s. By the end of Sarney's term in 1989 Brazil was immersed in what some called its worst economic and political crisis of recent decades. In Argentina, the excitement surrounding Alfonsín's assumption of power faded steadily as the Argentine economy failed to revive. In 1989, the final year of Alfonsín's presidency, a terrible economic crisis marked by spectacular hyperinflation demoralized the country completely and forced Alfonsín to turn power over to Carlos Menem, his elected successor, before the end of his constitutionally mandated term. In Peru, Alan García's wunderkind reputation collapsed within just a few years because of the unrelenting economic crisis aggravated by the worsening problem of the Sendero Luminoso guerrillas. By 1989 García was a besieged and largely discredited president, barely holding onto power.

As the political strains generated by the economic situation in

South America increased, South American leaders pressed the Reagan administration to adopt a more forthcoming economic policy, particularly with regard to the debt crisis. Their general argument was that the Reagan administration was failing to recognize or acknowledge the political effects of the economic crisis in South America and they urged the administration to back up its stated commitment to democracy in the region with real economic deeds. South American leaders, particularly Presidents Alfonsín, Sarney, and Sanguinetti made this point at every possible opportunity with high-level U.S. officials and their message was reinforced by a steady stream of policy papers, op-eds, and statements by liberal and moderate members of the U.S. foreign policy community.[32]

The general message about the inevitable connection between the economic problems and the future of democracy was usually accompanied by specific urgings that the administration adopt a debt policy aimed at debt reduction rather than just increased lending and economic growth. Proposals for debt reduction policies emanated from both South America and the United States. Senator Bill Bradley, for example, proposed a comprehensive debt strategy incorporating the goal of debt relief that for a time in 1987 and 1988 appeared to be gaining force as an alternative to the fading Baker Plan. The Reagan administration resisted these pressures, however, and stuck to its noninterventionist approach. It was only with the departure of the Reagan administration and the arrival of the Bush administration that a new policy appeared. In 1989 Bush's Treasury Secretary, Nicholas Brady, launched a new debt policy, known as the Brady Plan, which incorporated a debt reduction element.

## The Separation of Economics and Politics

It is interesting to examine why the Reagan administration remained steadfastly attached to its noninterventionist approach to the economic crisis in South America in the face of the rather obvious failure of the policy and the broad-based criticism it received. The main reason the administration did not adopt a more responsive policy was that most high-level administration officials (though certainly not all the career staff within the Treasury Department and State Department) were sincerely convinced that debt relief would have harmful consequences for the debtor countries (by hurting their long-term creditworthiness) and that the essentially free market approach of renewed lending and structural reform would eventually succeed. The policy also reflected the administration's tendency to separate the economic and political aspects of the situation in South America and not formulate economic policy on the basis of political considerations. The question of economic adjustment measures by South American governments, for example, was seen by the administration as an almost purely economic issue. For the South American leaders confronted with the task of trying to cut budgets and reduce public sector employment, however, it was almost a purely political issue. The U.S. officials behind the debt policy often did not seem aware of the degree to which austerity measures were politically difficult for the new democratic governments of South America. Instead they shook their heads over what seemed to them to be the stubborn ignorance of the South American leaders and despaired of ever seeing the prescribed structural reforms carried out.

More generally, the administration showed little appreciation of the damaging effects of the endless economic crisis in South America on the recently revived democratic political life of the region. Among some officials there was a strong, somewhat self-righteous sense that the debtor nations had made their bed (by borrowing so heavily in the 1970s) and would just have to lie in it. Often combined with that was the belief that some of the South American nations (particularly in the Southern Cone) were not as bad as they let on and that another few notches worth of belt-tightening would not really hurt them.

When confronted with the charge that the administration's debt policy was jeopardizing the democratic gains, U.S. officials tended to respond by pointing out that no military coups had occurred. This response reflected a short-term "quarterly report" style of political analysis that unfortunately characterized the administration's attitude about democracy in South America. As long as the Reagan administration could make it to January 1989 with no coups or sharp political reversals occurring in South America, it could claim that its prodemocracy policies were successful. Missing from this outlook was any sophisticated consideration of the longer-term political consequences of the decapitalization of South America and the recognition that consolidating democracy was not simply a matter of getting these first democratic governments through to the next election but a generation-long effort of building the necessary economic and political foundations for stable democratic societies.

The separation of economics and politics in the administration's debt policy was also to some extent due to bureaucratic factors. U.S. debt policy is primarily made by the Treasury Department. Treasury officials, both because of their training and professional orientation, tend to conceive of debt issues in economic terms; political issues are considered to be extraneous or external factors. The State Department, or more particularly the Bureau of Inter-American Affairs, did make a minor attempt to exert some influence over the policy and frame the issue in more political terms. In 1986 Deputy Assistant Secretary of State James Michel directed the Office of Regional Economic Policy in the Inter-American Affairs Bureau to study the debt issue from the point of view that the U.S. government greatly values the return of democracy to South America and wants to do everything possible to support it, rather than from the usual noninterventionist tenets of the debt policy as it stood. The regional economic office did come up with some new ideas, which involved a greater level of U.S. interventionism, but was unable to exercise any influence on the overall policy.[33] The Bureau of Inter-American Affairs was blocked in the first place by the Bureau of Economic and Business Affairs at the State Department, which held to the more purely economic view of the issue. And it was blocked by Secretary of State Shultz himself. Shultz, a former Secretary of Treasury, strongly believed that debt policy was Treasury's issue not the State Department's. And to the extent he did take a position on the issue, it was an even more conservative one than Secretary of Treasury Baker.

The administration's unwillingness to let political considerations intrude into its economic policy toward South America was also the result of relative priorities. The administration's debt policy was rooted both in the administration's policy convictions and its strongly held desire to protect U.S. lender banks.[34] The political interest in question—the well-being of the nascent democratic systems of South America—was simply not that important to the administration. Despite its numerous statements of support for the return of democracy to South America, the administration had little real interest in South America's political situation. As a general matter, the Reagan administration's only really strong interest in Latin America was preventing the spread of leftism in the region. That interest led to a high level of involvement in Central America for the duration of the Reagan years, owing to the presence of a leftist government in Nicaragua and of leftist rebels in El Salvador. In South America it led to an initial attempt to rebuild relations on the foundation of shared U.S.-South American anticommunist concerns. After that effort failed, for reasons discussed above, the administration had no real impetus for paying much attention to South America.[35]

The administration did welcome the democratic trend in South America but largely as a spectator applauding a distant occurrence. The dominant characteristic of Reagan's South America policy was the remarkably low level of attention to the region that it entailed. Despite the fact that South America contains the bulk of Latin America's territory, population, and wealth, the Reagan administration essentially ignored it, devoting what interest it had in Latin America to Central America, particularly Nicaragua. It is difficult to quantify this lack of interest in South America. It is evident, however, if one looks at any measure, such as the number of speeches given about the region, the time and energy the policy-making apparatus devoted to it, or the U.S. government funds committed to it. President Reagan gave more speeches about Nicaragua in one year (1986) than he gave about any or all of the South America countries in his entire presidency. Possibly only Africa and a few parts of Asia were of less interest to President Reagan and his foreign policy advisers than was South America.

In sum, the administration's Latin American debt policy remained an economic policy rooted in economic interests external to the region; concern over South America's political fate was not sufficiently great to constitute a major factor in the policy. To the extent that the Reagan administration did draw a connection between its economic policy toward South America and the political situation there, it believed that its advocacy of free market policies would actually strengthen the cause of democracy in South America. This outlook was based on the notion of a natural link between free market economics and democracy, or in the terms often used by administration officials, between "economic freedom" and political freedom. High-level administration officials, such as Secretary of State Shultz and Deputy Secretary of State John Whitehead, frequently lectured South American leaders on the value of adopting free market policies, arguing that such policies would not only lead to rapid development but would also contribute to the strengthening of democracy. As Shultz put it on one occasion:

> I believe freedom and economic development go hand in hand. . . . Our support for democracy complements our support for economic development and free markets—and vice versa.[36]

This credo regarding the natural complementarity of free market economic policies and democratic development was adopted by AID, which in the early 1980s had adopted an emphasis on private sector development in U.S. economic assistance and in the mid-1980s sought to connect this economic approach to the sweeping democratic trend in the region.

If the administration had simply been arguing that democratic political systems are almost always associated with capitalist economic systems broadly defined, there would be little to question.[37] In fact, however, what administration officials were telling Latin American governments was that a particular type of capitalism, the Reagan administration's free market version, is more compatible with democracy than any other kind of economic system. This argument was more ideological and much less well-founded. In Western Europe, many variations of capitalism, including social-democratic ones, have combined quite well with democratic political systems. Given that many Latin Americans look to Western Europe more than to the United States for political and sociocultural models, the Reagan administration's argument was not particularly persuasive.

Furthermore, administration officials were not merely asserting that democracy and a certain type of capitalism usually occur together, but that free market capitalism will tend to promote democratic development. This argument entails a considerable empirical leap of faith. The historical record is that democracies are almost always capitalistic, not that capitalistic countries are almost always democratic. There are no solid grounds for arguing that countries with a weak or absent tradition of democracy will tend to become democratic if they adopt free market policies. Free market policies have proven to be fully compatible with highly authoritarian governments in many developing countries, such as in many Asian countries since World War II.

The administration's argument was weak not only in general theoretical terms but also in relation to the specific historical experience of Latin America. Free market economic policies in Latin America have traditionally been associated with dictatorships, not democracies. The private sectors of many Latin American countries bear little resemblance to the mythical ideal of hard-working, hard-headed entrepreneurs that Reagan administration officials subscribed to. They are usually economic elites, often quite anti-democratic in conviction and in practice, usually held together by class affiliations and often enmeshed in deeply corrupted cooptive relations with the state. In the past at least, free market policies in Latin American countries have often meant allowing these dubious private sectors a free rein to exploit their structural advantages in order to enrich themselves further at the expense of a working class that is confined to a subsistence level existence. Free market policies have also meant reducing the already minimal protective net for the working class, which, when combined with the additional hardships and dislocations produced by free market policies, has greatly aggravated existing sociopolitical tensions. In the past, only dictatorships have been able to control those tensions—through violent repression.

A recent major study of economic development strategies in Latin America highlights this troubled relationship between free market capitalism and democracy:

> This more modern kind of repression [South American authoritarian governments of the 1970s] has very special characteristics: it combines free-market economics with destruction of democratic institutions and systematic use of terror to paralyze opposition. At the very least, the combination suggests that democracy and capitalism do not easily go together in contemporary Latin America. To put it

more strongly, the fundamental issue may be that informed majorities given the chance to express their preferences can usually be expected to vote for promises to control markets, shut off international competition and foreign investment, and use government rather than private enterprise as the main force shaping economic development.[38]

In the late 1980s a trend arose in which Latin American majorities did vote for political leaders promising free market policies, a phenomenon that may be interpreted either as an evolution of Latin American societies or simply the result of desperate populaces frustrated with all other solutions to their economic plight. In any case, in arguing for a simplistic equation of free market policies and democracy in Latin America, the Reagan administration displayed considerable ignorance of the troubled reality of that issue in Latin American history.

## MINIMAL EFFECTS

Despite its low level of interest in South America, the Reagan administration did not shy from taking credit for the resurgence of democracy there. In 1985, for example, Assistant Secretary of State Abrams asserted that the Reagan administration's policy was one of the principal causes of the redemocratization of South America.[39] This claim was repeated in later years as part of the administration's general claim to having played a key role in the resurgence of democracy throughout Latin America. Administration officials did not explain exactly how U.S. policy toward South America had fostered the democratic trend; their arguments about a U.S. role seemed to rest on the vague notion that frequent expressions of support by the administration for the democratic trend somehow translated into a powerful assist. Was the claim of a significant U.S. role valid?

With respect to the administration's early policy of rapprochement with the military governments of South America, the answer is a clear no. There is no basis for believing that improved relations with the South American military leaders of the early 1980s contributed to the democratic trend in the region. If anything, the policy worked against the trend. In the early 1980s the military governments in Brazil, Argentina, Uruguay, and elsewhere were struggling to maintain legitimacy in the face of economic decline and growing demands for political liberalization. They were delighted to receive respect and praise from the new U.S. administration and tried to parlay it, albeit with little success, into a domestic political boost. The administration's apparent abandonment of Carter's human rights policy gave these dictatorships hope that the external pressure for political liberalization had just been a passing phase and that the United States would no longer be an ally of the forces of change. The only exception, as discussed above, was Bolivia, where the Reagan administration (or at least the U.S. embassy in La Paz) did actively support and contribute to the civilian transition.

The administration's later policy, what has been called here the policy of verbal support, was certainly more prodemocratic than the earlier policy. Nonetheless there is little indication that it had any significant impact on the progress of democracy in South America. The words of support from the United States, the visits to Washington, and the generally respectful treatment by the U.S. government were all welcomed by the new democratic governments of South America. But improved political relations with the United States were really only a psychological boost to governments confronting the monumentally difficult task of rebuilding civil institutions, maintaining order, mollifying unhappy militaries, and trying to restart stalled economies. What the South American governments really wanted—substantial U.S. economic support to help alleviate the region's debilitating economic crisis—was not forthcoming. Although U.S. officials sometimes believe that verbal support by the United States for a South American government is of great consequence to that government, for the most part this is an outdated belief reflecting the assumptions of an earlier era.

Similarly, the administration's clear stand against military coups was appreciated by the new democratic governments but was of little significance. The United States has only very limited influence over the militaries of South America (with the possible exception of Bolivia). These militaries do not generally look to the United States for large amounts of training, supplies, or assistance. Despite the wishes and beliefs of some people in the U.S. government, the days when the United States exercised strong political influence over the South American militaries are gone. The near absence of military coups in South America in the 1980s was the result of internal factors—not U.S. policy—such as the militaries' ability to maintain their sovereignty despite civilian rule and the continuing economic stagnation, which acted as a strong disincentive against the retaking of power.

More generally, the decade-long resurgence of democracy in South America was an internal development, not the result of U.S. policy.[40] Economic problems were one important cause. The South American militaries had staked their claim to rule in significant part on the promise of economic discipline and growth. When the economic situation in South America began to deteriorate soon after the onset of the recession in the industrialized countries in 1979 (or in some cases, such as Peru, several years before) the militaries faced a serious crisis of legitimacy. Another major factor was the ideological evolution of the region. Many of the military governments of the 1960s and 1970s came to power as a reaction to growing leftist movements. And once in power they eradicated those movements, usually by brutal, repressive means. By the late 1970s, most of these movements had been decimated and the ideological ferment that contributed to their rise in the 1960s and early 1970s had largely disappeared. Thus, the anticommunist raison d'etre of the military governments was greatly weakened.

These two general causes—economic problems and ideological changes—by no means applied equally or even constituted the dominant factors in all the different countries. Although the resurgence of democracy was a regional trend, in each country it unfolded differently and was the result of a unique and highly complex set of political, economic, and social trends. In Argentina, for example, the defeat in the Falklands War was a major factor, but one obviously particular to Argentina. In Uruguay, the resilience of previous democratic habits and attitudes was of great importance in the transition. In Brazil, the military's difficulty in managing the socioeconomic changes brought on by the rapid economic growth of the late 1960s and 1970s was of particular relevance. For the purposes of evaluating the effects of U.S. policy, the important point is that the redemocratization of South America of the 1980s was the result of internal, not external, causes.

This negative assessment of the effects of the administration's stated policy of support of democracy in South America should not be taken to imply that the policy was either illusory or pointless. During the mid-1980s, some liberal commentators failed to recognize that the early policy of rapprochement had quickly faded and been replaced by a genuinely prodemocratic policy. They continued to condemn the administration's Kirkpatrickian approach long after it had largely been abandoned, at least in South America. It is true that the later policy of verbal support was only a vague and incomplete policy. It neglected the all-important economic area and did not have a significant effect on the political development of the region. Nonetheless it represented a break with the long-standing pattern of sympathy in U.S. conservative circles for military takeovers in Latin America and, together with the Carter administration's human rights policy before it, helped reduce the traditional reputation of the U.S. government in South America as a friend of reactionary political elites.

# 5

# DEMOCRACY BY PRESSURE

## CHILE, PARAGUAY, PANAMA, AND HAITI

In the late 1980s, the Reagan administration found itself embroiled in a series of controversial confrontations with a scattering of dictators in Latin America and the Caribbean. In Panama, the administration waged a vigorous but ultimately fruitless campaign to oust the notorious General Manuel Antonio Noriega. In Chile, the Reagan administration surprised many observers by exerting pressure against General Augusto Pinochet to carry out the long-awaited plebiscite on continued military rule. In Haiti, the administration helped engineer the departure of President-for-Life Jean-Claude Duvalier and struggled unsuccessfully to steer the post-Duvalier government to an electoral transition. And in Paraguay, the administration urged Latin America's most enduring dictator, General Alfredo Stroessner, to hold elections and permit the evolution of democratic rule.

The policies in these four countries evolved separately, in response to specific events in each country. Yet they shared important features. They were targeted at leaders who, although very different in many ways, had one common characteristic—they were the four remaining right-wing dictators in Latin America and the Caribbean, the four holdouts on the right against elected civilian rule. Furthermore, each case entailed a similar method—the administration exerted economic and diplomatic pressure for political change, pressure that was stronger than mere criticism but short of military force. Finally, each policy was cast in terms of promoting democracy. The administration declared that it was not just seeking the ouster of repugnant dictators but the establishment or

**149**

restoration of democratic rule. Given these common features, the policies can be understood as instances of a general policy category, the fourth and final category of democracy-related policies in the Reagan years—exerting economic and diplomatic pressure for democratic change against the remaining right-wing governments in the region.

This policy of pressure against right-wing dictators is of particular interest in that it was the farthest point of evolution of the Reagan administration's Latin America policy with respect to promoting democracy. The Reagan administration ended up working to weaken or even undermine pro-U.S. anticommunist leaders, employing the same methods and goals that just several years before it had excoriated the Carter administration for using in its human rights policy. The policy of pressure flatly contradicted the Kirkpatrick dictum that the United States must tolerate or support anticommunist authoritarian leaders in order to avoid their being replaced by left-wing governments. Furthermore, the policy of pressure on the right in Latin America and the Caribbean came to be linked with changing policies toward right-wing dictatorships in other parts of the developing world, such as the Philippines and South Korea, giving rise in the final years of the Reagan administration to the idea of a new, less tolerant U.S. policy toward "friendly tyrants."

## CHILE

### *Reembracing General Pinochet*

In the early 1980s, the Reagan administration sought warm relations with Chile's military dictator, General Augusto Pinochet, as part of its larger policy in South America of replacing the Carter administration's human rights policy with "quiet diplomacy" and rebuilding relations with anticommunist military dictatorships. The early Reagan team was particularly sympathetic to Pinochet, a forceful anticommunist who had ousted the leftist President Salvador Allende in 1973. Pinochet faced a large communist opposition, including an active guerrilla movement, and appeared to the Reagan administration to be a clear example of an anticommunist leader who merited U.S. support. The administration also favored Pinochet for economic reasons. Almost alone among South American leaders, he followed free market economic policies.

The administration took many steps in 1981 and 1982 to improve political relations between the United States and Chile, including lifting the 1979 ban on Export-Import Bank financing,[1] dropping its opposition to loans to Chile from the multilateral development banks,[2] and opposing U.N. human rights resolutions critical of Chile.[3] High-level diplomatic contacts were also reestablished. In the first half of 1981, General Fernando Matthei of the Chilean junta came to Washington and Vernon Walters, an aide to Secretary of State Alexander Haig, went to Chile. U.N. Ambassador Jeane Kirkpatrick stopped in Chile in August and had what she described as a "most pleasant" visit with General Pinochet in which she expressed the U.S. government's "desire to fully normalize our relations with Chile."[4] Administration officials spoke positively about Pinochet, emphasizing his successful fight against communism and the achievements of Chile's economy while downplaying the bothersome issues of human rights and democracy.[5] The administration appointed James Theberge, a conservative who was openly sympathetic to Pinochet, as U.S. Ambassador to Chile.

The administration also sought improved military relations with Chile. Regular visits between Chilean and U.S. military officers were reestablished and Chile was invited to take part in the annual UNITAS joint United States-Latin America naval exercises, after having not been invited in 1980.[6] U.S. military officials solemnly but vaguely invoked the "important security interests which necessitate close military-to-military cooperation with Chile."[7] When Senator Jesse Helms, Pinochet's best friend in Washington, moved to repeal the 1977 ban on military assistance and sales to Chile, the administration supported the effort vigorously. Congress did remove the ban but imposed a requirement that the President must certify, among other things, an improved human rights situation in Chile before assistance and sales can be initiated.[8] In early 1982, Secretary of State Haig and Assistant Secretary Enders almost went ahead with a certification in order to restart military assistance and sales to Chile. They ended up deciding not to, however, based on tactical considerations. They surmised that the Democrats in Congress would strongly object to military aid to Pinochet and that pushing for such assistance could get mixed up with and ultimately derail the administration's already shaky campaign to get approval for large-scale military assistance to El Salvador.[9]

The administration began to shift away from a uniformly pro-Pinochet policy in 1983. In that year serious civil unrest broke out in Chile, in response to the country's first sharp economic downturn in many years and a growing frustration with the continued absence of any real political space. Pinochet harshly suppressed the unrest, responding to each wave of strikes and demonstrations with overwhelming military and police force. The administration was put on the defensive by the political violence in Chile as critics in Congress and the U.S. public pointed to Chile as an example of the failure of "quiet diplomacy." The administration distanced itself somewhat from Pinochet, issuing cautious statements of regret over the events in Chile and sending communiques urging the Chilean leader to continue a dialogue with the opposition.[10]

Pinochet ignored the administration's messages on human rights and maintained his hard-line approach as the political turbulence continued in 1984. To many observers in Chile and the United States, it began to look as though the constitutionally mandated process of a democratic transition was in jeopardy. Under the 1980 Constitution (approved by a plebiscite of uncertain legitimacy), Pinochet was to rule as president and commander in chief of the armed forces until 1989. A plebiscite on his continued rule was to be held before the end of his term. If Chileans voted yes he would serve until 1997; if they voted no, presidential elections would be held in 1989. This transition process was to involve the gradual restoration of civilian political life, a restoration that Pinochet seemed to be ruling out with his unrepentant approach to the civil unrest of 1983 and 1984.

The administration fumbled for a policy that would balance its continuing sympathies toward Pinochet with some kind of support for the transition process. The search for a policy was complicated by serious divisions within the administration over Pinochet's nature and the appropriate U.S. tack. At least three differing views existed, personified at the senior policy-making level by Ambassador James Theberge, Assistant Secretary of State for Inter-American Affairs Langhorne Motley, and Assistant Secretary of State for Human Rights and Humanitarian Affairs Elliott Abrams.

Theberge was strongly pro-Pinochet. He highlighted the communist threat to Chile and argued that Pinochet was doing what was necessary to keep order and that the U.S. pressure on Pinochet needlessly alienated him and the Chilean military.[11] Motley was also sympathetic to Pinochet but became convinced in 1984 that the Chilean leader was going further than necessary in stifling political dissent and that the United States should play a role in supporting the constitutional transition process. Motley deeply disliked public criticisms of friendly governments, however, and maintained that whatever pressure the United States exerted, it must exert quietly, behind closed doors.[12] Elliott Abrams took a very different view. In the human rights bureau he had been working to temper the early Reagan administration's friendly policies toward right-wing dictators, arguing that such policies weakened the administration's credibility as a supporter of democratic change in communist countries. He argued forcefully within the administration for a vigorous policy of pressure against Pinochet on human rights and democracy issues.[13]

Theberge, Motley, and Abrams, and their respective supporters in different parts of the bureaucracy, argued intensely over Chile policy in 1983 and 1984. On the whole, Motley carried the day, both because he was in the more central policy position than Abrams or Theberge and because his views reflected a natural middle ground. The administration maintained a basically friendly policy toward Pinochet but began leavening it with more pointed private discussions with Chilean officials regarding U.S. human rights concerns and a somewhat less uniformly positive public line.

### Pinochet Loses Favor

In early 1985, U.S. policy began evolving clearly away from its pro-Pinochet orientation. In November 1984, Pinochet imposed a state of siege, the first in Chile since the 1970s. The state of siege convinced Motley, Shultz, and even Theberge that Pinochet was headed in the wrong direction and that the United States must send strong signals of its disapproval. The administration abstained on three multilateral development bank loans between February and May 1985, and made it clear that it abstained because it felt "it was time to send a signal" to protest the state of siege.[14] The administration also made it known that it was likely to abstain on several World Bank loans coming up for approval later that year. Pinochet lifted the state of siege on June 17, the day before the vote on the first of these loans, a $55 million investment loan. The administration, in turn, voted for that loan and for the others that came up for approval that year.

Two key personnel changes in 1985 turned the nascent policy shift into a full-fledged one. Elliott Abrams replaced Langhorne Motley and brought to the Bureau of Inter-American Affairs the perspective on Chile he had developed at the human rights bureau. And Harry Barnes replaced James Theberge as U.S. ambassador to Chile. Barnes, a senior career foreign service officer, had none of Theberge's sympathy for Pinochet and had sufficient stature and skill to become a major policy actor.

The policy shift was also facilitated by events in Chile. In August 1985, a group of major opposition parties in Chile signed the Accord for a Full Transition to Democracy (Acuerdo Nacionál para la Transición a la Democracia) in which they said they would accept the constitutionally mandated transition process (dropping their demand for early, open elections) in exchange for certain constitutional reforms concerning political activity.[15] The Accord did not succeed, but signaled a less confrontational and more unified approach by the opposition, strengthening the hand of those in the administration who were arguing that Chile did have a viable centrist alternative, that the United States was not faced with a stark choice between Pinochet and the communists.

The administration's post-1985 policy of support for a democratic transition in Chile had two halves: pressuring Pinochet to adhere to the formal transition process and permit the political conditions necessary for a fair plebiscite; and persuading the moderate opposition to abandon confrontational strategies and to accept the formal transition process. From 1985 on administration officials frequently declared that the United States supported a democratic transition in Chile, highlighted the contrast between the authoritarian state of Chilean politics and the wave of democratization in Latin America, and linked Chile policy to its overall support for democracy in Latin America.

The administration took a variety of political and economic steps to generate pressure on the Chilean government, although for reasons discussed below, these steps were not consistently pursued. At the United Nations, the administration stopped reflexively supporting Chile on human rights issues. In March 1986 the United States even initiated a resolution of the U.N. Human Rights Commission criticizing Chile's human rights practices.[16] Between December 1986 and March 1988 the United States voted four times at the United Nations on human rights resolutions criticizing Chile. The United States supported or abstained on three of the resolutions and voted against one. The administration also voted against or abstained on several multilateral development bank loans to Chile.

The effort to encourage the moderate opposition in Chile was primarily carried out by Ambassador Barnes and his staff in the U.S. embassy. Upon arriving in Chile, Barnes immediately established himself as an energetic and effective supporter of a democratic transition. He developed good relations with the major opposition parties and succeeded in convincing a very skeptical group of Chilean opposition leaders that the United States was sincerely committed to a democratic transition. He assisted the opposition parties in their negotiations with the government and in their ongoing effort to work together constructively.[17]

Barnes also developed contacts with the other major sectors of Chilean society, notably the military and the business sector, and conveyed to them the importance the United States attached to the democratic transition. Barnes complemented his work in Chile with effective consensus building in the U.S. foreign policy community. Liberals in Congress and in the Washington policy community deeply distrusted the Reagan administration with respect to Chile. Barnes gained their trust, however, and helped convince them that the administration was sincere in its prodemocracy policy and that a bipartisan democracy policy was both possible and necessary.

The administration's support for a democratic transition in Chile was a notable departure from its earlier policy. It was nonetheless a very cautious policy, which in 1986 and 1987 came in for considerable criticism by U.S. liberals.[18] Unlike most of the Chilean opposition and U.S. liberals, the administration did not advocate advancing or holding open elections but rather accepted the constitutional transition process. And the administration combined its support for a democratic transition with continued statements of concern about the threat of communism in Chile and Cuban support for the Chilean guerrilla movement.[19] These frequent references to the communist threat tended to mitigate the pressure on Pinochet by strengthening his own much-used anticommunist justification for the halting transition process.

The administration's policy was not only extremely cautious, it was weakened by persistent internal divisions. Motley and Theberge were gone but numerous officials remained in the administration who opposed a policy of pressuring Pinochet. They were a scattered group that included Vernon Walters (who had become U.N. Ambassador in 1985), National Security Adviser John Poindexter, NSC staff members José Sorzano and Jacqueline Tillman, and a variety of officials at the Defense Department and CIA, and of course, Senator Jesse Helms. These hard-liners held fast to the position that Pinochet was set on carrying out the transition, that his repressive domestic practices were necessary to fight the communists, and that U.S. pressure, particularly the activities of Ambassador Barnes, was counterproductive. They saw the administration's new policy as warmed-over Carterism and were horrified that the Reagan administration had ended up adopting virtually the same sort of policy they had worked so hard to reverse in 1981 and 1982.[20]

The hard-liners fought constantly with the State Department over Chile policy. Each U.N. vote and multilateral development bank vote on Chile was the subject of a furious internal tug-of-war in which decision memos with sharply contrasting options went up to the President. The hard-liners claimed to have President Reagan on their side, and they were probably right. Elliott Abrams himself acknowledges that on Chile, "the President's instincts were not good," meaning that Reagan continued to think of the Chilean leader as a loyal anticommunist friend who deserved U.S. support.[21] In one White House meeting in late 1987 or early 1988, where Secretary of State Shultz raised a specific question about policy toward Pinochet, Reagan looked up at the mention of Pinochet's name and said, "Pinochet saved Chile from communism, we should have him here on a state visit."[22] Everyone present was astonished at the idea; Shultz and his staff managed to bury it quietly.

Despite Reagan's views, the State Department was largely able to win out over the hard-liners on Chile. The hard-liners did win a few of the battles over votes at the U.N. or the multilateral development banks, weakening the policy somewhat. The hard-liners also fed Pinochet's hopes and led him to believe, incorrectly, that he could play off the contending factions in the U.S. government. But on the whole, the policy of pressure on Pinochet went ahead, particularly in Chile through the efforts of Ambassador Barnes.

How was it possible for the State Department to carry out a policy that the President seemed not to favor? Much of the answer lies in President Reagan's role in foreign policy. President Reagan had "instincts" on most issues, not well-developed, detailed views. The vagueness of those instincts and his lack of close involvement in policy-making resulted in his exercising little influence over many policies. When two factions within the administration clashed over policy, the victor was not always the one whose views accorded with the President's instincts but the one who had the most institutional clout. With respect to the Chile policy, the State Department outweighed the hard-liners. The State Department had the main responsibility for the day-to-day implementation of policy and Ambassador Barnes and the embassy were in direct control of much of its real substance. The hard-liners were on the margins of the policy process and, except for the very few particular issues that required specific presidential decisions, they were confined to kibitzing and fighting rearguard actions against the State Department's policy.

An additional factor was U.S. public opinion. In part because of the notorious U.S. involvement in Chilean politics in the early 1970s, General Pinochet was a well-known and much-hated figure among most Americans interested in Latin American affairs. As civil unrest rose in Chile in the 1980s and Chile policy became a headline issue again, U.S. public opinion clearly favored a policy of strong pressure. Thus, in the struggle between the State Department and the hard-liners over Chile policy, the State Department could make the inevitably appealing argument that a policy of pressure would win the administration some much-needed approval on a controversial Latin American issue, whereas the hard-liners could point to no significant base of public support in the United States for a tolerant policy toward Pinochet.

## The Plebiscite

The administration's support of a democratic transition in Chile clarified and intensified as the plebiscite campaign finally got underway in late 1987 and early 1988. On December 17, 1987, the Department of State released a statement, explicitly endorsed by President Reagan, stating that "the United States believes that a climate of freedom and fair competition must be established many months before the actual balloting takes place" and stipulating numerous political rights necessary for a fair campaign.[23] Several days later, Reagan signaled U.S. unhappiness with the early campaign climate by removing Generalized System of Preferences benefits for approximately $60 million worth of Chilean exports to the United States and suspending OPIC guarantees for the nearly $300 million of U.S. corporate investment in Chile.[24] That same month, Congress, with the administration's backing (and particularly at Ambassador Barnes's urging), approved a special $1 million appropriation to the National Endowment for Democracy for the promotion of democracy in Chile.

In Chile, the moderate opposition gave up its call for early elections and devoted itself to the plebiscite campaign. The opposition's strategy was straightforward: get as many voters registered as possible and convince them to vote against continued Pinochet rule. A number of new and existing organizations in Chile devoted themselves to the voter registration effort, including labor unions, the Catholic Church, and the newly formed National Committee for Free Elections, and the Crusade for Civic Participation. To campaign for the no vote, sixteen major opposition parties formed a coalition, the National Command for the No, in which they set aside their many specific platforms to focus on their common objective of defeating Pinochet.

The U.S. policy became very active as the plebiscite campaign advanced. Ambassador Barnes pushed hard on the all-important issue of the procedural fairness of the plebiscite, speaking out in favor of specific campaign and voting conditions, such as media access for the opposition, fair voting procedures, and a balloting system that would ensure voting secrecy and fair counting. Barnes's efforts were complemented by an increasingly active U.S. technical assistance effort funded by the National Endowment for Democracy and AID. AID gave a $1.285 million grant to CAPEL, a Latin American electoral assistance organization, for use in Chile. CAPEL in turn gave the money to the Crusade for Civic Participation, a nonpartisan Chilean organization formed in 1987 to promote voter registration for the plebiscite. The National Endowment spent $1.6 million in Chile in 1988 (the $1 million special congressional appropriation plus $600,000 of NED's regular funds) on programs involving

Chilean civic organizations, universities, trade unions, newspapers, and youth centers for activities related to the plebiscite, primarily voter registration and civic education projects.[25]

Some of the NED funds were used by the National Democratic Institute for International Affairs (NDI), a component organization of the Endowment, to assist the National Command for the No in its campaign against Pinochet. NDI funds helped the No Command design campaign materials, formulate campaign strategies, and organize an independent vote-counting system.[26] NDI funds were also used to purchase computers and other materials for the No Command to use in the campaign. NDI resisted accusations that it was taking sides in a foreign election with the argument that helping the No Command was just a way of compensating for the stacked deck held by the Chilean government. Although the deck was indeed stacked against the opposition, almost everyone at NDI, NED, and AID who worked on the Chilean plebiscite, believed or at least hoped that their technical assistance would help defeat Pinochet. As one AID official exclaimed, "We've helped register millions of voters and we consider each one of those a vote against Pinochet."[27] This high level of direct U.S. involvement in a Latin American election was not widely criticized in the United States in the way that U.S. involvement in earlier Central American elections had been, in large part because of the widespread antipathy for Pinochet among liberal critics of U.S. policy.

Administration officials in Washington backed up the active U.S. efforts in Chile with public and private affirmations of support for a fair plebiscite. Assistant Secretary Abrams and Assistant Secretary of State for Human Rights and Humanitarian Affairs Richard Schifter spoke out on the issue, attempting to make clear to doubters in the U.S. foreign policy community and to the Chilean government that the administration was serious about its commitment to democracy in Chile. In the final days before the plebiscite, the State Department received some intelligence information from Chile indicating that Pinochet was seriously considering calling off the plebiscite at the last minute.[28] Deputy Secretary of State John Whitehead called in the Chilean ambassador and told him how much importance the United States attached to the plebiscite. The State Department also gave the intelligence to the British government (the British government had good relations with Pinochet ever since the Falklands War when Chile, alone among Latin American states, did not side with Argentina) which also held a last-minute, high-level meeting with Chilean officials to convey the British government's desire to see the plebiscite take place.[29]

## A Motivational Stew

There is no simple answer to the question of why the Reagan administration shifted to an anti-Pinochet, prodemocracy policy in Chile. A mix of motivations was at work, falling into two general categories. On the one hand were two utilitarian motivations reflecting little interest in democracy per se. First, the administration promoted democracy in the interest of consistency via-à-vis its stated policy of promoting democracy in Nicaragua. During the mid-1980s the administration became increasingly aware that its efforts to use democracy arguments to win approval for contra aid were weakened to the extent that the administration was not perceived as promoting democracy with equal vigor in Chile. Administration officials going before Congress to lobby for contra aid had to have a good answer to the question, "If the administration is so concerned about democracy in Latin America, why doesn't it care about Chile?" The administration also supported the Chilean transition to keep ahead of Congress. Senator Kennedy and a number of other prominent Democrats had a strong interest in Chile and were constantly looking for ways to pressure the administration into adopting a more anti-Pinochet policy. The administration wanted at almost any cost to avoid losing control of its Latin America policy (or any area of its foreign policy) to Congress and sought to head off congressional attempts to establish specific policy mandates on Chile, such as country-specific legislation with respect to multilateral bank loans or economic sanctions. The State Department often tried to persuade the White House, the Treasury Department, or other agencies to go along with anti-Pinochet measures using the argument that if the administration did not go at least part way, Congress would step in with more far-reaching measures of its own.[30]

On the other hand, the administration also acted out of a real interest in democracy. Many administration officials gravitated toward the policy of promoting Chilean democracy in the belief that it was simply the right thing to do, that it accorded with basic U.S. values. During the second Reagan administration this belief in democracy was held by much of the Latin America policy team. As one of the few holdouts against the democracy trend, Chile was a natural focus of attention. Additionally, some administration officials advocated a prodemocracy policy toward Chile out of fear that Pinochet was leading Chile down a path of increasing polarization, heightening the long-term possibility of a violent leftist takeover. In their view, a democratic transition was necessary to stop this polarization and defuse the pressure for radical political change.

Given this complex mix of motivations, commentators analyzing the administration's Chile policy while it unfolded tended to ascribe to the administration whatever motivations fit the commentator's own ideological view of the administration. Liberal analysts highlighted the administration's concern for even-handedness vis-à-vis Nicaragua, discounting the possibility that the administration had any real interest in Chilean democracy. Supporters of the administration argued that the Chile policy was just another example of the administration's deep-felt commitment to democracy in Latin America. In fact, all four motivations mentioned above, and probably numerous others, were at work in a kind of motivational stew that varied over time and in the mind of particular policymakers. Harry Barnes, for example, was little concerned about balancing the Nicaragua and Chile policies. Elliott Abrams, however, the State Department's point man on Nicaragua, was quite concerned about that balance, but he was also motivated by the belief that the United States should promote democracy worldwide on principle, as an expression of U.S. values. The mid-level foreign service officers who worked on the policy in Chile and Washington probably tended to be more concerned about the long-term deterioration of Chilean politics and the need for a transition as a means of preventing long-term political instability. And a good number of the people working on the technical assistance projects were motivated by the belief that the United States had done a terrible wrong in intervening in Chilean politics in the early 1970s and that promoting democracy now would help make up for that wrong.

## A Bipartisan Success

The plebiscite turned out as the administration had hoped. Pinochet lost, but respected the results, setting in motion presidential elections for 1989. The presidential elections also came off peacefully and cleanly. A coalition of centrist, center-left, and leftist parties defeated the Chilean right, and Patricio Aylwin of the Christian Democratic Party became President. With the exception of Senator Helms and a few of the hard-liners in the administration, the entire U.S. foreign policy community was delighted by Pinochet's defeat. The administration and the National Endowment of Democracy indulged in a bracing round of self-congratulation, crediting themselves with having played an important role in the transition.

The United States was certainly on the side of democratic change in Chile from 1985 on. Whether or not U.S. policy had a significant effect on events in Chile, however, is another matter. The first question is whether U.S. policy had an effect on Pinochet's decision to go ahead with the plebiscite. In the mid-1980s, when it was being pressed by critics to do more to support a democratic transition in Chile, the administration repeatedly stressed the limits of U.S. influence on the Chilean government.[31] Once events in Chile began to go the right way, however, less was heard about these limits. In fact, the administration was correct in its earlier assertions that the United States had little economic or political leverage over Pinochet short of drastic measures such as a trade embargo or military force. The U.S. economic and political pressures exerted against Pinochet were as much symbolic as substantive. Pinochet went ahead with the plebiscite primarily for domestic reasons. The plebiscite was a constitutionally mandated process. Much of the military and most of the population supported the holding of the plebiscite. Pinochet could have called it off only at great risk to his ability to maintain his support in the military and to keep peace in the country. What the U.S. government would have said or done if he called off the plebiscite was almost certainly only a peripheral concern.

A second question, however, is what effect the U.S. policy had on the conditions in which the plebiscite was held and the activity of the opposition. Pinochet was probably going to hold the plebiscite in any case. Whether he planned to hold an even minimally fair one, however, is open to doubt. The opposition parties were greatly limited in their campaign by restrictions on access to the media and on many civil liberties, such as the freedom of assembly. The U.S. government's outspoken attention to the conditions of the plebiscite probably helped the opposition win concessions from the government and strengthened the opposition's campaign. And the U.S. technical assistance to the opposition helped get more voters registered and bolstered the No Command's campaign.

It is impossible to quantify the effects of U.S. involvement in the plebiscite process. It is probably safe to say that it was important but by no means decisive with respect to the outcome. Even this obviously cautious assessment should be tempered by some broader considerations. The plebiscite was one element of a very long transition process in Chile. If Pinochet had won, many Chileans would have believed it was due to unfair election conditions or vote-counting fraud. The struggle for a democratic transition would not have ended, it would have continued just as it had for over a decade. The success of the transition was the result of a number of deeply rooted internal factors, including a decade of persistent activism by the Chilean opposition, the genuine constitutionalism held to by most sectors of the Chilean society, and the country's long tradition of democracy. The U.S. assistance in the closing months of the plebiscite campaign was a minor factor occurring at the tail end of a very long, and thoroughly Chilean, process.[32]

## PARAGUAY

### Turning Against Stroessner

U.S. policy toward Paraguay also underwent a decisive shift during the Reagan years. During the 1980s Paraguay was ruled by General Alfredo Stroessner, who had taken power in 1954 and held on to become Latin America's longest-lasting dictator. In the Carter years, the traditionally friendly relations between the U.S. government and Stroessner had deteriorated when Carter criticized Paraguay's dismal human rights record. The early Reagan administration turned the clock back to friendlier times as part of its general effort to rebuild relations with the military dictatorships of South America. During the second administration, however, the policy shifted toward an increased emphasis on promoting human rights and democracy.

As with Chile, the later prodemocracy policy was led by the

State Department. In Washington, State Department officials, particularly Assistant Secretary Abrams, spoke out on human rights issues in Paraguay and the need for a democratic transition. In June 1987, for example, Abrams declared:

> We have been particularly critical of limits on freedom of the press and assembly [in Paraguay]. We have strongly protested the closing of Paraguay's independent newspaper, *ABC Color*, as well as restrictions or harassment of independent radio stations. We have urged the Paraguayan government to create the conditions conducive to dialogue, free expression, and free association. . . . We urge the Government of Paraguay to allow the people of that country to join in Latin America's democratic wave.[33]

A new, activist U.S. ambassador, Clyde Taylor, arrived in Asunción in late 1985 and undertook a vigorous effort to convey the U.S. government's support for a democratic transition. Taylor made a point of meeting with opposition group leaders and spoke openly of the desirability of political change in Paraguay. His activities drew harsh, negative reactions from the Paraguayan government, which was surprised that a Reagan administration ambassador was engaging in the sort of public human rights diplomacy they had suffered through in the Carter years. Taylor was insulted and threatened by the Paraguayan government and in one instance Paraguayan police broke up a reception given in Taylor's honor by a Paraguayan women's group.[34]

The administration lacked significant political and economic leverage over Paraguay and the new policy was largely confined to verbal declarations and moral suasion. The United States had only a minor aid relationship with Paraguay in the 1980s (between two and five million dollars of economic aid per year and fifty and one hundred thousand dollars of military training assistance per year) and so potential aid leverage was minimal. Economic relations between the United States and Paraguay were relatively unimportant to both countries and did not constitute a fertile area for U.S. pressure. The administration did suspend Paraguay's access to trade benefits under the Generalized System of Preferences in 1987 to protest the Paraguayan government's restrictions of the right of labor unions to organize, but this was the only significant economic measure taken.

The National Endowment for Democracy carried out a variety of small democracy assistance projects in Paraguay from 1985 to 1988, including support for Radio Naduti, an independent radio station, Women for Democracy, a prodemocracy women's group, the Center for Democracy, another nonpartisan, prodemocracy group, the Paraguayan Institute for International and Geopolitical Studies, a public policy institute, and several other such organizations. Although the Endowment's work was carried out separately from U.S. policy, it was encouraged by the administration, particularly by the U.S. embassy in Asunción.

In contrast to its Chile policy, the administration's Paraguay policy was not the subject of serious internal divisions. Stroessner did not have the support within right-wing American circles that Pinochet had and no other U.S. government agency had any particular interest in maintaining good relations with him. The State Department was able to make policy toward Paraguay largely unhindered by competing agencies.[35] Unlike Chile, however, Paraguay had no history of democracy and a lower level of economic and political development. Although the Paraguayan political situation was somewhat in flux in the second half of the 1980s, the fledgling Paraguayan opposition bore little resemblance to the well-organized, politically sophisticated opposition pushing for an electoral transition in Chile. The U.S. policy of supporting political change in Paraguay was, accordingly, a more basic campaign.

The motivations behind the policy of pressure in Paraguay were similar to those in Chile. The State Department was concerned with being even-handed in its overall democracy policy and was increasingly annoyed by Stroessner's unwillingness to join his neighbors in permitting a transition to elected civilian rule. The State Department was also concerned with the long-term political consequences of a stagnant dictatorship in Paraguay. For example, Abrams contended in 1987 that "any other practice [except democracy] not only portends more tensions with the United States, but protests, divisions, and, ultimately, unrest in Paraguay itself."[38] Ambassador Taylor expressed the same sentiment in an interview in early 1987: "We believe democracy is the best defense against instability."[37]

To the surprise of many, General Stroessner fell from power in February 1989. He was ousted by General Andrés Rodríguez, a longtime loyalist who represented a faction within the ruling Colorado Party that had for some years opposed the too-close identification of the party with General Stroessner. Stroessner's fall was the result of various causes, including the division within the Colorado Party, as well as Stroessner's advanced age (seventy-six) and increasing personal weakness.[38] The political liberalization Stroessner had begun to permit in the mid-1980s may also have contributed to his fall, although the stirrings of the opposition groups and the strengthening of organized labor accomplished in that liberalization were still only minor forces in early 1989. The U.S. policy of pressure against Stroessner may also have played a role, but probably only a small one.[39] Stroessner had long boasted of the backing of the U.S. government and the clear signals of dissatisfaction from the administration may have weakened his political base. Nonetheless, the ouster was at root the work of the traditionalist faction of the Colorado Party. Whether or not the ouster portends a full democratic transition in Paraguay remains to be seen. Presidential elections were held on May 1, 1989 and General Rodríguez was elected President by a wide margin. Since then he appears to have maintained a notably less-repressive rule than Stroessner but has not yet changed the long-entrenched hold of the military and the Colorado Party.

## PANAMA

### The Reagan Administration and General Noriega[40]

In December 1977, President Carter and Panamanian President Omar Torrijos signed the Panama Canal treaties, creating a framework of joint U.S.-Panamanian management of the Canal until the year 2000 and full Panamanian control after that. The Panama Canal treaties were a major diplomatic breakthrough that ended years of tension and unrest in Panama over U.S. control of the Canal and appeared to establish a basis for decades of harmonious relations between the two countries. In fact, however, the 1980s proved to be the stormiest decade of U.S.-Panamanian relations ever, and in December 1989, just twelve years after the Canal treaties were signed, the United States launched a major military invasion of Panama, the first large-scale, direct U.S. military intervention in Latin America

(Grenada being in the Eastern Caribbean) since the invasion of the Dominican Republic in 1965.

In the early 1980s U.S.-Panamanian relations were quiet, despite the unexpected death of Torrijos in 1981. In the wake of Torrijos's death, the Panamanian National Guard assumed control of Panama and the top officers of the Guard, including General Manuel Antonio Noriega, wrestled behind the scenes for primacy. Neither the Canal treaties nor the U.S. military base rights (Panama is the home of the United States Southern Command, the U.S. military's Latin American headquarters) were disturbed by the leadership transition in Panama and the Reagan administration was confident that U.S. interests were in good hands with the National Guard. Torrijos had initiated a process of transition to formal civilian rule in the late 1970s with national elections projected for 1984. The Guard pledged to adhere to this transition timetable; a pledge the administration noted approvingly but appeared to care about only marginally. Panama's relatively calm domestic political situation and low levels of human rights violations contrasted favorably with the turbulent Central American countries to the north, giving the administration little reason to concern itself with Panama's internal affairs.

In 1983, Noriega pushed aside the last of his rivals and became head of the National Guard and de facto ruler of Panama. Although Noriega was scarcely a household name outside of Panama, he was well known within the U.S. government. He had worked for the CIA and U.S. military intelligence almost continuously since his days in military school in the late 1950s. As chief of intelligence under Torrijos in the 1970s, he had worked closely with the CIA to build up the Panamanian intelligence service. Noriega was notorious for his ruthlessness, cunning, and pure love of power. He was uninterested in ideology and throughout the 1970s had sold his services simultaneously to Cuba and the United States (as well as to many other foreign intelligence services), skillfully playing enemies off each other and constantly coming out the winner. Noriega's involvement in many international criminal enterprises, including gunrunning and drug trafficking had almost led him to be indicted in the United States in the late 1970s but he was protected by his friends in the U.S. military and intelligence communities and by a Carter administration concerned about not taking any steps that might upset the U.S. Senate's approval of the Panama Canal treaties. In 1981 Noriega was put back on the CIA payroll, at a rate of around $200,000 a year, about the same as President Reagan's salary.

Having gained the leadership of the National Guard, Noriega began running Panama as his personal fiefdom, enriching himself tremendously and consolidating the loyalty of the Guard officer corps, loyalty that was based both on fear and self-interest, as many of the officers were themselves getting rich under Noriega's rule. Noriega recognized the importance of form in political life and allowed the long-planned 1984 presidential elections to proceed. He supported Nicolás Ardito Barletta, a technocratic economist and former vice president of the World Bank, against Arnulfo Arias Madrid, the populist mainstay of Panamanian politics for over fifty years. Arias had the distinction of having been elected president three times in the past and having been ousted by the military each time, the last time in 1968 after holding office for only eleven days. Barletta ran a solid campaign but was going down to defeat against Arias until Noriega's chief of staff, Colonel Roberto Díaz Herrera, set in motion a plan to rig the vote-counting in Barletta's favor. Eleven days after the election Barletta was formally declared the winner by a very narrow margin. U.S. intelligence picked up on the fraud and transmitted the information to Washington. The Reagan administration kept the information under wraps and invited Barletta to Washington in July where he had a cordial meeting with President Reagan, Vice President Bush, and Secretary of State Shultz. And in an important gesture of support, Secretary of State Shultz (as well as Jimmy Carter) attended Barletta's inauguration October 1984.

Two years later it became publicly known in the United States that Barletta's victory was fraudulent and that the U.S. government had known of the fraud almost immediately after it occurred. Secretary of State Shultz was asked by U.S. journalists about his decision to attend the inauguration in light of his knowledge about the electoral fraud. Schultz replied:

> Panama had an election that marked a transition from military to civilian, something we had been encouraging. . . . And the election was close. It was thought to be close by polling results, and in general everybody thought it would turn out close and it did. . . . We basically stayed out of it. It's their election, not our election. We don't go around the world certifying elections.[41]

Shultz's decision to attend the inauguration reflected the State Department's view that the United States faced a choice between backing an honest and skillful economist who might consolidate civilian rule or shunning Barletta and risking an out-and-out military coup. The State Department decided to downplay the electoral fraud and back Barletta.[42] As former Deputy Assistant Secretary of State Frank McNeil has argued, however, the administration was sending mixed signals to Noriega:

> The policy backed by Ambassador Briggs and Assistant Secretary Motley, was to try to avoid a new Somoza and to support real civilian rule. The body language that Noriega saw from the CIA, military intelligence, and some in DOD suggested otherwise; that if he could consolidate his hold, his friends in Washington would take care of things. The State Department could be safely ignored.[43]

Noriega was in any case well on the way to consolidating his hold. In September 1985, the Panamanian Defense Forces (the new name of the Panamanian National Guard), at Noriega's direction, murdered Hugo Spadafora, a prominent Panamanian political figure. Spadafora had been returning to Panama after a long period abroad, possibly with the intention of exposing Noriega's and the Panamanian Defense Forces' involvement in international drug trafficking. The brutality of the murder (Panamanian military personnel beheaded Spadafora alive) and relative rarity of such brazen acts of political violence in Panama shocked Panamanians and caught the attention of many people in the United States and elsewhere. When Barletta began to form an independent commission to investigate the murder, Noriega promptly locked him into Noriega's own office and kept him trapped there until he signed a resignation statement. Barletta was replaced by Eric Arturo Delvalle, who was known as a weak politician compliant to Noriega's direction.

The Reagan administration scarcely blinked at Barletta's ouster. Noriega was not only an old friend and current asset of the U.S. military and the CIA, he had gained the Reagan administration's special friendship by helping out with the contras. He had allowed the contras to use some airfields in Panama, provided them some funds, and agreed to train some contras for the southern front in Costa Rica that the United States had been attempting to develop in conjunction with Eden Pastora. For the Nicaragua-obsessed Reagan administration, this assistance vastly outweighed Noriega's authoritarian political behavior at home and even his increasing involvement with drug trafficking, knowledge of which was becoming more extensive within the U.S. government in the mid-1980s. Noriega met with CIA Director William Casey on November 1, 1985, just a few months after ousting Barletta. Casey criticized some of Noriega's Cuban-related activities but did not mention Barletta's ouster or the drug trafficking issue. Noriega apparently left the meeting reassured of his good relations with the Reagan administration.[44]

In June 1986 the *New York Times* ran two front-page stories by Seymour Hersh setting out a mass of damaging information about Noriega leaked from U.S. intelligence sources.[45] Noriega was reported to be or have been involved in drug trafficking, illegal reexports of U.S. high technology products to Cuba and Eastern Europe, sales of arms to the leftist M-19 guerrillas in Colombia, and the Spadafora murder. The stories also revealed Noriega's CIA connections. The revelations brought Noriega into the U.S. public eye for the first time and instantly created the image, accurately enough, of a dangerous, sadistic figure with sinister ties to the U.S. government. The negative publicity prompted an internal policy review in the administration. Noriega's utility with respect to the contras still dominated the administration's outlook, however, and no change in policy was made.

Although Noriega was still on good terms with the administration, his growing notoriety was beginning to create pressure in other circles for the United States to distance itself from him. Senator Jesse Helms began to question the U.S. relationship with Noriega in 1986 and was soon joined by Senator John Kerry. The ultra conservative Helms and liberal Kerry, an ideological odd couple, were both concerned by Noriega's ties to international drug trafficking. In addition, Helms was a staunch opponent of the Panama Canal treaties and saw Noriega as the sort of unreliable Latin tyrant to whom the Canal should never have been turned over. Helms successfully sponsored an amendment to an intelligence appropriations bill in late 1986 calling for the CIA to provide a report on the various allegations of criminal activity by the Panamanian Defense Forces and Kerry directed the Senate Subcommittee on Terrorism, Narcotics, and International Communications (which he headed) to begin investigating Noriega's involvement with international drug trafficking.

Despite the growing pressure from Congress and the heightened awareness of Noriega's shady character among the U.S. public, the Reagan administration began to move away from its close relationship with Noriega only in mid-1987 and even then more in response to events in Panama than to domestic pressure. In early June, Noriega's chief staff, Díaz Herrera, broke with Noriega and publicly accused him in Panama of many wrongdoings, including fixing the 1984 elections, directing the murder of Hugo Spadafora, and even planning the plane crash that killed Torrijos in 1981. Díaz Herrera's accusations created a furor in Panama and provoked massive demonstrations against Noriega and the military, the first such demonstrations since Noriega gained power. A group of opposition leaders and parties formed a coalition called the National Civic Crusade and organized a general strike on June 10. On June 11, the Panamanian government declared a "state of urgency" and suspended many civil and political rights.

The administration initially took a cautious line toward the chaotic events in Panama. After several weeks of serious civil unrest in Panama, the U.S. Senate passed a resolution calling for a public accounting of the allegations against Noriega and the Panamanian Defense Forces as well as for Noriega and any other implicated officers to relinquish their duties pending an investigation. Noriega was infuriated by the resolution and four days later a surging mob of pro-Noriega demonstrators in Panama stoned the U.S. embassy. The Panamanian police guarding the embassy had been withdrawn shortly before the demonstrators arrived, indicating Panamanian government complicity in the attack. The attack on the embassy outraged Secretary Shultz and finally moved the State Department to criticize Noriega openly and to suspend economic and military aid. The civil unrest in Panama continued through July then faded as the opposition was unable to shake Noriega's tight grip on power. The events of June and July spurred the belief that had been building up for years in the State Department that Noriega was a danger to Panama and a liability to the United States and that the administration must pressure him to step down. The CIA and the Defense Department acknowledged that Noriega was corrupt and repressive but were reluctant to forsake someone who had been useful for so long and in so many ways. The Drug Enforcement Agency also backed Noriega, contending that the allegations of his involvement in drug trafficking were overstated and that he had actually been very helpful to U.S. drug enforcement officials in the region.

Out of this divided internal alignment emerged a weak consensus that Noriega should step down but that this goal should be pursued in a cautious, behind-the-scenes manner. No strong methods for dislodging Noriega were agreed upon. In this autumn of 1987, Noriega learned that criminal indictments against him were being prepared in Florida and sent out feelers through José Blandón, the Panamanian Consul General in New York, as to the possibility of some arrangement whereby he would step down from power but remain in Panama and receive immunity from prosecution in the United States. Blandón half-negotiated, half-conspired with Gabriel Lewis, an influential Panamanian (and former Panamanian ambassador to the United States) who had been plotting in the United States for some time to find a way to force Noriega out. The Reagan administration participated indirectly in the negotiations but sent mixed signals to Noriega about whether the administration really wanted him out. Noriega turned defiant and the nascent "Blandón Plan" went nowhere.

In December, the administration, partly as a result of Gabriel Lewis's intensive lobbying, decided to send an official envoy to meet with Noriega and deliver a tough message on the need for his departure. After much interagency back-and-forth about who should go, reflecting the still deeply divergent views of Noriega within the administration, Assistant Secretary of Defense Richard Armitage was sent in late December. Armitage was not given a strong, clear message to convey, however, and just outlined to Noriega a plan whereby Noriega would retire and elections would be held. Armitage delivered no ultimatum and Noriega came away unfazed.

The Reagan administration shifted to a forceful anti-Noriega policy only in February 1988 and the shift came as a result of two events outside the administration's immediate control. On February 5, the U.S. Attorney's Office in Miami announced that two Florida federal grand juries had indicted Noriega on multiple counts of drug trafficking. The indictments were the work of several independent-minded federal prosecutors who had relentlessly pursued the case on their own. The administration had been informed of the indictments while they were in preparation but because of bureaucratic distraction had paid relatively little attention to them, despite their obviously powerful policy implications. The indictments were front-page news in the United States. In the public's mind they confirmed the long-festering rumors about Noriega's drug ties and officially branded Noriega as an untouchable. They had an immediate, major effect on the administration's policy: in an election year in which the drug problem had already become an important campaign issue, the administration could not afford to be seen tolerating an apparently known drug trafficker. An adamant anti-Noriega policy became an unquestionable political necessity.

As the administration geared up to take more aggressive steps against Noriega, the President of Panama, Eric Arturo Delvalle, split with Noriega and attempted to dismiss him as military chief of staff on February 25, 1988.[46] Delvalle's attempt failed badly. The pro-Noriega National Assembly met within hours of Delvalle's announcement, voted him out of power and voted in a Noriega lackey, Education Minister Manuel Solis Palma, as president. Although Delvalle's move failed, it gave the administration a visible handle for an anti-Noriega campaign. The administration backed Delvalle, continuing to recognize him as the legitimate president of Panama even as he went into hiding. With the close assistance of Arnold & Porter, a major Washington law firm, Delvalle and Panamanian Ambassador to the United States Juan Sosa fought back against Noriega, imposing a freeze on all Panamanian government assets in the United States. The administration provided the certification of Delvalle's and Sosa's status necessary to make the measures work under U.S. law. The administration added its own set of economic sanctions on March 11, placing the U.S. government's monthly Canal payments to the Panamanian government (approximately $7 million per month) and all other U.S. government payments to Panama into an escrow account "for the Delvalle government on behalf of the Panamanian people," and suspending trade preferences for Panamanian goods.

The State Department was optimistic that the combination of Delvalle's asset freeze and the U.S. sanctions would paralyze the Panamanian economy and rapidly drive Noriega out of power. Administration officials stated privately that Noriega would be out in a matter of weeks, if not days. White House spokesman Marlin Fitz-water warned Noriega ominously that "there are limits to our patience."[47] Two State Department officials were sent to Panama in mid-March to negotiate with Noriega over his departure, offering that the United States would not pursue extradition if Noriega left Panama. Noriega, however, had deftly rallied his many financial resources, and called for assistance from his many friends abroad, such as Muammar Qaddafi, and was holding up surprisingly well against the economic pressure. He rejected the U.S. offer and defiantly denounced the Reagan administration.

In late March and early April, the administration attempted to settle on new measures that would drive Noriega out. A serious interagency division plagued this already chaotic and hurried policy process. The State Department, led on this issue by Assistant Secretary Abrams, pushed for dramatic measures. The State Department floated various military-oriented proposals, including a plan to set up Delvalle and a dissident military officer in the Canal Zone, protected by U.S. troops, as leaders of a new Panamanian government, a military strike to topple Noriega, or a surgical "snatch" operation to capture Noriega and bring him to the United States to stand trial. The Pentagon, led by Admiral William Crowe, Chairman of the Joint Chiefs of Staff, firmly opposed any military action against Noriega. The Pentagon argued that using U.S. military bases in Panama in an attack on the Panamanian government would cause governments all over the world to call into question the presence of U.S. military bases on their soil and that any military action would endanger the lives of the 50,000 Americans living in Panama. Abrams and Crowe fought bitterly over Panama. Pentagon officials were amazed by the State Department's aggressive advocacy of what they saw as reckless military solutions. "Where are the voices of reason at the State Department?" one Pentagon official asked.[48] State Department officials in turn lamented what they saw as the Pentagon's excessive caution, ascribing it to post-Vietnam paralysis.

President Reagan did not step in and resolve this heated interagency debate, although by not taking an interest in the State Department's military proposals he effectively killed them. The only measures that the competing agencies could agree on were economic sanctions. On April 8, Reagan invoked the International

Emergency Economic Powers Act (IEEPA) to prohibit all payments to the Noriega/Solis Palma government by U.S. citizens, U.S. corporations, and their subsidiaries in Panama. The sanctions were fairly strong, but were far short of a total trade embargo, let alone the military measures that the State Department wanted. They represented, more than anything, the administration's desire to do something but its deep unwillingness to take serious risks and the continuing ambivalence about the anti-Noriega endeavor within the military and intelligence agencies. The State Department was intensely frustrated by the unwillingness of the rest of the administration to go all-out against Noriega. The other agencies felt the State Department was acting recklessly with little idea of what it was doing.

The economic sanctions further damaged the Panamanian economy but did not force Noriega out. He managed to keep the economy afloat, to suppress dissidents within the PDF officer corps, and keep the civic opposition cowed. Negotiations between Noriega and the administration continued in April and May. The administration opened the possibility that it would quash the indictments in return for Noriega's departure, provoking a controversy in the United States and a division between Vice President Bush and President Reagan. Bush, seriously concerned that U.S. concessions to Noriega could lead to him being branded soft on drugs in the U.S. presidential campaign, came out publicly against any deal that involved quashing the indictments. Reagan nonetheless approved the concession and Deputy Assistant Secretary of State Michael Kozak, the principal U.S. negotiator with Noriega, came within inches of getting a deal for Noriega's departure when Reagan and Shultz lost their patience and called off the negotiations in late May.

The negotiations were never restarted and the policy froze in place for the rest of 1988. On the one hand, the administration was unable to find any further methods of effective pressure against Noriega.[49] On the other hand, out of fear of being branded as soft on drugs, the administration could not back away from the sanctions that were continuing to hurt the Panamanian economy (and many Panamanians). As the presidential campaign got underway in earnest, the Bush camp imposed a single goal on the administration's Panama policy: keep the entire issue out of the public eye as much as possible and fight off attempts by the Dukakis campaign to make an issue out of Noriega's extensive connections with the Reagan administration.

## Drugs, Democracy, and the Canal

The Reagan administration generally explained its shift to an anti-Noriega policy as the result of antinarcotics and prodemocracy concerns. Some observers accepted those rationales at face value; others pointed to the United States's underlying interest in protecting the Panama Canal. The motivations behind the shift are difficult to reduce to any one factor or even cluster of factors. It is clear that in the 1980s the U.S. government saw its two dominant interests in Panama as being the maintenance of a stable Canal relationship and the continued right to maintain military bases there. For most of the decade, the Defense Department felt both of those interests were secure with Noriega in power and that Noriega gave the additional benefit of cooperation with the contra campaign. The CIA concurred with the Defense Department, and also favored Noriega as a useful intelligence asset. The State Department initially paid little attention to Panama, but in the mid-1980s became concerned that Noriega was well on the way to becoming a Marcos-style dictator who would lead Panama down a path of increasing repression and instability that would ultimately jeopardize the Canal relationship. As discussed above, the State Department was consistently outweighed by the Defense Department and the CIA and for a time at least was also won over by Noriega's assistance with the contras.

The shift to an anti-Noriega policy occurred in two stages. The first shift occurred in 1987 and was triggered by the civil unrest that hit Panama in June and July. The unrest persuaded the State Department that its concerns over the long-term consequences of Noriega's rule were valid and bolstered the State Department's case against U.S. agencies favorably disposed to Noriega. That first shift, however, proved to be only partial. The second shift occurred in early 1988 after the indictments against Noriega were handed down. Once Noriega was indicted he became an untouchable in U.S. policy terms. The Pentagon and CIA could no longer plausibly argue that his utilities outweighed his liabilities and the State Department was able to move the administration to an out-and-out anti-Noriega policy.

The drug issue was a crucial factor behind the Reagan administration's decision to turn against Noriega. But it must be understood that the anti-Noriega policy was not an antidrug policy per se. The administration had known of, and tolerated, Noriega's involvement in drug trafficking for years before it shifted to a policy of real pressure against Noriega. It was only when Noriega's drug trafficking became public that it was a major factor in the administration's policy calculations. In other words, the administration was moved to act against Noriega not so much because he was involved in drug trafficking but because his involvement became publicly confirmed and thus extremely embarrassing to the administration. In sum, the anti-Noriega policy was advocated by the State Department out of concern for long-term U.S. interests in Panama but came to be accepted by the White House and other foreign policy agencies because of the public relations problems stemming from the Noriega drug ties.

The Reagan administration also formulated its anti-Noriega policy in prodemocracy as well as antinarcotics terms. Administration officials declared that what the United States wanted was a democratic Panama and linked their demands for Noriega's departure to the holding of presidential elections there. In fact, however, the administration's policy was not a democracy policy, it was an anti-Noriega policy, and the two were not equivalent. Noriega was by no means the sole impediment to democracy in Panama. The Panamanian military, with or without Noriega, was a highly corrupt, repressive, and antidemocratic force that had maintained direct control over Panama for over twenty years. If the Reagan administration had actually wanted to promote democracy in Panama it would have had to attack the military's powerful hold on the country. The administration explicitly did not do that; it said that its quarrel was with Noriega, not with the Panamanian military. Pushing for an electoral transition to civilian rule was not a means of changing the military's dominant position. All that was likely to emerge from such an electoral process was the sort of formalistic, military-dominated civilian rule that had emerged in El Salvador, Guatemala, and Honduras.

## Humiliation in the Tropics

The Reagan administration's campaign against General Noriega was a startling failure, one of the most visible foreign policy failures of the 1980s. The administration's inability to oust the most insignificant of tyrants in a small country traditionally dominated by the United States made the U.S. government look inept and powerless in the eyes of Latin America and the world. The policy was riddled with flaws of planning and execution. To start with, the administration essentially backed into the policy. Throughout the turbulent mid-and late-1980s in Panama, the United States reacted to events rather than anticipated them. For example, the State Department finally spoke out against Noriega only when serious civil unrest had broken out in Panama and the U.S. embassy had been stoned by pro-Noriega demonstrators. And the administration finally moved to an openly anti-Noriega policy only after drug indictments had been handed down. Backing into the policy proved to be a perilous approach. The administration fell into the pattern of hurriedly announcing policy goals in response to fast-breaking events and then looking around after the fact for the tools and resources to achieve them.

The constant divisions and in-fighting within the administration greatly weakened the policy. In 1986 and 1987, when the administration was beginning to question its relationship with Noriega, the divisions within the administration resulted in Noriega receiving mixed messages, which he interpreted as a lack of real desire on the administration's part to see him leave. In the crucial weeks in early 1988 when the administration was groping to knock Noriega out, administration officials were mired in endless interagency disputes over policy formulation.

The administration's embarrassing overconfidence in its ability to force Noriega out stemmed from a vast overestimation of U.S. power. As it has done repeatedly in recent decades, the U.S. government greatly overestimated the political leverage that would derive from economic sanctions. The sanctions did have considerable economic impact (unusual for sanctions) but the economic harm did not make Noriega lie down and give up, as some in the administration thought it would. Noriega's support in the military, and even the populace, was greater than the administration had reckoned and his ability to withstand political and economic turbulence was also much greater than anticipated. The Reagan administration misjudged not only the political effects of economic sanctions but the general level of U.S. influence. Many U.S. policymakers harbored the out-of-date idea that if the United States turned against a government in a small Latin American country, such as Panama, that government would rapidly collapse.

A further flaw was the administration's tendency to go it alone. The administration worked poorly with the Panamanian opposition and tended to deal directly with Noriega or his representatives without cutting the opposition in on the process. The opposition was angered by the administration's methods and came to be suspicious of whether the administration wanted real change in Panama or just to solve its own domestic public relations problems. Similarly, in keeping with its diplomatic style in Central America, the administration had little time for the efforts of other Latin American countries with an interest in the Panamanian situation and paid little attention to the possibility of multilateral negotiations or serious OAS involvement.

These many policy flaws—the infighting, the overestimation of U.S. influence, and the go-it-alone style—made the administration look bad and weakened the policy. But even if the administration had been of one mind, had accurately assessed U.S. influence, and included the Panamanian opposition and the OAS in its efforts, the result would not likely have been much different. The fact is that short of military action, which President Reagan did not want to consider, the administration did not have the political or economic leverage to oust Noriega.

The core failure of the Reagan administration's Panama policy was not the ill-fated campaign to oust Noriega but the years of tolerance and even active cooperation with the Panamanian strongman as he consolidated his repressive hold on Panama and multiplied his involvement in a host of sordid and illegal activities. The administration stood by uncritically as Noriega destroyed the civilian political process that Torrijos had attempted to reinitiate. And the administration overlooked his growing involvement with drug trafficking, his many other criminal enterprises, and his relationship with Cuban intelligence because of his occasional assistance to the contras. The administration's disastrous policy toward Noriega was in fact only an extension of a relationship the United States had been cultivating for decades. It was a classic case of the historic tendency in U.S. relations with Latin America for the United States to develop close attachments with corrupt, repressive tyrants on the theory that their helpfulness on security issues will outweigh the many negative implications of such a relationship. And as has almost always been the outcome of such relationships, the Reagan administration paid a high price when Noriega's unsavory nature came to light and the administration was put in the difficult box of trying to exorcise a demon it had done much to create.

## Aftermath: Operation Just Cause

Along with the moribund contra policy in Nicaragua and the endless war in El Salvador, the failed anti-Noriega policy was one of President George Bush's least pleasant inheritances from Ronald Reagan in the foreign policy domain. President Bush's initial approach was simply to downplay the whole embarrassing mess and get on with more productive policy initiatives in other parts of the world. The May 1989 presidential elections in Panama, however, put Noriega back on the front pages of the international press. Noriega annulled the elections to stymie what observers were certain was an overwhelming victory by the opposition; days after the election Noriega's thugs brutally beat opposition leader Guillermo Endara in broad daylight on the streets of Panama City. Once again Noriega was the defiant, evil king and the U.S. government was the powerless onlooker. After the aborted elections, President Bush began openly proclaiming his desire to see Noriega ousted by the Panamanian Defense Forces but undertook no measures to help bring about such a result. In October a group of Panamanian military officers staged a coup attempt against Noriega that came close to succeeding but failed when expected U.S. assistance (primarily the blocking of roads leading to Noriega's headquarters) did not materialize. The Bush administration had contacts with the coup leader, Major Moisés Giroldi Vega, days before the attempt but was leery of providing assistance owing to uncertainty about Giroldi's sincerity and fear that the U.S. participation might violate the U.S. legal prohibition on assassinations of foreign leaders. The exact extent of U.S.

involvement in the coup attempt was uncertain at the time, but the U.S. public received a strong impression of unpreparedness and disorganization, bringing much criticism upon the Bush administration. Commentators portrayed the coup attempt as the Bush administration's first foreign policy failure, strengthening President Bush's resolve not to let the Noriega issue drag on indefinitely and prompting the White House and Pentagon to begin serious planning for military action against Noriega.

Tensions between the United States and Panama continued to mount in late 1989 and incidents of Panamanian harassment of U.S. military personnel in Panama multiplied. Finally, after one U.S. soldier was killed by Panamanian security personnel at a roadblock, and another serviceman was beaten and his wife threatened, President Bush ordered a full-scale invasion, codenamed, "Operation Just Cause." On December 20, 1989, thousands of U.S. troops landed in Panama, battled the Panamanian Defense Forces and within three days quelled the resistance and effectively controlled the entire country. Between five hundred and one thousand Panamanians, many of them civilians, and twenty-one U.S. soldiers were killed in the invasion. Guillermo Endara was sworn into the presidency on the day of the invasion and quickly formed a new government. Noriega eluded the U.S. military for four days then took refuge in the Vatican mission in Panama. After a tense ten-day waiting game, Noriega surrendered himself to U.S. forces. He was immediately whisked off to the United States and put on trial for drug trafficking.

The Bush administration justified the invasion of Panama as necessary to protect the integrity of the Panama Canal treaties, to protect U.S. lives, to fight drug trafficking, and to promote democracy. The democracy rationale became a particular favorite of President Bush's. He led off his 1990 State of the Union address with a glowing reference to the restoration of democracy in Panama. In fact, neither democracy nor any of the other stated rationales determined the decision to invade. The Canal was a long-range concern but not a pressing one; Noriega had not taken any significant steps to limit U.S. access. With respect to protection of U.S. lives, a large-scale military invasion resulting in the killing of close to one thousand people is an unusual response to the killing of one U.S. citizen. In any case, U.S. personnel were being harassed in response to the

U.S. policy of pressure against Noriega; it would have been enough to cease the pressure to ensure no further harassment of U.S. citizens in Panama. The antinarcotics rationale was, as discussed earlier, hollow. It was the public revelation of Noriega's drug trafficking and his ties to the United States, not the drug trafficking itself, that provoked the shift to an anti-Noriega policy.

Finally, regarding promoting democracy, the notion that a burning desire to bring democracy to Panama pushed the Bush administration to military action is groundless. The U.S. government managed to live with a nondemocratic government in Panama for decades before it turned against Noriega in 1988. And the Bush administration was obviously able to live with nondemocratic governments in other countries of importance to the United States. The fact that elections had recently been held in Panama and that the credible candidate had apparently beaten Noriega's candidate helped the Bush administration justify the invasion. But restoring democracy was not a major motivation in and of itself.

The true motivation behind the invasion was simple. President Bush and his advisers would not stand for public defiance of the United States by a small-time tyrant who had an embarrassingly long history of close involvement with the United States. Such defiance was personally aggravating to Bush; moreover, it was harmful to the President's image. General Noriega was above all a public relations problem. The events of 1989 demonstrated to President Bush that the problem would not go away and that it was taking a toll on his foreign policy reputation. Once the Pentagon came around to the idea that military action was feasible and not likely to bog the military down in a long-term potentially unpopular campaign, it was only a matter of time before President Bush took the only surefire way to end the Noriega headache.

## HAITI

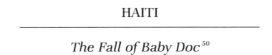

### *The Fall of Baby Doc* [50]

From 1981 to 1985 Haiti was almost a nonissue in the Reagan administration's Latin America and Caribbean policy. The administration perceived few political or economic interests in the world's oldest black republic and the poorest country in the Western hemisphere. There was no active communist movement in Haiti to excite the administration's attention. The country appeared to be in the firm grip of Jean-Claude Duvalier, known as "Baby Doc," who had taken over in 1971 at the age of nineteen, after the death of his notorious father, François Duvalier, or "Papa Doc." U.S. relations with Haiti had deteriorated in the late 1970s over human rights issues as well as the wave of Haitian refugees arriving in the United States in 1980. The Reagan administration saw Jean-Claude Duvalier as a net positive—although he was a corrupt, repressive, and inept leader, he was firmly anticommunist and pro-United States. The administration was disposed to improve relations with him and set out to increase U.S. economic aid to Haiti and include it in the newly established Caribbean Basin Initiative.

A 1981 amendment to the Foreign Assistance Act established that U.S. aid to Haiti could be provided only if the President certified that Haiti was making progress on human rights.[51] Limited political improvements were in fact occurring in the early 1980s as Duvalier carried out a confusing on-again, off-again set of political liberalization and economic reform measures. The administration highlighted the positive and downplayed the negative in its annual human rights certifications of Haiti. The small group of Congressmen interested in Haiti, primarily the Congressional Black Caucus, expressed skepticism at the certifications as well as frustration at the administration's superficial, positive view of Duvalier, but did not have the clout to change the policy.[52] U.S. economic aid increased steadily from $27.1 million in 1980 to $34.6 million in 1981 up to $55.6 million in 1985.

In November 1985, a series of riots broke out in Gonaives, a provincial city in Haiti's main agricultural region, and soon exploded into nationwide protests against the government. The outbreak of violence and unrest caught the Haitian government, and the United States, by surprise. Just four months before, Duvalier had affirmed his apparently solid hold on power by holding a referendum on his rule as President-for-Life and triumphantly announcing a 99.9 percent favorable vote. After the referendum, the administration had dutifully certified Haiti's human rights progress once again to permit more U.S. aid. The outbreak of protests in November had no obvious, immediate cause; they represented the accumulation of years of political and economic discontent and the rising tension caused by the gap between Duvalier's rhetoric of political liberalization and the reality of his absolutist rule. The protests gained force very rapidly and within a month observers in Haiti were speculating that Duvalier would soon fall. In January, Duvalier's position weakened and rumors of his departure began to multiply. On February 7, Duvalier and his family fled to France, abruptly ending the twenty-eight-year-old reign of the Duvaliers.

The United States played a cautious, reactive role during most of the period of the collapse of Duvalier's rule. In November and December the Administration stood back, making vague statements about possibly reducing U.S. aid and attempting to judge how far the protests would go. The U.S. embassy, led by Ambassador Clayton McManaway, concluded in early January that Duvalier was on the way out and convinced the State Department to accept that fact and adopt a policy of facilitating as peaceful and rapid a departure by Duvalier as possible. McManaway met with Duvalier in this period and pressed him on the gravity of his situation and the lack of realistic options for the maintenance of his power. In mid-January Duvalier sent a confidante to Washington to ask Elliott Abrams personally what the United States really wanted in Haiti. Abrams told him that Duvalier should step down from power and a transition to elected civilian rule should occur.[53] In late January Secretary of State Shultz called for a democratic transition in Haiti on the television program "Good Morning America." The State Department announced on January 29 that the administration would not certify Haiti for further economic assistance. And during late January the State Department looked all over Europe and Africa for a country that would accept Duvalier and his family. Every country contacted refused except France, which agreed to a temporary stay. When Duvalier decided to leave, a U.S. air force jet was hurriedly flown to Haiti for his exile flight.

## The Failed Transition

Within days of Duvalier's departure, an interim government was formed, headed by Lieutenant General Henri Namphy, a career military officer who was the military chief of staff in the period before Duvalier's departure. Namphy announced on February 10 that the interim government was fully committed to the development of a "real and functional democracy" and promised that free elections would be held.[54] The new government suspended the Duvalierist constitution and dissolved the rubber stamp national assembly. The administration praised the interim government and expressed optimism about Haiti's political future.

In the weeks immediately following Duvalier's departure, the administration formulated a new Haiti policy which was a two-part policy of promoting democracy: first, supporting the interim government and trying to guide it through an electoral transition; and second, pushing the civilian political sector to get organized and participate actively in the electoral process. The administration employed several tools to support and guide the interim government. The first was economic aid. The previously suspended aid was quickly restored and new aid was sought. U.S. aid increased from $55.6 million in 1985 to $77.7 million in 1986 and $101.1 million in 1987, making Haiti the largest recipient outside Central America of U.S. economic aid to Latin America and the Caribbean in 1987.

The aid was intended to serve a dual purpose. It was to help the interim government hold the country together during the rocky transition period. Economic discontent had been as much a cause of Duvalier's downfall as political discontent. If the interim government were to gain any credibility it had at least to prevent further economic deterioration. In addition, the aid was to give the administration leverage, both in the form of a carrot and a stick, to hold the interim government to its democratic promises. An example of the use of aid as a carrot came in June 1986 when violent anti-government protests broke out in Haiti in response to the government's perceived political and economic stagnation. The administration urged Namphy to respond positively. When he finally did so by setting out an electoral timetable, the U.S. government rewarded him by announcing an emergency grant of $20 million of economic aid. Aid was used as a stick in the summer of 1987 when Namphy tried to take control of the electoral process away from the independent Electoral Council. The U.S. government objected to Namphy's attempt and threatened to cut off economic aid. In response to U.S. pressure and a storm of domestic protests, Namphy yielded.

A second element of the effort to steer the interim government toward elections was "jawboning" of the government by U.S. officials, primarily those in the U.S. embassy in Haiti. The embassy threw itself into the situation, essentially appointing itself responsible for the transition process. Embassy officials from Ambassador Brunson McKinley on down (McKinley replaced McManaway in 1986) met constantly with Haitian government representatives to advise, cajole, demand, and beseech them to move ahead with the transition. At every stage of the transition, the embassy pushed the interim government to take the necessary steps and monitored the government's actions intensely. The AID mission matched the political campaign with its own intimate involvement in the interim government's economic planning process.

A third element was a multimillion dollar electoral assistance project, funded by AID and managed by the Costa Rica-based Center for Electoral Promotion and Assistance (CAPEL). The project, which was started in early 1987, aimed to help the Haitian government overcome its lack of technical expertise in elections and promote the massive civic education necessary to inform Haitians about the elections. The project provided technical assistance to the Haitian government on electoral issues such as organizing polling places, selecting ballots, and voter registration. It also sponsored a civic education effort carried out by nongovernmental Haitian organizations.

A fourth element, minor but very controversial, was U.S. military aid. The administration judged that with the departure of Duvalier and the break-up of the Tonton Macoutes (Duvalier's violent, corrupt legion of thugs) the remaining security forces might be unable to keep order. The administration thus decided that military and police aid was necessary and hurried $383,000 worth of nonlethal riot equipment to Haiti in March 1986. The following month, Assistant Secretary Abrams declared that the Haitian military must modernize and professionalize; the Administration soon announced that it would seek four million dollars in military aid to provide the Haitian army with trucks, training, and communications equipment.[55] The shipment of riot control equipment and the proposed military assistance caused a great stir in Haiti, including demonstrations at the U.S. embassy. The Haitian military and police were engaged in frequent clashes with a restless and bitter populace; the news that the United States was equipping those forces angered many Haitians. In the long run, only a small amount of military assistance ($3.2 million) was actually provided, but it generated widespread controversy and clouded U.S. policy for the duration of the transition period.

The administration's attempt to steer the interim government to an electoral transition rapidly fell into a downward spiral. At each of the many junctures in the transition process—setting up an electoral timetable, elections for a constituent assembly, the constitutional referendum, creating the Electoral Council, and preparing for the presidential elections—the interim government was increasingly inflexible, opaque, and even negative. At each juncture the United States pressed harder to persuade or induce General Namphy to take the necessary steps to keep the transition process on track. A cyclical process of increased efforts and diminishing returns set in. Administration officials strained to put a good light on Namphy's doubtful actions (or lack of action), and to hold to its optimistic public line on the interim government even though the factual basis for that line was steadily eroding. This cycle led the United States so far down what was at root a path of self-deception that when the electoral process fell violently apart in November 1987, the United States was caught looking dangerously out-of-touch with the reality of the Haitian political situation and overly attached to a disreputable "transitional" government.

The other half of the administration's policy was encouraging Haitian civilian politicians to organize and participate in the elections. The U.S. embassy served as an intermediary between the government and politicians on various electoral issues, attempting to lessen the high degree of mutual mistrust and facilitate the resolution of specific disagreements. The embassy also urged the candidates to campaign actively, form political parties, get out in the countryside, and generally act like "real" candidates. The embassy's goal was not simply to invigorate the electoral process but also to encourage what it saw as "the democratic center," a group of about a dozen candidates (there were well over fifty presidential candidates) who were generally wealthy, foreign-educated, and politically "moderate" (not too connected with the Duvalier elite but not associated with populist or fringe groups). The embassy believed that if this group could dominate the electoral campaign it would increase the chances of the elections coming off, and augment the likelihood of someone being elected whom the Haitian military would accept and the United States could work with.

The embassy's efforts with the presidential candidates were complemented by the National Democratic Institute for International Affairs (NDI). NDI put together a series of seminars on political party development and electoral campaigning for a group of Haitian politicians, approximately the same "democratic center" that the embassy was working with. The NDI project was more than simply a set of informational seminars; it was a coalition-building effort in which NDI facilitated the centrist candidates working together as a group to challenge the interim government on the many problems with the electoral process. The NDI effort worked toward the same goal as the embassy, that is, attempting to clarify the fragmented Haitian political field by promoting a coherent and somewhat unified center.[56]

After almost two years of a precarious, violence-scarred process, the transition broke down on election day, November 27, 1987. The elections were disrupted by a series of vicious attacks on voting stations, churches, and radio stations that left dozens dead and many more wounded. The attacks were carried out by mobs of what are believed to have been remnants of the Tonton Macoutes. Government soldiers ignored or even joined in some of the assaults. Namphy canceled the elections, dissolved the Provisional Electoral Commission, and abrogated all electoral legislation. The U.S. government responded by suspending almost all economic and military assistance. Yet the administration held to its seemingly unshakable optimism about the underlying democratic nature of the political process unfolding in Haiti. The White House, for example, commented on the election day slaughter in extraordinarily banal terms: "This regrettable situation will obviously set back the democratic processes."[57]

Presidential elections were eventually held, in January 1988, but were a shadow of the free and fair elections the United States had once hoped for and did not prompt the administration to lift the aid suspension. Leslie Manigat, the new president, lasted less than five months before being deposed by Namphy. Namphy was in turn ousted in a coup in September 1988 by General Prosper Avril, a long-time Duvalier aide, as the Haitian political scene lapsed again into violence and chaos.

*The Democracy Rationale*

It would be fanciful to propound any elaborate motivations for the administration's decision to encourage and facilitate the departure of Duvalier. The administration was not in a position to do much one way or the other during Duvalier's rapid fall. What it did do— the suspension of aid, the consultations with Duvalier, and the assistance in getting him out of the country—was a quick and sensible reaction to a crisis, not the implementation of a premeditated policy.

With respect to the policy of trying to guide the interim government to a democratic transition, the motivations were vague but uncontroversial. By 1985 promoting democracy had become the dominant theme of U.S. policy in Latin America and the Caribbean. When Duvalier began to fall, the administration saw Haiti as another case of the region's trend toward democracy and a logical place to pursue a prodemocracy policy. The absence of any strong geopolitical or economic interests in Haiti that might have called for more traditional security policies made it possible for the policy rhetoric and reality to merge. Once articulated as the U.S. goal in Haiti, promoting democracy dominated an empty sea and gave direction to what for years had been an essentially rudderless U.S. policy toward Haiti.

*A Costly Failure*

The administration's failed effort to guide Haiti to a democratic transition entailed at least two substantial costs for the United States—costs not acknowledged by the administration, or for that matter by Congress or the U.S. foreign policy community, both of whom supported the thrust of the administration's policy. The policy closely associated the United States with a government that was hated by most Haitians, tarnishing the image of the United States. The U.S. government started the post-Duvalier period with a reserve of good will among Haitians because of its role in facilitating Duvalier's departure. That good will steadily eroded during 1986 and 1987 when the United States served as the interim government's most loyal supporter, even though the government was steadily alienating and angering the Haitian public. Additionally, the wide gap between the administration's persistent optimism about the transition process and the unfortunate reality of that process made clear to the Haitian and international audiences the lack of realism in U.S. thinking about Haiti and the inability of the United States to exercise any meaningful power or influence there.

A fundamental flaw of the administration's policy was its mistaken assumption that the interim government was sincere about seeking to hand over power to an elected civilian government. The administration's willingness to take Namphy at his word in February 1986, when he proclaimed the goal of democracy, was remarkable. It is hard to understand why it should have been expected that a career officer in the Haitian military, who had served as the chief of staff of the armed forces under Duvalier, would suddenly become a committed democrat. Yet the administration rushed to embrace Namphy, characterizing him as a sober, technocratic, unambitious military man who had no goal other than presiding over an orderly electoral transition and returning quietly to military life. The administration was not alone in this early rhapsodizing about Namphy; the U.S. press and foreign policy community joined in as well. For example, the *New York Times*, reporting on Namphy's first press conference on February 10, spoke almost glowingly of Namphy's "whimsy" that it said was a "hallmark" of his personality.[58] The contrast between that upbeat story and the somber front-page article about two and a half years later on Namphy's overthrow of President Leslie Manigat, which reported that Namphy, "clutching a submachine gun and wearing a steel helmet, appeared angry and defiant as he spoke to the nation on television soon after securing control of the presidential palace," was instructive.[59] Furthermore, the administration's blind spot toward Namphy (and the interim government generally) was not merely an initial lapse but a persistent one. Over the course of the transition, Namphy repeatedly gave cause for doubt about his political agenda and character. Yet the U.S. embassy, in particular Ambassador McKinley, who was meeting regularly with Namphy, held fast to its view that Namphy was determined to carry out the transition and cede power.

It is worth pausing to consider the roots of the administration's unrealistically optimistic view of Namphy and the interim government. One cause was a general one: the ahistorical American approach to foreign cultures and events. For most Americans, Namphy was an unknown figure, a quiet member of the Duvalier regime suddenly thrust into the limelight. U.S. officials blithely assumed the best about Namphy, turning upside down his entire background so that what was stressed was not his long, close association with the deplorable Duvalier regime but the fact that it appeared he "didn't participate in its worst excesses."[60] Right from the beginning a deep gap existed between the Haitian and American views of the transition. Haitians started with deep distrust of Namphy and the interim government, whereas the United States assumed the interim government wanted to do good for Haiti.

Another cause of the U.S. optimism was a simplistic or misconceived view of what was entailed in the interim government "turning over power" to a civilian government. The crucial question of why those with power would simply give it up was assumed away or ignored. The administration acted on the apparent assumption that Duvalier's fall had ended the hold of the repressive Duvalierist elite on Haiti and created a power vacuum that the interim government would preside over until an elected civilian government was in place, ready to have power "handed over" to it by the interim government. In fact, however, the fall of Duvalier was just the collapse of one family's rule, not the dissolution of the deeply entrenched political and economic structures that upheld that rule. A transition to democracy would have required profound changes in those political and economic structures, an upheaval that would have dwarfed the civil unrest that drove the Duvaliers out. With the Duvaliers gone, the power in Haiti shifted to the interim government and was held by it quite firmly. There was no power vacuum or any real impending transfer of power to an elected government but rather a new governing arrangement based on essentially the same economic and sociopolitical structures as before.

U.S. officials involved in Haiti policy in the post-Duvalier period might respond to the charge that they misjudged the character of the interim government with the argument that they had their doubts about Namphy from the beginning, or developed them along the way, but that they believed they could steer the interim government toward an electoral transition. Even if one accepts that argument (and much evidence suggests otherwise), it merely points to a second fundamental problem with the policy: the U.S. government badly misjudged its ability to influence the interim government. The administration overestimated the potential leverage of the increased economic aid, a classic, recurring mistake in U.S. foreign policy all over the world since World War II. U.S. economic aid was important to Haiti but the elite was willing to do without it, if necessary, to keep its political prerogatives, especially because an aid cut-off worsened the lives of the poor more than the elite. The effects of the U.S. diplomatic interventions and jawboning were similarly overestimated. The embassy tried to assume the role of a crucial behind-the-scenes actor in the Haitian transition, but all the innumerable consultations, meetings, and harangues between embassy officials and the interim government were of little real consequence. The Haitian officials listened politely, then went off and did exactly as they pleased. The embassy and the State Department fell into the familiar trap of assuming that just because the United States had decided to exercise its political will in a hapless, seemingly dependent country (and one which the United States had militarily occupied several generations before), it would get its way.

A final serious problem with the policy was the almost exclusive focus on elections. The administration equated a democratic transition in Haiti with elections; the policy of promoting democracy was largely an effort to make sure presidential elections were held. Much less attention was paid to the question of whether any real change was occurring in the political and economic structures that made Haiti a profoundly antidemocratic country. For the U.S. government, the formal electoral process, particularly the near-mythical "electoral timetable," gained a reality of its own, increasingly separate from the actual political and economic situation in Haiti. The administration clung to that separate reality in the face of rapidly multiplying contradictions, insisting up to the last moment that the transition would come off, until the electoral process was finally shattered and the unpleasant, stagnant reality of Haitian political life was again the only reality at hand.

Was there an alternative to the U.S. policy? Most commentators, even traditional critics of the administration, approved of the pro-democracy emphasis of the policy. To the extent that the administration was criticized, it was for intervening too little rather than too much. Some U.S. liberals urged the administration to exert much harsher pressure on the interim government; some even proposed a U.S. military invasion or an OAS-organized invasion to assure a democratic transition.[61] It is extremely unlikely, however, that increased U.S. pressure, even military force, could have "made" Haiti a democracy. The United States might have forced the military and business elite to accept formal civilian rule but it was not within the United States's (or any other country's) capabilities to change the direction of Haiti's political history and reconfigure Haiti's economy, political culture, and social structure along the lines of a liberal Western democracy. The basic fault of the administration's policy was not that it was using insufficient tools to achieve its goal, but that it established as a goal something it did not have the wherewithal to achieve.

The only viable alternative was to do less, not more. After the fall of Duvalier, the United States could have pronounced its hope for a democratic transition in Haiti, but then adopt a wait-and-see approach to the interim government, offering the possibility of increased aid if concrete steps toward an electoral transition were taken. Elliott Abrams says that he has no regrets about having decided to back the interim government right away, arguing that it was incumbent on the United States to avoid any sort of power vacuum in Haiti that might lead to serious political instability.[62] But in February 1986 there was no power vacuum in Haiti—the departure of Duvalier was not a revolution that swept away an entire ruling structure. The business elite and the military remained in place and faced no significant competitors for power. The choice facing the administration was not between supporting an interim military government or risking anarchy. It was between embracing a dubious military government or taking a more cautious stance. A more cautious policy would not have had any better result with respect to Haiti's political process. It would, however, have spared the United States the costs of associating itself with an ultimately reprehensible government and of demonstrating vividly to the world the United States's inability to match its lofty stated goals with actual influence and capability.

## A NEW POLICY TOWARD "FRIENDLY TYRANTS"?

The Reagan administration's shift to a policy of pressure against the remaining right-wing dictators in Latin America and the Caribbean, together with its decisive shift away from supporting President Ferdinand Marcos of the Philippines in the mid-1980s, prompted some observers to posit a full-scale abandonment of the administration's initial Kirkpatrickian dogma regarding Third World dictators. Certainly the Reagan administration moderated its approach in these countries, but one must be careful about hypothesizing the emergence of a new, well-formed global policy toward "friendly tyrants" in the later Reagan years.

In the first place, the various policy shifts toward specific countries that did occur were largely reactive. In the Philippines, the administration came around to dropping Marcos only very slowly and in response to a long list of damaging events such as the murder of Benigno Aquino and the stealing of the 1985 "snap" elections.[63] In Haiti, the administration moved against Duvalier only once the country was in revolt and his position had become untenable. In Panama, the administration tolerated years of Noriega's drug trafficking and political criminality, turning against him only after serious civil unrest broke out and his wrongdoings became widely publicized in the United States. And in Chile, the administration warmly supported Pinochet until persistent domestic unrest in Chile and Pinochet's unyielding response raised concerns of a long-term polarization of Chilean society. The Reagan administration reacted to events rather than anticipated them, scrambling to accept the inevitable and then attempting to present that acceptance as a forward-looking, coherent policy.

The policy was also selective. The Reagan administration turned against Pinochet, Marcos, Duvalier, Noriega, and Stroessner. But with dictators in other parts of the world, such as President Mobutu of Zaire and President Suharto of Indonesia, the Reagan administration was content to maintain friendly relations. As long as a conservative dictator was not losing his grip on power or was not becoming a household name for evil in the United States, the Reagan administration was generally happy to be a friend.

Finally, the policy shift was at most only partial. The moderates in the administration, whose hand was growing in the later Reagan years, supported the shift strongly. The hard-liners, however, who were still important, were skeptical. The hard-liners fought the policy of pressure against Pinochet tooth and nail. They dragged their feet on the anti-Noriega policy, resisting a turn against Noriega until the drug indictments made it inevitable. President Reagan had to be dragged into cutting off support for Marcos and even after Marcos fell, Reagan maintained affection for him and a frosty reserve toward the new president, Cory Aquino. The moderates were able to carry the day in these various cases because of the progression of events in the countries themselves, the moderates' increasing weight within the foreign policy bureaucracy, and their ability to marshal congressional and public support for policies of pressure. Nonetheless it would be a mistake to see the administration as having clearly and completely shifted to a new policy with respect to right-wing dictators.

# 6

# THE REDISCOVERY OF
# POLITICAL DEVELOPMENT ASSISTANCE

In the 1960s, the United States developed a set of political development assistance projects to increase political participation and
strengthen democratic institutions in Latin America. Most of these
projects were abandoned in the early 1970s due to frustration with
inconclusive results and a shift in overall U.S. foreign assistance
goals and methods. To the surprise of many observers, political
development assistance made a comeback in the 1980s. The Reagan administration initiated a wide variety of assistance programs
explicitly aimed at democratic development in Latin America involving the Agency for International Development, the State Department, the United States Information Agency, the Justice Department, as well as the newly created National Endowment for
Democracy.

These political development programs constituted only a small
part of total U.S. assistance to Latin America but were nonetheless
substantial—in the Reagan years U.S. government democracy assistance programs to Latin America totaled approximately $100 mil-
lion and National Endowment for Democracy programs $25 million.
This democracy assistance received relatively little media or scholarly attention and constituted the quiet underside of the more
visible, declaratory elements of the Reagan administration's prodemocracy stance toward Latin America. This chapter gives an overview of these political development programs as well as an analysis
of their methodologies and a preliminary evaluation of their results.

By way of introduction, the chapter begins with a brief look at the antecedent programs of the 1960s and 1970s and President Reagan's Project Democracy initiative of the early 1980s.

## POLITICAL DEVELOPMENT ASSISTANCE
## IN THE 1960S AND 1970S

U.S. political development assistance to Latin America was primarily initiated as part of the Alliance for Progress launched by President Kennedy in 1961. The Alliance was one part of the large-scale expansion of U.S. assistance to the developing world. That broad assistance effort, aimed at producing rapid economic growth in developing countries, was based on W. W. Rostow's "take-off" theory of economic development—the idea that carefully targeted infusions of external assistance could spark economic "take-offs" in developing countries. The economic goals were linked to political goals. It was believed that rapid economic growth in developing countries would foster democratic development by expanding middle classes, politically empowering lower classes, and transforming traditional economic elites from reactionary landed classes to socially responsible industrial classes. These political goals were directly linked in turn to the primary overall purpose of U.S. foreign policy in that period, which was preventing the spread of communism. U.S. policymakers hoped that movement away from authoritarian governments to reform-minded democratic governments in the developing world would undercut populist pressures for radical leftist change.[1]

As the expanded U.S. foreign assistance effort unfolded in the 1960s, it met with some success in promoting economic growth in different parts of the world, including Latin America, but produced few results with respect to promoting democracy. A number of liberal Democrats in Congress observed this political shortcoming and concluded that the economic growth being fostered by U.S. assistance was too concentrated in the hands of traditional elites. They believed that the solution was for the United States to create assistance programs directly aimed at increasing political partici- pation and building democratic institutions. These Congressmen, after sponsoring several bills on the issue in the early 1960s, led Congress in 1966 to enact Title IX of the Foreign Assistance Act of 1961. Title IX directed AID to emphasize "assuring maximum partic- ipation in the task of economic development on the part of the people of developing countries, through the encouragement of democratic private and local governmental institutions."[2] Although Title IX did not create a particular set of programs or establish spe- cial funding sources, it was a significant commitment of the U.S. government to political development assistance:

> Title IX was the first explicit legislative injunction to the aid agency to concern itself directly and indirectly with politi- cal development in the Third World. . . . The intent and content of Title IX were to make political development, de- fined in terms of political participation and democratic in- stitutions, a goal of equal rank and salience with economic development.[3]

In Latin America, AID carried out four types of programs pur- suant to Title IX:[4] civic education programs to spread democratic ideas and attitudes and to foster the creation of democratic institu- tions such as community action groups, cooperatives, and rural as- sociations; leadership training programs to "create a corps of lead- ers dedicated to the proposition that progress in their respective countries should and can be achieved through the active and maxi- mal participation of the people in the tasks of government;"[5] pro- grams to support municipal government training institutes and other means of training local government officials; programs of technical assistance and training for national legislatures.

AID's experience with political development assistance in Latin America (and elsewhere) was not a happy one. To start with, AID believed itself unsuited to the task—AID saw itself as an economic development organization and engaged in political development assistance only with considerable reluctance and skepticism. AID found the programs troublesome to implement because of their po- litical nature and slow to produce results. Furthermore, democracy was in retreat in Latin America in the late 1960s, providing an unfriendly climate for democracy assistance. As the overall U.S. policy toward Latin America moved away from its earlier emphasis on supporting democracy to a fairly open toleration of authoritarian regimes in the late 1960s, the political development assistance programs lost any coherent relation to U.S. policy as a whole.

Political development assistance was largely abandoned in the early 1970s. The specific cause was the shift in the United States's foreign assistance strategy from the economic growth model to a basic human needs approach. The deemphasis on economic growth implied a deemphasis of the related political development component. More generally, the retreat from political development assistance was part of the larger shift in U.S. foreign policy away from the self-confident, expansionistic view of the U.S. role in the world in the 1960s to the post-Vietnam outlook of self-doubt, non-interventionism, and political relativism.

Political development assistance resurfaced in a minor way in the late 1970s as part of the growing emphasis in U.S. foreign policy on promoting human rights abroad. In 1978 Congress added Section 116(e) to the Foreign Assistance Act of 1973, authorizing AID to carry out programs to promote civil and political rights abroad. AID created some small human rights projects in Latin America, largely focused on legal aid for indigents. AID had little interest in human rights programs in this period, seeing them as political distractions foisted on it by Congress and as an unwelcome reminder of the political development efforts of the late 1960s.[6]

## Project Democracy

To understand the U.S. political development assistance programs in Latin America in the 1980s, it is necessary to examine briefly President Reagan's "Project Democracy," a global foreign policy initiative of the early 1980s that had some effect on the rise of political development assistance to Latin America. Project Democracy has been the source of considerable confusion both because the rhetoric surrounding the project greatly exceeded the dimensions of the actual project and because in the mid-1980s, NSC staffer Oliver North used the same name for the secret U.S. resupply program to the Nicaraguan contras.

## Toward a Global U.S. Government
## Democracy Program

Project Democracy is usually associated with the June 1982 speech by President Reagan before the British Parliament. In that speech, entitled "Promoting Democracy and Peace," Reagan urged the West to support the growing "democratic revolution" in the world and committed the United States to developing a global program of democratic assistance:

> The objective I propose is quite simple to state: to foster the infrastructure of democracy, the system of a free press, unions, political parties, universities, which allows a people to choose their own way to develop their own culture, to reconcile their own differences through peaceful means.[7]

The June 1982 speech reflected planning for a democracy initiative that had been going on since the start of the Reagan administration. When President Reagan took office in 1981, members of his early foreign policy team were concerned not only that the United States was slipping behind the Soviet Union militarily but that the United States was losing "the war of ideas" to the Soviet Union. These advisers look worriedly at the generously funded programs of book distribution, radio broadcasting, student scholarships, study tours, and the like that the Soviet Union was using to spread the gospel of Marxism-Leninism worldwide and feared the United States was doing far too little to publicize the virtues of democracy. They believed that the idea of democracy was insufficiently understood and admired around the world; Secretary of State Haig warned that "too many are denigrating democracy as weak and indecisive, unable to cope with the challenge of the Eighties."[8] These advisers were determined to fight the war of ideas aggressively and they decided to create a global "Project Democracy" which, according to a project proposal later submitted to Congress, would "advocate the principles of democracy, support those people and institutions committed to democratic development, build and reinforce bonds based on shared values between people and nations, and counter the spread of totalitarianism through the active interchange of ideas and vigorous democratic institutions."[9]

The early plans for Project Democracy envisaged a large and diverse set of democracy-related assistance projects carried out by different U.S. government agencies but funded from a centralized budget at the United States Information Agency (USIA). In the second half of 1981 a small group of officials, primarily on the staff of the National Security Council and at USIA, began hastily assembling information on all existing U.S. government foreign assistance projects that could plausibly be seen as democracy-related and generating ideas for new projects. They decided to present to Congress a budget request for a centralized democracy assistance program that would expand existing democracy-related projects and create a set of new ones. USIA, rather than AID, was chosen as the operational base for the initiative because of USIA Director Charles Wick's good relationship with President Reagan and because the thrust of the initiative was spreading the *idea* of democracy, not fostering long-term developmental processes in other countries. As the U.S. government agency responsible for disseminating ideas and information about the United States abroad, USIA was seen as the logical center for an idea-oriented democracy initiative.

The planning for Project Democracy was one element of a larger process in the early Reagan administration of reexamining and reinvigorating the general set of U.S. public diplomacy activities around the world. The early Reagan team interpreted the concept of public diplomacy more broadly and somewhat more aggressively than previous administrations: public diplomacy was to consist not simply of outreach activities to shape foreigners' opinions about the United States but of efforts to influence foreigners' domestic political beliefs in ways favorable to U.S. foreign policy. Getting foreigners to believe in democracy or to understand democracy better was seen as an important goal. Thus, for example, a training conference on the role of political parties in democratic societies in which foreign participants from nondemocratic societies were taught basic methods of party organization and operation would be a form of public diplomacy.

To increase the institutional base for public diplomacy in the government, President Reagan signed National Security Decision Directive 77 (NSDD 77) in January 1983 creating four interagency committees to plan and coordinate the implementation of public diplomacy programs. One of these committees, the International Political Committee (IPC), chaired by the Deputy Secretary of State, was specifically assigned the task of planning and coordinating democracy promotion activities. Although the IPC was to have ties with the planned USIA-based Project Democracy, the precise relationship between the two was left unclear. The basic idea appears to have been that USIA would serve as the central operational agency of Project Democracy while the IPC would be a high-level interagency steering committee that would set out general initiatives and help ensure the implementation of that Project Democracy.

## Toward a Democracy Foundation

In the same years that the Reagan administration was planning Project Democracy, work was going on in other circles in Washington toward the establishment of a quasi-autonomous, government-funded foundation for the promotion of democracy abroad. The idea for such a foundation had been bouncing around Washington for over ten years and had attracted the interest of a variety of people including Representative Dante Fascell, Lane Kirkland (AFL-CIO), William Brock (Republican National Committee), Charles Manatt (Democratic National Committee), Michael Samuels (U.S. Chamber of Commerce), George Agree (a political scientist), Allen Weinstein (a historian), and others. The idea for such a foundation was based in substantial part on the West German political party foundations through which each major West German political party carries out activities to support fraternal parties and promote democracy in other countries. The valuable role of the West German party foundations in the democratic transitions in Spain and Portugal in the mid-1970s was noted by various U.S. observers and the question was increasingly raised in Washington as to why the United States had no similar organizations. Impetus for some kind of democratic foundation also came from the AFL-CIO whose international wing had been looking for a steady new source of funds ever since losing its CIA funding in the late 1960s.

The idea began to gain momentum in 1979 when William Brock, Charles Manatt, and George Agree formed the American Political Foundation to study the issue seriously. Over the next several years they talked up the idea in Washington and began to build a base of bipartisan interest and support in Congress. They pushed for a democratic foundation that would have four component organizations, representing the Republican and Democratic parties, the U.S. labor movement, and U.S. business. In early 1982, the American Political Foundation requested U.S. government funds for a major study to map out a plan for the creation of a democracy foundation. The early Reagan administration, itself in the midst of planning Project Democracy, was sympathetic to the idea, because of the explicit emphasis on promoting the *idea* of democracy abroad and the expansive, pro-American hubris surrounding the project. In his June 1982 British Parliament speech, President Reagan said he looked forward to receiving the results of the American Political Foundation's study. The APF received $400,000 from the government and initiated the study in November 1982 in the form of the "Democracy Program" which was a kind of pilot organization with a board made up of interested persons including William Brock, Charles Manatt, Lane Kirkland, Dante Fascell, Michael Samuels, and George Agree, as well as a director (Allen Weinstein) and a staff of twenty.[10]

## Project Democracy Goes to Congress

In February 1983, after about a year and a half of preparatory work, the administration presented to Congress its proposal for a U.S. government global democratic assistance program. The "Project Democracy" proposal, as it was called, was a $65 million request[11] consisting of forty-four ongoing and proposed projects to be funded through USIA and managed primarily by USIA, AID, the State Department and the AFL-CIO. Most of the projects were educational—study tours, exchange programs, book publication, university programs, and conferences. All were aimed at promoting a greater understanding of democracy and/or the United States.

Project Democracy did not fare well before Congress.[12] Many of the proposed projects appeared to be simplistic efforts to convince foreigners of the evils of communism and the virtues of American democracy. Congressmen feared that the overall initiative would be little more than "a multimillion dollar American propaganda effort."[13] Many of the projects were obviously hastily designed and the initiative as a whole was not informed by any sophisticated political development ideas or analysis. Furthermore, the organizational form of the initiative confused and displeased Congress. It was unclear whether Project Democracy was just a repackaging of existing projects under a USIA umbrella or a genuinely new initiative. Neither USIA Director Charles Wick nor Secretary of State Shultz was able to clarify the proposal much in testimony before Congress.

Two months after the administration presented the Project Democracy request, the Democracy Program of the American Political Foundation issued an interim report entitled, "The Commitment to Democracy: A Bipartisan Approach." The report called for the establishment of a bipartisan, private, nonprofit organization to be called the National Endowment for Democracy (NED) and to be funded by annual U.S. government appropriations. The Endowment would be an umbrella organization that would disburse most of its funds to four subcomponent organizations operated by U.S. labor, business, and the Democratic and Republican parties (U.S. labor already had an international outreach organization, the other three subcomponent organizations were to be created once the National Endowment for Democracy funds became available). Congress was much more favorable to the idea of a National Endowment for Democracy than it was to the administration's Project Democracy proposal. The multipartisan nature of the proposed National Endowment appealed to many Congressmen in the same measure that the potentially one-sided and propagandistic Project Democracy worried them. And the National Endowment, being separate from the Executive Branch, would likely be more subject to Congress's influence than would Project Democracy.

The two proposals, Project Democracy and the National Endowment for Democracy, ended up as rivals for congressional funding. During consideration of the State Department Authorization Act for fiscal years 1984 and 1985 (the bill in which Project Democracy had been inserted), the House Foreign Affairs Committee and the Senate Foreign Relations Committee added specific legislative authority for funding a National Endowment for Democracy. The House Foreign Affairs Committee saw the NED as a "structure better able to carry out new [Project Democracy] initiatives."[14] After much deliberation, Congress eventually funded the creation of the NED and essentially rejected Project Democracy, approving only a few of the specific projects in the Project Democracy request. NED's initial funding ($18 million for fiscal year 1984) was much less than NED's backers had hoped for but was enough to get the organization underway.[15] The National Endowment for Democracy was inaugurated by President Reagan on December 16, 1983, and began operation in 1984.

Having failed to gain congressional support, Project Democracy was essentially stillborn. The various democratic assistance projects already underway at different agencies continued, but no central democracy assistance program was created. The International Political Committee established as part of the NSDD 77 public diplomacy organizational framework to coordinate democracy assistance efforts did meet off and on from 1983 to 1986 but without any Project Democracy budget it had no real influence or impact within the government. And the larger public diplomacy initiative of which the Project Democracy proposal had constituted one part also gained little substance. Its most concrete achievement was the creation of a public diplomacy office in the State Department that spent most of its time and resources mounting the vast anti-Sandinista, procontra publicity campaign.

Several years after Project Democracy went down to defeat in Congress, the term "Project Democracy" reappeared. Oliver North had nicknamed the secret contra resupply operation "Project Democracy" and during the Iran-contra investigations in 1987 this fact emerged, prompting speculation of links between the illicit Iran-contra activities and the original Project Democracy initiative. The only actual such link was in the public diplomacy realm—the secret NSC/CIA contra supply operation appears to have had some ties to the anti-Sandinista public diplomacy operation,[16] which had grown out of the broader effort to expand U.S. public diplomacy activities abroad but was not directly tied to the original Project Democracy proposal or to the National Endowment for Democracy.

## U.S. GOVERNMENT DEMOCRACY PROGRAMS IN LATIN AMERICA

Although Project Democracy failed to result in a global U.S. government democracy assistance program, it did contribute to the creation of a varied set of democracy assistance projects in Latin America. The planning process for Project Democracy brought together officials working on Latin American affairs from the State Department, USIA, AID, and elsewhere and encouraged them to think of ways the United States could promote democracy in Latin America. After Congress rejected the administration's Project Democracy initiative, these officials kept meeting and began developing democracy projects for Latin America and obtaining the necessary region-specific funding. The Project Democracy initiative, with its high-level White House backing, made clear to those mid- and low-level officials that despite the early Reagan administration's negativism on human rights, democracy was an acceptable, even priority, cause. They learned to invoke the project or at least its spirit to persuade reluctant superiors to support programs of democracy assistance in Latin America.

These new democracy assistance programs for Latin America generally entered the planning stage during the latter half of the first Reagan administration and got underway during the second administration. The programs developed as a patchwork of initiatives reflecting the interests and initiatives of particular individuals in different agencies. They were not coordinated by any one committee or agency and were not funded by any central democracy budget. In rough terms these programs fell into three categories: human rights and democratic participation programs, elections assistance, and judicial assistance.

### Human Rights and Democratic Participation Programs

In the late 1970s, pursuant to Section 116(e) of the Foreign Assistance Act, AID developed some human rights projects in Latin America, primarily involving support for Latin American legal aid organizations. The initial set of high-level Reagan appointees at AID were suspicious of human rights projects, seeing them as left-wing political activism cloaked in apolitical garb. They were particularly hostile to legal aid projects. President Reagan opposed public funding of legal aid in the United States; his AID appointees extended that position to oppose all U.S. funding of legal aid abroad. The various legal aid projects were quickly shut down and AID's Section 116(e) human rights programs in Latin America shrank from $1,028,000 in 1979 and $813,000 in 1980 to $408,000 in 1982, (with $200,000 of those 1982 funds going to the international observer mission for the 1982 elections in El Salvador).[17]

The very small group of AID career officers who were interested in the human rights programs feared that the Reagan administration would cut off human rights programs altogether and searched for a way to prevent that. With the advent of the high-level discussion and planning for Project Democracy in 1981 and 1982, they saw that although the human rights theme was in decline, the democracy theme was ascendent. They deduced that political development programs cast in terms of promoting democracy rather than human rights could be sold to the Reagan team. Beginning in 1983 they began developing a new set of programs that emphasized the concept of democratic participation rather than human rights, using the Section 116(e) funds and some new funds that became available with the rapid increase of economic assistance to Central America.

These new democratic participation projects focused on assistance to small-scale, nongovernmental organizations or groups in Latin America, usually through intermediate U.S. nonprofit organizations, to carry out civic education and community action programs. One such project was support to OEF International (a U.S. nonprofit organization) to carry out a multiyear program of training and education for community groups in Central America. Another was a grant to Partners of the Americas (also a U.S. nonprofit organization) for a program of training, technical assistance, and exchange programs between local groups in Central America, such as community organizations, youth groups, and public service agencies, and counterpart groups in the United States. Other projects dealt with specific sectors or issues that were seen to be related to democratization, such as training journalists or improving civil-military relations. Only a few projects entailed assistance to governmental institutions and they were small projects aimed at parts of the governments other than the executive branches, primarily at national legislatures and municipal governments.

In a few cases these programs maintained an explicit focus on human rights, such as a multimillion dollar grant to the Costa Rica-based Inter-American Institute of Human Rights for human rights advocacy work. Some projects reflected a conscious repackaging of human rights concerns into democracy terms. For example, during the 1980s AID funded two projects in Latin America run by Cultural Survival, a Massachusetts-based organization devoted to protecting indigenous people worldwide. The early project was described as an effort "to promote human rights and grassroots development among the Indians of Latin America."[18] The later project, which appears to have been essentially similar, was characterized instead as "a two year program to strengthen democratic participation among Indian communities and organizations in Central America."[19] Overall, AID obligated close to $20 million for human rights and democracy participation programs from 1983 to 1988, with almost all of the funds going to Central America, due to the availability of funds for that region and the lack of funds for South America.

## Elections Assistance

AID also became significantly involved in elections assistance to Latin America in the 1980s. This was a new area of activity for AID; AID had traditionally stayed clear of elections-related assistance out of a desire to avoid politically charged areas. The door to election assistance opened in El Salvador in the early 1980s. The State Department wanted to ensure that the 1982 Salvadoran Constituent Assembly elections achieved some international legitimacy and asked AID to fund an international observer mission (organized by the State Department). The officials who managed Section 116(e) funds at AID hesitated, greatly reluctant to get entangled in the political side of the controversial U.S. policy toward El Salvador. Secretary of State Haig insisted that the funds be provided, however, and they were.

After the election, the AID mission in El Salvador began assisting the Salvadoran electoral commission to develop a computerized electoral registry, as described in chapter 1. The election assistance effort mushroomed once the 1984 elections drew near. AID contributed several million dollars of local currency assistance for the purchase of electoral supplies.[20] AID and State Department officials in the U.S. embassy in San Salvador involved themselves closely in the actual election planning and administration.

AID got involved in a similar way in the 1985 presidential elections in Honduras. As in El Salvador, credible elections in Honduras were an important U.S. policy goal and the State Department pushed for larger amounts of U.S. assistance to the Honduran electoral commission as the elections drew near and technical uncertainties persisted. The AID mission in Honduras gave a very large quantity of local currency assistance, probably over $5 million, to the Honduran electoral tribunal, as well as $680,000 from AID in Washington for elections supplies.[21] State and AID officers in the U.S. embassy in Honduras threw themselves into the technical aspects of the electoral process, to the point of assembling ballot boxes in their offices and assuring the distribution of the boxes to polling sites.[22]

AID also gave elections assistance to Guatemala for its 1985 presidential elections but it was a much smaller effort than in El Salvador and Honduras, reflecting the perception in the U.S. government that the Guatemalan Electoral Tribunal was relatively well organized and was not in danger of fumbling away the elections through administrative incompetence. The smaller program also reflected the reticence of the AID mission in Guatemala about getting involved in the political process there. AID gave $234,000 to the Guatemalan electoral tribunal to finance the purchase of ballot paper and $321,260 for a training program for poll workers and poll watchers.[23]

In addition to direct funding of Central American electoral tribunals, AID also supported elections in the region through the Inter-American Center for Electoral Promotion and Assistance (CAPEL), a Costa Rica-based organization affiliated with the Inter-American Institute of Human Rights. CAPEL was founded in 1983 by some Latin Americans who saw that with the resurgence of democracy in Latin America there was a growing need for a Latin American electoral assistance organization. Their project was supported by AID human rights and democracy officers in Washington who hoped to channel the administration's strong desire to promote elections in Central America away from unilateral interventionist efforts into a Latin American organization. AID funded CAPEL from its inception and by the end of 1988 had provided more than $4 million of assistance, almost all of CAPEL's budget. CAPEL carried out many different activities, in South America as well as in Central America, including technical assistance to electoral tribunals, conferences for electoral officials, training courses in electoral processes, electoral research, and election observer missions.

Elections assistance also spread beyond the borders of Central America. As discussed in chapter 5, AID established an ambitious elections assistance project in Haiti in 1987 as part of the U.S. effort to guide post-Duvalier Haiti to an electoral transition. And in Chile, electoral assistance was also an important component of the later U.S. policy of promoting a democratic transition. AID supported the Chilean plebiscite by giving a $1.285 million grant to CAPEL which CAPEL in turn granted to CIVITAS, a Chilean organization carrying out voter registration programs.

## The Administration of Justice Program

The largest set of U.S. democracy assistance projects in Latin America in the 1980s was the administration of justice program, an interagency initiative implemented by AID, the State Department, USIA, and the Justice Department.[24] The main element of this program was assistance to the judicial systems of Latin America and the Caribbean to help them improve the administration of justice in their respective countries. A related emphasis was training in criminal investigative skills for the police forces of the region. Planning for the administration of justice program got underway in 1983, the first project was initiated in 1984, and by 1987 the program's annual budget had reached $20 million. By the end of 1988 over $60 million had been obligated under the program, approximately $50 million for judicial systems and $10 million for police training.

The idea of U.S. judicial assistance to Latin America and the Caribbean was first broached in the Reagan years in 1981–1982 by John Bolton, a high-level political appointee at AID. Bolton was unable to garner support within the AID bureaucracy, however, and the idea gained no momentum. The idea soon resurfaced in a particular context—El Salvador. Throughout the early 1980s, Congress maintained pressure on the State Department to "do something" about the Salvadoran government's lack of progress on the cluster of high-profile murder cases of special interest to the United States, such as the nuns case (the December 1980 murder of four U.S. churchwomen), the Sheraton murders (the 1981 murder of the head of the Salvadoran land reform program and two AFL-CIO officials advising on that program), and the 1980 murder of Archbishop Romero. The State Department officials following those cases were astounded by the incompetence and disorganization the Salvadoran judicial system demonstrated in the cases. U.S. officials became convinced that the civil war in El Salvador had led to a breakdown of the judicial system and that this breakdown was a major cause of the death squad violence wracking the country. They concluded that the best way to achieve progress on the high-profile murder cases was to help El Salvador repair its judicial system.

In 1983 this idea was translated into action. The State Department formed an interagency working group on the administration of justice in Latin America and the Caribbean, headed by Principal Deputy Assistant Secretary of State for Inter-American Affairs James Michel. The working group began planning a judicial assistance program for El Salvador. It also examined the judicial systems of other countries in Central America and decided that judicial assistance should be implemented throughout the region. The working group's decision to extend judicial assistance beyond El Salvador was based on the view that because independent, competent judicial systems are an integral part of Western democratic governments, judicial assistance is a logical, even necessary component of an effort to promote democracy in any country with historically weak civil institutions. Thus, although the decision to pursue judicial assistance was sparked by a specific need to address right-wing political violence in El Salvador, from the beginning the administration of justice program was conceived as a long-term, region-wide democratic development program.

The interagency working group studied the previous U.S. legal assistance program to Latin America, the law and development program of the late 1960s and early 1970s, in order to avoid repeating the mistakes of the past. From this retrospective analysis a set of operational principles for the administration of justice program were derived[25]: first, help Latin American governments improve their judicial systems on their own terms rather than try to export U.S. legal models; second, support existing local institutions rather than create new institutions; third, focus on concrete, practical goals that have a clear link to the overall developmental objectives; and fourth, give judicial assistance only to countries that have elected civilian governments. These principles have informed all the specific projects created under the administration of justice program.

The El Salvador Judicial Reform Project was hurriedly launched in 1984, using congressional earmarks for its $9.2 million funding. The project combined an immediate concern over obtaining progress in the high-profile political murder cases with the administration's longer-term prodemocracy interest in a general improvement of the Salvadoran judicial system. Reflecting the former concern, the project foresaw the establishment of an investigative commission, which was to consist of an elite police unit under civilian control (the Special Investigative Unit) and a forensic team to provide the Salvadoran government the means to solve high-profile political murder cases. It also called for the formation of a judicial protection unit to protect participants in trials of sensitive cases. Reflecting the latter, more long-term concern, the project provided for the establishment of a law reform commission and a judicial training program. AID was the implementing agency of the El Salvador project, although State Department officials were heavily involved in the planning of the program and maintained a role in monitoring its implementation.

With the Salvador project underway, the administration of justice program broadened into a regional undertaking. After some lobbying by Deputy Assistant Secretary Michel and other administration officials, Congress established a legislative foundation for judicial assistance in 1985, authorizing the use of up to $20 million per year for programs to strengthen the administration of justice in Latin America and the Caribbean.[26]

In January 1985, AID created an administration of justice office in its Latin America and Caribbean bureau and folded into it the existing democratic assistance programs, in particular the human rights and democratic participation programs and elections assistance projects described above. In March 1985 AID launched the Regional Administration of Justice Project, a $9.6 million, five-year judicial assistance program based at a small U.N. institute in Costa Rica (the United Nations Institute for the Prevention of Crime and Treatment of the Offender [ILANUD]). Under this program, ILANUD offers training courses for judges, prosecutors, and other legal personnel as well as a range of technical assistance to courts and justice ministries on such issues as case management, legal data bases, and law libraries. The original participants in the regional program were Costa Rica, El Salvador, Honduras, the Dominican Republic, and Panama. Over the course of the program Panama was dropped (and then readded after the 1989 U.S. invasion), Guatemala was added, funds were made available to include some South American participants, and the overall funding was increased to over $12 million.

The administration of justice program continued to expand rapidly. A $10 million Caribbean regional project was initiated in 1986, based at the University of West Indies in Barbados, to provide assistance for the judicial systems of various Eastern Caribbean states and Jamaica. From 1986 on, single country projects ranging in size from $1 million to $5 million were established in many countries including Costa Rica, Guatemala, Peru, Honduras, Bolivia, and Colombia, generally focusing on judicial training, technical assistance, and the provision of materials and supplies for the judiciary. A variety of small-scale legal assistance projects were also created, including assistance to bar associations in the region, tie-in programs with U.S. law schools, and exchange visits and study tours for Latin Americans involved in the administration of justice.

A major subcomponent of the administration of justice program was police training. State Department officials grappling with the problem of the Salvadoran government's lack of progress on the high-profile political murder cases in the early 1980s were struck not only by the incapacities of the Salvadoran prosecutors and judges, but also by the almost complete lack of investigative skills on the part of the Salvadoran police. As a result, the officials planning an administration of justice project for El Salvador decided that training police in investigative techniques must be a part of the project. This decision to include investigative training of foreign police was extended to the administration of justice program as a whole, based on the view that since police are an integral element of any criminal justice process, it makes no sense to exclude them from a general assistance effort to improve that process.

The U.S. officials developing the administration of justice program drew a line between assistance to police to improve investigative skills and assistance for operational matters such as crowd control or arrest methods. Maintaining this line was seen as a way of avoiding the more controversial areas of police assistance, thereby improving the chance of getting past Congress's long-standing opposition to police aid. State and Justice Department officials lobbied Congress to include a provision in the 1985 authorization of the administration of justice program for police aid programs. They succeeded in obtaining authorization for "programs to enhance investigative capabilities, conducted under judicial or prosecutorial control." This phraseology emphasized the neutral-sounding notion of "investigative capabilities," artfully avoiding the word "police." The phrase "under judicial or prosecutorial control" was compromise language intended to limit U.S. aid to foreign police operating within the rule of law in their country. The administration interpreted the phrase loosely and in practice police aid was given to any country with an elected civilian government, even if, as in Guatemala and El Salvador, the police's adherence to the rule of law was very partial at best.

With the authorization obtained, the International Criminal Investigative Training Assistance Program (ICITAP) was rapidly created. AID transferred $160,000 to the Justice Department in September 1985 for start-up funds. In 1986 ICITAP received $1.36 million, which was increased to $2.75 million in 1987 and $6.4 million in 1988. The program was housed at the Department of Justice both because the Justice Department had more expertise in police matters and because AID wanted nothing to do with it. AID had been badly burned by its association with the Public Safety Program in the late 1960s and early 1970s and was determined not to get involved in police aid again. Even just transferring funds to ICITAP caused considerable unhappiness at AID, leading the State Department to arrange a redelegation of the administration of justice authorization in 1987 so that ICITAP would receive its funds from the State Department instead.

ICITAP rapidly put together an ambitious program of short training courses for police officers in Central America and the Caribbean in basic investigative skills, such as crime scene search, collection and preservation of evidence, fingerprinting, and interviewing. ICITAP also included judges and prosecutors in some of its courses to increase their knowledge of investigative methods and to increase understanding and communication between the police and the judicial sector. In addition to these training courses, ICITAP also sponsored a series of regional conferences for the police commissioners of Central America and the Caribbean at which the commissioners discussed with ICITAP trainers and with each other issues of police management, police standards and accreditation, coordination of law enforcement efforts, and sharing of facilities. These conferences were related to ICITAP's longer-term goal of going beyond simply training investigative skills to modernizing and professionalizing police forces in Latin America and the Caribbean.

ICITAP was not the only police training program the U.S. government carried out in Latin America during the 1980s. The State Department's global Anti-Terrorism Assistance Program provided operational training to several Central American police forces. The Defense Department furnished military equipment and military-related training to the Salvadoran police during the Duarte years. The Drug Enforcement Agency trained a number of Latin American police forces in drug enforcement methods. These other training programs differed from ICITAP, however, in that they concentrated on the operational side of police work. ICITAP saw its larger mission as helping Latin American police separate themselves from the military forces and guiding them toward a more "modern" conception of the role of police in a democratic society. ICITAP was the only police training program that was explicitly part of the democracy assistance programs; the other programs implicitly accepted the police they dealt with as subdivisions of the militaries and simply tried to make them stronger and more effective in their operational capabilities.

## Democracy Assistance and Macrolevel Policy

The democracy assistance programs were consistent with the dominant stated theme of the Reagan administration's Latin America policy. It would be a mistake, however, to assume that the programs derived directly from or formed an integral part of the macrolevel policies described in the preceding chapters. The only area where such a close relationship obtained was the elections assistance programs. The intensive elections assistance efforts in El Salvador and Honduras in the mid-1980s were part and parcel of the administration's policy of fostering the emergence and maintenance of elected civilian governments. Similarly, the elections assistance programs in Haiti and Chile were integral elements of the multifaceted policy to promote an electoral transition.

The relation between the bulk of the democracy assistance programs—the administration of justice program and the democratic participation programs—and the administration's broader policies in the region was less close. The administration of justice program was born in El Salvador as part of the administration's effort to strengthen the civilian government there. The program spread to the rest of Latin America and the Caribbean, however, not as a result of any high-level policy directives but rather through the efforts of an informal group of mid- and low-level officials who happened to have an interest in the idea. Some of them believed that the stated theme of promoting democracy was a genuine concern of the high-level policymakers in the administration. Others were cynical about the administration's real commitment to promoting democracy but saw the stated emphasis on democracy as an opportunity to carry out programs they thought would be good for the region. These latter officials were often not especially sympathetic to the administration's overall Latin America policy—particularly the contra policy in Nicaragua and the general emphasis on military assistance—but they were career officials who were inclined to make the best of a difficult period by developing programs that conformed to their own views while being consistent with the administration's stated policies. Similarly, the human rights and democratic participation programs were developed under the democracy umbrella of the administration's Latin America policy but were in fact the work of a few career officials who felt themselves to be on something of a lone crusade within the administration rather than implementing directives from above.

At AID, the relation between the democracy assistance programs and the overall policies toward Latin America was particulary loose. Most of the small group of AID officials involved saw the democracy programs as the silver lining of a Latin America policy they considered overly militaristic and interventionist. They implemented the democracy programs essentially in isolation from the administration's overall policies. One AID official involved in the democracy programs, for example, when asked about the relationship between the Office of Democratic Initiatives in the Latin America Bureau of AID and the policymakers in the State Department's Inter-American Affairs bureau replied, "They don't interfere with us too much."[27] Another put it simply, "We keep as far from Elliott Abrams as possible."[28]

## Limited Results

Evaluating the specific achievements of the democracy assistance programs would require a large-scale empirical study, which is well beyond the scope of this book. AID itself, as well as all the other institutions carrying out democracy assistance programs, has not yet solved the dual problem inherent in evaluating political development assistance programs: finding coherent, measurable indicators of democratic progress and isolating the causal effects of such assistance programs from the thicket of factors bearing on the political development of any country. And in any case, the programs are relatively new, making it perhaps premature to assess their results.

Retreating to a level of general impressions, it can be said that the democracy programs are a positive set of initiatives. They reflect a genuine attempt to contribute to the sociopolitical good of Latin America by persons who have some working familiarity with Latin America and who are sincere in their desire to promote democracy. The programs are having some limited positive effects. The human rights and democratic participation programs have raised awareness in Central America about human rights issues and helped activate some local civic education groups. The elections assistance projects did generally improve the technical quality of elections in the target countries. And the administration of justice program has in some countries led to increased training of judges and police, improved technical capabilities of judicial systems, and generally heightened attention to what are traditionally badly ignored judicial systems. There is no significant evidence, however, that the democratic assistance programs of the 1980s had or are having any profound effect on the political development of any Latin American societies.

In the 1980s, just as in the 1960s, the United States invested its political development assistance in Latin America with high expectations. Administration officials portrayed the democratic assistance programs as major initiatives to promote democratic change in Latin America and the public debate over the programs focused on whether the programs were in fact having profound effects, with both proponents and opponents implicitly accepting the notion that such programs should and could have such effects. In fact, this assumption was misguided. Even if the problems of execution and design discussed below were absent, the U.S. political development assistance to Latin America initiated in the 1980s would not have had and will not have profound political effects on Latin America. Why? Because the magnitudes of the task and of the solution are vastly out of proportion with one another.

Problems in Latin America such as political violence, the weak rule of law, and the absence of real democratic norms are problems that go to the core of the societies. They represent deep-seated economic and social structures, long-standing political habits, and fundamental cultural patterns. The notion that some modest amount of training seminars, exchange programs, and technical assistance can solve these problems has no logical foundation. One way to appreciate the mismatch of problem and solution is to turn the tables and consider an example with the United States as the target rather than the recipient of foreign aid.

Suppose for example that Sweden announced it was very concerned about the problem of racism in the United States, in particular the threat racism poses to U.S. social stability, and initiated a five-year aid program to help eliminate American racism. Then over the next five years Sweden funded several nonprofit institutes in the United States to hold one- to two-week seminars for government officials on racial awareness, helped several local government councils study the problem of racism in their communities, subsidized the distribution of antiracist books and pamphlets, and brought selected American community leaders to Sweden on study tours to learn about race relations.

If at the end of the five years a team of Swedish aid officials came to evaluate the project and asked the aid recipients whether the project had eliminated or at least quantifiably reduced racism in the United States, the U.S. recipients would be astonished at the notion that such a program could have any significant impact on the problem. They would likely acknowledge that the program was well designed and that the participants found it interesting and useful; but they would tell the Swedes that racism in the United States is a centuries-old problem that goes to the core of American society and is not something that can be "fixed" in a few years or even a few decades, particularly by a foreign country. What then should we expect Salvadorans or Guatemalans to say after we fund some democracy assistance programs in their countries and then return in several years to ask whether our programs have made their societies democratic?

It is worthwhile to reflect on why Americans tend to make this startling leap of faith about the significance of political assistance programs. To start with, Americans bring to the task an implicit belief that the United States has extraordinarily strong powers of influence on the domestic life of Latin American countries. Part of this belief derives from the crude sense that because the United States is big and rich and many Latin American countries, particularly Central American countries, are small and poor, the United States can fairly easily exert a decisive influence on their domestic evolution. Part of it also stems from a mistaken view of the past. In previous decades the United States was able to dictate its political will on Latin America in many cases. Not only has this power declined significantly in the past twenty years, but to the extent the power did exist, it was the negative power to get rid of leaders we did not like, not a positive power to bring about the evolution of political forms such as democracy.

This overestimation of America's capacity to effect political change in Latin America is also rooted in a remarkable faith in the power of training to change people, institutions, and societies. The most common operative feature of the democracy assistance programs of the 1980s was training. Americans tend to believe that individuals can be shaped and socialized through modern, rational education, a belief reflecting our liberal heritage and our immigrant-oriented culture. This view is taken to an extreme in the Latin American programs, where we expect that occasional or even repeated one- or two-week courses can reverse attitudes and practices, such as the violence of the Salvadoran and Guatemalan security forces, that have been ingrained for generations.

The failure of past U.S. training efforts to establish democratic values in various Latin American institutions is simply ignored in the push to establish new training programs. The Panamanian military, for example, was extensively trained by the U.S. military over a period of decades in a sustained, multilevel training program that none of the training programs in the recent democratic assistance programs comes even close to matching in scope. Yet the Panamanian military in the 1980s displayed few of the values, such as discipline and lawfulness, that were cardinal to that earlier training effort. Similarly, the Guatemalan and Salvadoran security forces received vast amounts of U.S. training in the 1960s and early 1970s, directed at least in part to instilling discipline and lawfulness. Yet those forces acted savagely in the civil conflict that occurred just a few years after the training programs ended. These past efforts are generally not even considered in the habitual American rush to tackle the future and ignore the past in Latin America. To the extent they are considered, they are ususally dismissed as irrelevant because they involved assistance to nondemocratic governments whereas the programs of the 1980s were conducted only with democratically elected governments. This distinction may have some limited validity but it is irrelevant to the basic point that training is not an easy route to producing genuine value changes in foreign institutions.

Finally, American attitudes about democracy itself also foster the great belief in political development programs. Americans tend to view democracy as a natural political state; nondemocratic systems are aberrations from a norm. This view of democracy leads to the view that political development (defined by Americans as progress toward U.S.-style democracy) is a relatively easy process. Americans confronting a nondemocratic country such as Honduras or El Salvador tend not to ask, "I wonder whether this country might ever become democratic?" but rather, "I wonder why democracy hasn't succeeded?" The implicit assumption is that democracy should naturally succeed and that success is just a question of making the right adjustments. Political development assistance programs are thus seen more as attempts to adjust something that has gone wrong or remove obstacles in an already cleared path than to build something from scratch or fundamentally alter the existing state of affairs.

## Bureaucratic Problems

Although the democracy assistance programs were basically a positive, albeit limited, initiative, they were afflicted by at least two types of shortcomings—bureaucratic problems and methodological uncertainties. The bureaucratic problems were many. The AID planning process for such programs was aimed more at designing out any possible small failures than creating significant successes. Implementation of the programs was plagued by constant slowdowns and inefficiencies. It was also hampered by a lack of coordination within the different offices and agencies involved, too little support from higher-level officials, and a pervasive shortage of impetus and support from the bureaucratic process as a whole. Interim evaluations of the programs functioned more to validate existing approaches than genuinely to examine what had been tried and to find more effective alternatives.

These many difficulties reflected a fundamental underlying problem: there is no natural home in the U.S. government for political development assistance. Most of the democracy assistance of the 1980s was implemented by AID. Unfortunately, however, AID as an organization does not like to do political development work and is not good at it. AID's persistent disinclination toward political development assistance was obvious to all involved. The human rights and democratic participation programs came about only because of the persistence of a handful of low- to mid-level program officers working with little support from their bosses. AID got into the elections assistance field only against its better judgment, because of State Department pressure. Similarly, the State Department was responsible for organizing the administration of justice program and essentially forcing it on AID.

Why does AID not like to do political development work? The reasons are the same now as in the 1960s: AID sees itself as an economic development organization, not a political development one. Most AID officers have no expertise or interest in political development work. In the 1980s AID felt pressed for staff just to carry out its economic programs and did not feel it could devote staff to a whole new area of work. And the AID bureaucracy fears that political development work will harm AID's close economic relationships with many governments and involve AID in damaging political controversies both at home and abroad.

Even if it were disposed to commit itself strongly to political development assistance, however, AID would not be a good base for such activity. AID is staffed by many well-trained and dedicated people, but for a complex set of reasons is a startlingly inefficient and ineffective organization. In simple terms, AID has become a dinosaur; it is a bloated, slow-moving organization unable to adapt rapidly to changes either abroad or at home. The particular demands of political development assistance coincide almost exactly with AID's most glaring weaknesses. Although political development must be a long-term effort, it nonetheless requires an ability to move quickly to seize trends and opportunities as they arise. No U.S. government agency is more incapable of quick action than the almost incomprehensibly bureaucratic AID. Political development assistance also demands risk-taking, which by nature is neither safe nor uncontroversial. Yet after decades of congressional scrutiny, AID has become almost paralytically risk-averse. Finally, political development assistance requires a deeply sophisticated understanding of the process of political change in diverse foreign cultures. AID lacks such political capabilities and has shown no interest in acquiring them.

Not only is AID ill-suited to political development work but there are no obvious alternative bases within the U.S. government. The State Department has considerable political expertise abroad but is not a development organization, that is to say, it does not carry out long-term aid projects in foreign countries (the exception being the recently created antiterrorism and antinarcotics programs that are development projects in a certain sense). USIA deals largely with the dissemination and exchange of information related to foreign opinion of the United States and U.S. foreign policy, not with hands-on, long-term development programs. The CIA has hands-on abilities but operates covertly, an operational mode that has consistently proved to be ill-suited to political development assistance.

## *Methodology*

A second problem with recent U.S. democracy assistance programs has been the developmental methodology they employ. In the late 1960s, U.S. political development assistance to Latin America followed a "bottom-up" conception of democratization, that is to say, it emphasized increasing mass participation in political life with the idea that democracy results from the political empowerment of all members of a society. Much of the political development assistance in that period went to private groups rather than to governments, private groups dedicated to civic education and leadership training. What governmental institutions the programs did assist were on the more participatory end of the scale—local government and national legislatures.

In contrast, much of the political development assistance of the 1980s followed a "top-down" approach to democratic development. The assistance programs aimed to make governmental institutions in the target countries conform to democratic norms and practices, with the idea that democracy occurs when the government of a country behaves in accordance with democratic principles. The bulk of the democracy assistance programs, that is, the administration of justice program and the elections assistance programs, entailed direct assistance to governmental institutions, in particular judicial systems, police, and electoral tribunals. The exception was the human rights and democratic participation programs, which utilized the 1960s bottom-up methodology. Those programs, however, constituted only a small part of the political development assistance programs of the 1980s.

The difference in methodology between the 1980s and 1960s programs was a consequence of the differing bureaucratic origins of the two programs. In the 1960s the impetus to create political development assistance programs came from congressional liberals, who were concerned with ensuring that the large classes of poor people in developing countries not be left out of the economic development process. They believed that increasing political participation as broadly as possible would give the poor a political role and foster a process of democratic development that would render more just and harmonious the process of economic development.

In the 1980s, the impetus toward political development assistance came primarily from the State Department, in particular from the State Department's policy in Central America of resisting the spread of leftism by promoting incremental transitions from right-wing military governments to moderate, elected civilian governments. The policy aimed to maintain order in Central America by gradually shaping the existing governments into more democratic forms. The political development assistance programs embodied this idea of incremental change from the top. The political development assistance programs were extended outside of Central America to the Caribbean and parts of South America but remained rooted in the top down approach developed in Central America in the early 1980s.

In both the 1960s and 1980s, AID had primary responsibility for implementing democracy assistance programs. This operational continuity did not, however, bring about any methodological continuity—AID basically did whatever it was told to do (reluctantly), whether by the Congress in the 1960s or by the State Department in the 1980s.

If one looks from some distance at the political development programs of the 1980s, what is striking is that the broad impulse to use U.S. assistance funds to promote democracy in Latin America got translated into such a narrow program effort—over half of U.S. democracy assistance was devoted to aiding the courts and police of Latin America. Of all the many sectors of Latin American societies that might be targeted in a democratic promotion campaign, the law enforcement sector is obviously a rather limited focus. The emphasis on aiding the law enforcement sectors of Latin American countries reflected the close connection between maintaining order and promoting democracy that has long permeated U.S. Latin America policy. The traditional pattern of U.S. involvement in the internal affairs of Latin American countries has been for the U.S. government to espouse an interest in promoting democracy while having as its main concern maintaining order, more particularly, preventing the rise of leftist governments. The Reagan administration came to its stated interest in promoting democracy through its concern over the threat of leftism in Latin America, particularly Central America. Thus the interest in promoting democracy was closely tied to an interest in keeping order. Assisting the law enforcement sectors of Latin American societies was a natural consequence of such an outlook.

The problems with a political development assistance strategy oriented toward law enforcement institutions and toward governmental institutions generally are essentially the same as those of the overall policy of promoting democracy by transition in Central America. The assistance tends to ignore the profoundly antidemocratic underlying political and economic structures of the societies and to focus on modifying institutional forms that are often of peripheral importance in real terms. It also tends to encourage the general tendency of the United States to concentrate its political attention on the elite ruling groups and not to involve itself with the many other sectors of society that have long been disenfranchised and must be incorporated into a participatory political process for democracy to take root.

These weaknesses of the "top-down" approach were well demonstrated by the El Salvador Judicial Reform Project. As discussed above, the State Department created a judicial assistance project in El Salvador in the belief that the problem of right-wing violence there was substantially due to the lack of an effective law enforcement system—the high-profile political murder cases were not being solved because the police had no investigative skills and the prosecutors and judges were incompetent. State Department officials repeatedly stated that El Salvador suffered from a breakdown of its justice system and until that system was repaired, the problem of political violence could not be solved.

Creating a judicial assistance program to get at the problem of right-wing political violence was a way of addressing the problem without confronting the fundamental issue of the configuration of power in El Salvador. Political violence from the right was caused by the long-standing existence of a whole sector of Salvadoran society that held almost all of the military, political, and economic power in the country, that was opposed to any change in its privileged position, and that was willing to use violence to stop such change. The law enforcement system failed to bring to justice the perpetrators of the high-profile political murder cases (or any of the tens of thousands of more pedestrian political murders) primarily because it was either a captive of that sector or even an active part of it (as was the case of some of the Salvadoran police), rather than because of its technical weaknesses. The Salvadoran justice system did not break down as a result of the civil war and thereby cause the torrent of political violence of the late 1970s and early 1980s. The justice system has never exercised independent authority over the dominant sector of Salvadoran society. The massive political violence that occurred in the civil war merely highlighted the justice system's long-standing inadequacy; it did not result from it.

The notion then that the political violence from the right could be controlled by technical improvements in the justice system rather than by breaking up the Salvadoran's right's traditional position of power was fundamentally flawed. And the El Salvador Judicial Reform Project, which incorporated that notion, predictably failed to help the Salvadoran government bring to justice any perpetrators of right-wing political violence. By the end of the 1980s not a single high-level Salvadoran military officer had yet been convicted in any of the thousands of cases of right-wing violence. After the judicial reform program had been operating several years and this failure became evident, State Department officials began backing away from the program's original justification, arguing that technical improvements in the justice system would at least help clarify where the real roots of the problem of bringing to justice perpetrators of right-wing political violence lay, by giving police the capability of developing cases and identifying suspects even if the cases did not ever lead to conviction. This was a significant retreat from the original conception and was in fact an empty idea—the sources of right-wing political violence were already quite clear.

## THE NATIONAL ENDOWMENT FOR DEMOCRACY

After its formal creation in 1983, the National Endowment for Democracy (NED) began operating in 1984 and rapidly developed a diverse set of democracy assistance programs in Latin America. Although some of these programs resembled the U.S. government activities analyzed above, the National Endowment programs are considered separately here because NED is not part of the U.S. government. The precise relation between NED's activities and U.S. policy in Latin America is explored below. The National Endowment and its four component organizations devoted a significant share of their budget to Latin America in the 1980s, reflecting the widespread perception that Latin America was a fertile ground for democracy assistance: the Endowment's expenditures on Latin American activities ranged between $4 million and $6 million per year between 1984 and 1988 (out of the annual Endowment budget of between $15 million and $21 million), totaling approximately $25 million in those years. This was certainly a very significant figure, but it is useful to remember that it is less than one-quarter the size of the U.S. government democracy assistance programs in Latin America in the same years. The National Endowment's activities in Latin America received somewhat more media attention than the U.S. government's democracy assistance programs, but the National Endowment was in fact a far less significant actor on the democracy assistance stage.

## Activities and Methods of the National Endowment

To analyze the Endowment's work, the activities of the four component organizations of the Endowment, the Center for International Private Enterprise, the Free Trade Union Institute, the National Republican Institute for International Affairs, and the National Democratic Institute for International Affairs, must be considered separately. Each of these component organizations has its own budget (most of which comes from annual grants from the National Endowment's central budget), as well as its own board of directors and staff, programs, and operational approach.

The Center for International Private Enterprise (CIPE), a division of the National Chamber Foundation, which is a private, nonprofit corporation affiliated with the U.S. Chamber of Commerce, is the U.S. business component of the Endowment. CIPE funds projects in Latin America to promote private enterprise and free market policies. These programs aim to increase Latin Americans' understanding of the benefits of private enterprise and to strengthen private Latin American institutes that advocate free market policies. Most of the projects to date have consisted of short courses or seminars by the grantee institutes, both for the general public or more specialized audiences. A typical example is a 1986 project in Chile

to assist the Centro de Estudios Publicos (CEP) in conducting a series of seminars on privatization for academics, journalists, government leaders, and the business community in Chile. The seminars, coupled with CEP's new "Punto de Referencia" quarterly bulletin, aim to expose the myth that Pinochet's government has pursued market-oriented policies when, in fact, the role of the state and state-owned enterprises has expanded considerably in recent years. By building support for a competitive private enterprise economy, CEP seeks to enhance the economic role of the individual and encourage the inclusion of private enterprise principles in the democratic transition process.[29]

CIPE's heart clearly lies with economic issues rather than political development per se. Its programs in Latin America are almost exclusively oriented toward influencing the economic policies of the host governments. CIPE sees its economic programs as a form of democracy assistance according to its credo that "economic freedom" (that is, free markets and private enterprise) goes hand-in-hand with political freedom and that, therefore, promoting free market policies is a way of promoting democracy. This credo has a strong appeal to the U.S. business community. As discussed in chapter 4, however, historically in Latin America there has been only a weak or even negative correlation between democratic governments and governments that pursue free market economic policies and there is no solid basis for arguing that free market policies are generative of democracy. Nonetheless, in the latter half of the 1980s many of the newly democratic governments are attempting to pursue more market-oriented policies and CIPE's programs are useful to increase the general understanding of such approaches.

The Free Trade Union Institute (FTUI), a private, nonprofit corporation sponsored by the AFL-CIO, represents the labor component of the National Endowment.[30] FTUI works to advance free trade unionism abroad, a long-standing activity of the U.S. labor movement. In Latin America most of its projects are carried out by the AFL-CIO's Latin American regional institute, the American Institute for Free Labor Development (AIFLD). FTUI's Latin American projects are union-building activities such as training union organizers and strengthening union infrastructures. Some of the projects also include public education activities on the role of unions in democratic societies. An example is a 1986 program in Uruguay

to provide support for a program designed to strengthen the democratic labor movement in Uruguay and provide an alternative to communist domination. The program involves training in organizing techniques, education at the

Venezuelan Workers Confederation labor school, and professional assistance to new unions or those already in existence. A small team of professional advisors provides legal,
organization and bargaining expertise on an as-needed
basis.[31]

The prodemocracy rationale for FTUI's programs in Latin America is the same rationale that has been asserted for generations by
the AFL-CIO in relation to its international work: promoting free
trade unionism will deter Marxist control of labor unions and help
ensure non-Marxist unions, which in the view of the AFL-CIO are a
vital ingredient of democracy. The AFL-CIO's ardent anticommunist
orientation in Latin America has in past decades led it to positions
of questionable democratic fidelity; like the U.S. government, it has
lapsed into supporting dictators for the sake of their anticommunism.[32] In the 1980s the orientation of the AFL-CIO's work in Latin
America has become somewhat less dominated by anticommunist
concerns and more clearly related to supporting democracy for democracy's sake. This evolution has occurred both because of the diminishment of the perceived threat of communism in South America and a generational change away from the AFL-CIO's traditional
cold war view of Latin America.

The two political party institutes, the National Republican Institute for International Affairs and the National Democratic Institute
for International Affairs, work with political parties and the political
process in Latin America. They do so, however, in very different
ways.[33] The Republican Institute takes an explicitly partisan approach, backing what it calls "like-minded" institutes and political
parties that espouse a set list of conservative values, including "free
market economics, individual liberty, rule of law, family values."[34]
In Argentina, for example, the Republican Institute supported the
Union del Centro Democratico (indirectly through an institution affiliated with the UCD), a small conservative party to the right of the
dominant Peronist and Radical parties:

The Republican Institute is assisting an institution affiliated
with the newest Argentine political party, the Unión del
Centro Democratico (Democratic Center Union) which after
four years has become the alternative voice against social-

ism and a government-controlled economy. The program is assisting the party in grassroots political organization and institution building so that the message of free enterprise and responsible, limited government can be communicated throughout the country.[35]

The National Democratic Institute (NDI), in contrast, pursues an explicitly nonpartisan approach. Its projects aim "at strengthening democratic systems and not at supporting a particular political ideology, policy agenda or candidate."[36] NDI's particular focus is electoral transitions from nondemocratic to democratic governments. In such situations, as in Haiti in 1987 and Chile in 1988, NDI tends to pursue two kinds of assistance efforts: projects to help multiparty, prodemocracy coalitions campaign against nondemocratic ruling parties, and international election observer missions. The observer missions have grown beyond the bounds of simple observation efforts to become very sophisticated monitoring efforts aimed at preventing vote fraud, particularly at the vote-counting stage. NDI also carries out projects, usually seminars or conferences, on what it calls "governance" issues related to the consolidation of democracy in newly democratic societies, issues such as constitutional reform, improved civil-military relations, and the rationalization of national budgeting processes. NDI's 1986–1987 Haiti program is an example of the nonpartisan, process-oriented approach. That program conducted

a three-day Party-Building Workshop for approximately twenty rising Haitian political and civic leaders as well as party representatives from democratic countries in the Caribbean, Latin America, and Africa. . . . Participants discussed the roles and responsibilities of political parties in developing civic awareness and participation, the benefits of a loyal opposition to democratic development, constitutional choices and electoral codes and procedures. Workshop sessions focused on the technical aspects of party-building such as organizational development, party management, issue formulation, constituency building, and budgetary strategies. The second phase of this program was a multinational survey team visit to Haiti in December, 1986 to analyze the country's technical needs in holding national elections.[37]

The prodemocracy rationale of the Republican Institute's work is somewhat indirect. NRIIA's projects are not specifically directed toward countries in transition from nondemocratic to democratic rule; they are generally carried out in countries that already have elected civilian governments. The basic aim of the projects is to increase the strength of the conservative side of the existing political spectrum. Such projects can be considered prodemocratic as opposed to just proconservative in the limited sense that they help strengthen at least one part of the formal democratic infrastructure of the various countries and potentially contribute to the strengthening of civil society and the spread of a democratic civic education. In some instances the NRIIA's efforts appear to be almost purely proconservative as opposed to prodemocratic, such as the project to support the conservative party in Costa Rica, a country that already has a very well-established civil society and democratic infrastructure.[38] In other cases the prodemocratic quality of the NRIIA's approach is more evident, such as in Bolivia, where the Republican Institute has been assisting what it considers the prodemocratic side of the traditional conservative sector against what it considers to be the unreconstructed, nondemocratic side of the Bolivian right.

The National Democratic Institute's approach, in contrast, has a clear prodemocracy rationale. NDI's assistance to multiparty coalitions campaigning against nondemocratic ruling parties are explicitly aimed at promoting transitions to democracy. Similarly, the election observer missions are targeted at transitional elections in which a country is moving from nondemocratic to democratic rule. NDI's democratization focus is heavily election-oriented, opening it to the same criticisms as many of the U.S. government's prodemocracy policies of overemphasizing elections relative to the other features of democracy. As a political party institute rather than a developmental organization, however, it is almost inevitable that NDI's focus will be on electoral processes.

Alongside the activities of its four component organizations, the National Endowment itself directly funds some projects in Latin America. Unlike the business, labor, and political party institutes, the Endowment has no obvious counterpart organizations in recipient countries nor any obvious functional approach to the issue of democracy prevention. The Endowment's projects have generally focused on civic education and involved Latin American citizens action groups or U.S. universities or policy institutes with ties to civic groups in Latin America. The Endowment has taken the path of emphasizing projects that aim to spread the idea of democracy itself and that try to reach as broad a cross-section of the target society as possible.

## How Autonomous is the National Endowment?

The relation between the National Endowment for Democracy and the U.S. government remains poorly understood outside the small circle of persons directly involved with the Endowment. Many people assume that the Endowment is simply an arm of the U.S. government foreign policy bureaucracy. In fact this is not the case. The Endowment is primarily funded by the U.S. government but is an autonomous, nongovernmental organization that makes its own decisions about programs, staff, and methods. The Endowment is required to clear projects with the State Department before implementing them but in practice that is a pro forma requirement which largely serves to ensure that the State Department and the relevant U.S. embassy abroad are aware of the Endowment's activities. The Endowment staff (including the staff of the component organizations) do consult from time to time with State Department, AID, and USIA officials about project development and implementation, but such consultations are exchanges of ideas and information, not directives from the government to the Endowment.

   Although NED is not part of the U.S. government, a sort of informal concordance obtains between the Endowment's activities and U.S. foreign policy, particularly in terms of the geographic areas of emphasis, the concepts with which political developments are analyzed, and the general conception of the United States's role abroad. This concordance is not due so much to direct methods of governmental influence as to the fact that NED is a mainstream Washington organization whose directors and staff are from the same sociopolitical milieu as the policymakers in the government and who share the same assumptions as they do about U.S. interests abroad and the nature of U.S. political influence in foreign countries.

To the extent that NED is directly influenced by the government, it is Congress much more than the executive branch that is the relevant actor. Congress controls NED's funding and NED accordingly is extremely sensitive about not offending congressional sensibilities and maintaining good relations with key members of Congress. When Congress believes that the United States should be promoting democracy actively in a particular country and that the executive branch is not addressing the task adequately or is not suited to it, Congress turns to NED. The various component organizations of the Endowment as well as the Endowment itself concentrated on Chile during the 1988 plebiscite and on Nicaragua during the 1990 presidential elections because of strong congressional interest and special funding from Congress for programs in those countries.

## *Problems and Prospects*

As with the U.S. government democracy programs, it is still too early for any definitive assessment of the National Endowment for Democracy's programs in Latin America. At a general level it is evident that they suffer from the same problem of scale as the U.S. government programs. It would be unrealistic to expect that a few conferences, training programs, and seminars will change the historical path of any country's political development. Yet like the U.S. government, NED projects a certain hubris regarding the importance of its programs, reflecting similar assumptions as those held by U.S. government policymakers, such as the belief that the United States has a great ability to influence domestic political systems in Latin America, that significant change can be achieved in foreign institutions through a very modest set of training programs, and that democracy is a kind of natural outcome toward which countries can evolve fairly quickly and easily.

Even the three most concentrated instances of NED involvement in Latin America in recent years reveal a limited impact on the actual political evolution of the countries concerned. In Chile in the late 1980s all the component organizations of NED participated in a highly positive effort to facilitate the transition away from military rule to democracy. As discussed in chapter 5, however, the entire U.S. involvement was at best only a minor part of the democratic transition. In Panama, the National Endowment, primarily through the activities of the National Democratic Institute, played a highly visible and successful monitoring role in the 1989 elections. The election monitoring made Noriega's fraudulent interference with vote-counting clear to Panamanians and the international community and gave the Panamanian people and Bush administration a solid factual foundation for rejecting the election. Nonetheless the electoral fraud would almost certainly have become known without the observer mission (perhaps not so quickly or definitely) and the elections were just one of many junctures on the road to the end of Noriega's rule. In Nicaragua, the Endowment was directed by Congress to get deeply involved in helping the opposition in its campaign against the Sandinistas in the 1990 presidential elections. Owing to bureaucratic delays in Washington and obstacles imposed by the Sandinista government, however, very little of the Endowment's aid to the opposition got through until the last minute and few observers credit (or blame) the Endowment with having had significant effect on the campaign.

The National Endowment's democracy assistance to Latin America shares the same problem of scale as the U.S. government programs but does not suffer from the same bureaucratic problems that they do. The National Endowment is a much smaller organization than AID or any of the federal agencies involved in democracy assistance programs. The process of designing and implementing projects is much more streamlined at the Endowment. This allows it to respond more quickly to fast-breaking political situations, such as elections. It also allows for more variation and innovation in project design. The AID project design process is so cumbersome and negativistic that once a certain type of project has been approved, successive projects tend to be replicas of the initial project simply because as replicas they will stand a better chance of getting through the approval process. In general, the National Endowment has the advantage of being an organization whose sole purpose is to promote democracy. Unlike agencies of the United States, it does not have to weigh democracy programs against other programs and does not see democracy promotion as a sidelight to its main activities.

The National Endowment does face one important disadvantage relative to AID, USIA, and the State Department. Because of its limited budget, the Endowment does not have a network of employees abroad who can get to know local political scenes intimately and work directly with recipient organizations. The Endowment and its component organizations have very small, Washington-based staffs and tend to rely on a narrow range of contacts in any one country. Usually the Endowment has known those contacts only a short time and once it establishes an acceptable working relationship with them it usually makes little effort to broaden its circle of contacts and relationships. From the perspective of the foreign country, this narrow footing often raises questions in the minds of the various local political actors as to why "the Americans" (which is how the Endowment is usually conceived of abroad) are supporting a particular person or institution so heavily and paying little attention to everyone else.

A striking feature of the Endowment's operations, and a negative one, is the publicity consciousness that pervades the Endowment and its programs. The National Endowment is under constant pressure to justify its funding to an impatient and still-skeptical Congress and is obliged to play to the Washington audience heavily. The Endowment tends to concentrate its efforts on countries that are "hot" in U.S. policy terms rather than those that may be the most fertile ground for democratic development. Endowment projects are designed to get the most "bang for the buck," but the bang is often that of publicity and attention in Washington (by associating with fashionable international political figures or holding high-profile conferences with strong VIP participation) rather than true developmental achievements.

Perhaps the most serious shortcoming of the Endowment's activities to date is that, with the exception of the National Democratic Institute, which has focused on facilitating electoral transitions, the Endowment and its component organizations have not yet developed clear prodemocratic methodologies. The labor institute funds noncommunist labor unions, the Republican Institute backs conservative political parties, and the business institute promotes free market economics. In Latin America at least, these activities bear only an uncertain relation to democratic development. As with the U.S. government democracy assistance programs, the Endowment exports ideas based on U.S. experience to a very different Latin reality, and has, in particular, a tendency to assume that fostering institutions characteristic of U.S. democracy is the key to democratizing traditionally nondemocratic societies.

# **7**

# CONCLUSIONS

---

It is possible now to return to the general questions that have framed this study and examine the answers that have emerged: Why did the Reagan administration adopt promoting democracy as the central stated theme of its Latin America policy? What was the balance of rhetoric and substance in the policies that went under the heading of promoting democracy? What did the Reagan administration mean by democracy in Latin America? Did U.S. policy contribute significantly to the decisive trend toward democracy in Latin America in the 1980s? In addition, some general lessons about the suitability of promoting democracy as a goal of U.S. policy toward Latin America can now be drawn.

## *An Evolutionary Policy*

The Reagan administration characterized almost all its policies toward Latin America as efforts to promote democracy. The mix of rhetoric and reality in the administration's pervasive use of the democracy theme was complex. Four different types of policies were carried out under the democracy promotion rubric. Each had its own mix of style and substance. Considerable evolution in the content of the policies occurred during the decade, generally reflecting a movement away from purely rhetorical invocations of the democracy theme to more substantive prodemocracy involvement.

The democracy theme first appeared in the Reagan administration's Central America policy. One-half of the Reagan administration's intensive anticommunist campaign in Central America was bolstering the governments of the countries it saw as threatened by internal or external leftist aggression—El Salvador, Honduras, Guatemala, and Costa Rica. Very early on the administration adopted the line that it was not just bolstering existing Central American governments against leftist threats, it was promoting democratic change in those countries. The adoption of the democracy theme reflected two quite different motivations. On the one hand, the administration recognized that it would not be possible to secure congressional approval for the ambitious military assistance programs contemplated for those countries unless there was movement away from military rule to elected civilian governments. On the other hand, some persons in the administration, generally the moderates who dominated the State Department's Latin America team, believed that anticommunist military efforts in El Salvador, Guatemala, and elsewhere would not be successful if the underlying political and economic problems that created pressure for radical change were not solved.

Although the Reagan administration cast its policies toward these Central American countries as democracy promotion campaigns, in fact the fundamental policy was anticommunism. Promoting democracy, which the Reagan administration interpreted as fostering elected governments, was one component of the anticommunist policy (along with military and economic components), though it was not the totality of the policy. The priority of the political component relative to the military component varied over time in each country. In the early 1980s, the military component was clearly the administration's highest overall priority. The hard-liners in the administration dominated the Central America policy and they were interested in the political component largely for its utility in the domestic policy arena; their commitment to it even for that purpose was essentially rhetorical. The moderates were genuinely interested in the political component but they had only limited influence. This balance shifted somewhat in the mid-1980s. As the leftist insurgencies in El Salvador and Guatemala were brought under control and elected governments emerged, the military component of U.S. policy toward those countries lost its urgency and the political component grew in relative importance. In Honduras no such evolution occurred because the high-intensity military component of U.S. policy toward Honduras was tied to the unbending Nicaragua policy rather than to internal developments in Honduras.

The theme of promoting democracy spread to the other half of the Reagan administration's Central America policy, the anti-Sandinista campaign in Nicaragua, soon after it appeared in the policy toward the other countries of Central America. In 1982, the Reagan administration adopted the "internal democratization" of Nicaragua as one of its conditions for a bilateral security accord with Nicaragua. This adoption was a move by the hard-liners to insure that no security accord was negotiated between the United States and Nicaragua that left the Sandinista government intact. The hardliners believed that the Sandinistas were hardened communists and would therefore never accept an accord that provided for democracy in Nicaragua. In short, the hard-liners settled on the "internal democratization" of Nicaragua as a principled, publicly acceptable formulation of their basic desire to oust the Sandinistas.

As the militaristic policy toward Nicaragua developed, the stated emphasis on promoting democracy grew. The administration increasingly packaged the policy as a noble democratic crusade, devoting a great deal of time and energy to denouncing the Sandinistas as brutal totalitarians and praising the contras as heroic freedom fighters. The intensification of the democracy rhetoric reflected the administration's continual effort to win support for its policy in the U.S. Congress and from the U.S. public. Promoting democracy was the most effective sales pitch for a military-oriented, anticommunist policy.

Promoting democracy figured as a theme of the October 1983 U.S. invasion of Grenada. The invasion was an anticommunist intervention aimed at rolling back one small part of the outer fringe of the Soviet Union's sphere of influence. The Reagan administration made restoring democracy one of the main stated rationales for the invasion; as with the Nicaragua policy, promoting democracy was an alternative to presenting the policy in naked anticommunist terms. Having stressed democracy promotion during the invasion, the administration kept U.S. troops on the island long enough to oversee the establishment of an electoral process and the election of a government with plausible democratic credentials.

After it became established as the overarching theme of all of the Reagan administration's Central America policy, promoting democracy emerged as the dominant stated theme of the administration's South America policy as well. In the initial years of the Reagan administration, promoting democracy did not appear as an important element, either rhetorical or substantive, of U.S. policy toward South America. The Reagan administration was preoccupied with trying to rebuild relations with the military governments of the region, particularly in Brazil, Argentina, and Chile, and there was little place in this anticommunist policy for democracy concerns. Between the 1982 Falklands War and the end of the first Reagan administration, however, U.S. policy shifted away from the renewal of relations with military governments toward a low-profile policy of support for the newly emerging democratic governments of South America. The policy shift was primarily the result of the strong democratic trend in South America itself; military governments were on their way out, and the early policy of removal went out with them. The administration characterized the new policy as a policy of promoting democracy. This prodemocratic cast of the later South America policy was genuine, but the administration put so little real economic or political weight behind it that the administration's prodemocratic commitment made little impression in South America or in the U.S. policy community.

During the second half of the 1980s, the Reagan administration developed policies of economic and diplomatic pressure against the four remaining right-wing dictators in the region, Pinochet in Chile, Stroessner in Paraguay, Noriega in Panama, and Duvalier in Haiti. In each case the administration was seeking to induce the dictator to step down and permit a transition to elected rule. The policies developed quite separately from one another but the administration portrayed them as multiple examples of a policy of promoting democracy in right-wing as well as left-wing countries. The policies were rooted in a mix of symbolic and substantive motivations in which promoting democracy was a genuine motivation but not always the dominant one.

Although the Reagan administration embraced the promoting

democracy theme for its rhetorical value, there is no question that over the course of the Reagan years the theme gathered some real substance and that an administration initially unsympathetic to what it saw as moralistic crusades abroad became sincerely interested in being a force for democracy in Latin America. This shift was the result of a number of factors; three major ones stand out. The first was the consistent pressure on the Reagan administration from many Democrats in Congress to pay attention to democracy and human rights in Latin America. This pressure forced the administration to engage itself with the issue and in some cases shaped U.S. policy in ways favorable to the promotion of democracy and human rights. The pressure affected all different areas of the Reagan administration's Latin America policy.

The deep-seated opposition of many Democrats in the House of Representatives to military assistance for Central American countries with military governments was crucial in convincing the hard-liners in the administration to add a political component to its military-oriented, anticommunist policy in those countries. Throughout the 1980s, congressional interest in human rights and democracy in Central America obliged the administration to address questions of the day-to-day reality of the political process in El Salvador, Honduras, and Guatemala and to incorporate at least some concern for human rights into its policy.

Congressional resistance to the contra aid program was obviously a major factor in the evolution of the administration's anti-Sandinista policy in Nicaragua. The Reagan administration expended incalculable quantities of time and energy in an only partly successful effort to get congressional approval for contra aid. The concern of many Democrats in Congress that in Nicaragua the Reagan administration was arming antidemocratic, reactionary forces for an anticommunist crusade led the Reagan administration to cast the contra program in prodemocracy terms and to some extent even to try to mold the contras into a more democratic shape.

Congressional pressure also affected the Reagan administration's South America policy. Congressional Democrats blocked most of the administration's early attempts to restart military assistance to South America, effectively taking the wind out of the incoming administration's policy of renewing relations with the military governments of South America and speeding the transition to a policy of support for the growing democratic trend there. Congress also had a role in the emergence of the administration's later policy of pressure against the remaining right-wing dictatorships in the region. Congressional interest in promoting a democratic transition in Pinochet's Chile, distancing the United States from General Noriega in Panama, and backing the precarious democratic trend in post-Duvalier Haiti contributed to the prodemocratic evolution of the administration's policies in those countries.

The prodemocracy influence of the congressional Democrats on the Reagan administration's Latin America policy can be understood as the extension into the 1980s of the human rights consciousness that gained a place in U.S. foreign policy in the 1970s. Although Ronald Reagan's election in 1980 represented a repudiation of Jimmy Carter's foreign policy, the belief that human rights should be an important concern in U.S. foreign policy did not disappear from the American political consciousness. The human rights agenda was closely associated with Carter but in fact predated the Carter administration and arose out of broader trends, including the post-Vietnam desire to put U.S. foreign policy on a clear moral footing and the impact of increasing interest and knowledge of the U.S. public (produced by the increase in international communications and travel) about political conditions in other countries. When President Carter was defeated, this growing human rights consciousness lost its chief spokesperson but not the public basis of its support. The Democrats in Congress, or more specifically, a small set of liberal senators and representatives, became the repository of this human rights concern within the U.S. government.

The incoming Reagan administration sought to turn the clock back on U.S. foreign policy to the pre-Vietnam era, to an old-fashioned cold war approach in which the United States would accept the need to support unsavory dictators as an inevitable component of the global struggle against Soviet communism. The Reagan administration discovered fairly quickly, however, that it was not possible to forge a bipartisan foreign policy on this basis; a concern for human rights and democracy also had to be factored into the policy. Throughout the 1980s, congressional Democrats, as well as many interest groups in the U.S. policy community, pushed the administration on the issue, obliging the Reagan administration to develop its foreign policy as a blend of its cold war instincts and this newer U.S. concern for human rights.

A second cause of the rise of promoting democracy in the Reagan administration's Latin America policy was the changing balance between the moderates and hard-liners in the policy-making process. The moderates tended to be interested in promoting democracy as a necessary component of anticommunist policies and as a valid policy goal in and of itself. The hard-liners were less interested in promoting democracy and much more focused on military-oriented anticommunist campaigns. In the early 1980s, the hard-liners controlled or at least strongly influenced almost all of the Latin America policy, both in Central America and South America. By the late 1980s, however, the moderates were in control of almost all Latin America policy with the large but nonetheless singular exception of Nicaragua, where the hard-liners maintained their hold. The later Reagan administration's policies toward Latin America were largely implemented by the same career officers at the State Department, AID, Defense Department, CIA, and elsewhere who had carried out Latin America policy in the 1970s. And with the exception of the anti-Sandinista policy in Nicaragua, the policies were not substantially different from those of the Reagan administration's recent predecessors.

The shift from hard-liner to moderate predominance was the result of a general thinning of the hard-liners' ranks that occurred in the second Reagan administration. The latter Reagan administration was much more moderate than the first with respect to foreign policy. Hard-liners still occupied the key senior Latin America policy-making positions during the second Reagan administration but most of their deputies and staff were moderates. And above them, President Reagan was no longer breathing fire at the Soviet Union. The increasingly small group of hard-liners involved in Latin America policy concentrated their time and energy on the issue they cared most strongly about—Nicaragua—and let the rest of the Latin America policy fall into the hands of the moderates. This tendency was reinforced by the decline of the perceived leftist threat to Latin America that occurred during the 1980s. The Reagan hard-liners had become engaged in Latin America policy largely because they saw the region as the subject of a concerted Soviet-Cuban campaign to spread communism throughout Central America and even

South America. As the insurgencies in El Salvador and Guatemala were brought under control and South America evolved peacefully toward moderate elected governments, the hard-liners' fear of a regional communist takeover faded and they lost most of their interest in the region, except for Nicaragua, where fighting communism was still an active concern.

The rise of promoting democracy in the Reagan administration's Latin America policy was also the result of a third cause, the tendency in U.S. foreign policy-making for rhetoric to influence reality. Government officials sometimes set out lofty rhetoric on a foreign policy issue and then find that, almost without their intending it, the actual policy begins to gravitate toward that rhetorical line. This effect occurs in part because once senior officials state particular goals, even if only for rhetorical purposes, they will find that they are held to them. Critics and commentators in the public, as well as other agencies and branches of the government, will begin asking what the government is actually doing to achieve the stated goals. Faced with such inquiries, senior officials tend to respond by telling their subordinates to start doing something in pursuit of the goals, if only to give the impression that they are serious about them.

This phenomenon was of great importance in the Reagan administration's Latin America policy. In the early 1980s President Reagan and his top advisers adopted promoting democracy as a useful rhetorical line for their Latin America policy—it unified diverse policies in a single, clear framework and put a pleasing, principled face on military-oriented realpolitik policies. The stated emphasis on promoting democracy also allowed the Reagan administration to associate itself with the growing trend toward democracy and to champion Latin America's successes as the administration's own. Having made democracy the stated goal of its policy, however, the Reagan administration soon found that its policy was evaluated in those terms, that Congress and the public pressed the administration on the status of democracy in Latin America and asked what the administration was really doing to promote it. And so, predictably enough, senior officials began signaling the foreign policy bureaucracy to take up the issue actively. This opened the way for an evolution toward policies with real prodemocratic substance.

This interactive effect renders impossible any simple characterization of a policy or set of policies as rhetoric versus substance. Rhetoric and substance constantly interact in the policy-making process with rhetoric leading to substance, which may in turn generate new rhetoric that will have yet further effects on the policies. The Reagan administration talked endlessly about promoting democracy in Latin America. That talk inevitably had significant effects on the policy.

## The Reagan Administration's Conception of Democracy in Latin America

What did the Reagan administration mean by democracy in its many invocations of the term with respect to Latin America? The answer to this question is not especially complex. The Reagan administration was quite consistent in its view of democracy in all the different policies that went under the title of promoting democracy. The administration's view was that a country is a democracy when it has a government that came to power through reasonably free and fair elections. A corollary of this view was that the process of democratization in a country is the organization and implementation of a national electoral process. Promoting democracy was thus primarily conceived of as encouraging or assisting a country to hold national elections and then helping whatever government emerged from the elections to maintain and consolidate power.

The gap between this formal, institution-oriented view of democracy and the concept of Western pluralist democracy that informs conventional Western political science analyses was significant. To begin with, the Reagan administration's "elected government equals democracy" formula ignored the crucial question of how much actual authority any particular elected government had, whether, for example, an elected government's authority was largely curtailed by traditional power groups in the country, such as the military or an economic elite, or whether certain attributes of the elected government itself, such as its own gross ineptitude or corruption, effectively negated its claim to being a functioning representative government. Given the traditional weakness of the civilian political sector in most Latin American countries, the Reagan administration's unwillingness to inform its pronouncements on democracy with any assessment of the real authority of a particular elected civilian government rendered those pronouncements of little value.

Moreover, the Reagan administration made little attempt to go beyond its institutional view of democracy to consider the degree or kinds of political participation that existed within particular countries. The administration treated voting as the definitive form of political participation and paid little attention to the question of whether a continuous, multidimensional process of political participation—a process involving the uninhibited formation and mobilization of interest groups, the free expression by groups and individuals of their political interests and attitudes, and a process of day-to-day interaction and responsiveness between the government and the citizens of the country—was actually existent or at least developing in countries attempting to make a transition to democracy.

Interestingly, in one country the administration did give considerable attention to a gap between the existence of an elected government and real democracy. That country, of course, was Nicaragua. After Nicaragua held presidential elections in 1984, the Reagan administration was determined to show that despite having an elected government, Nicaragua was not a democracy. The approach the administration took for the task paralleled that used by U.S. liberals asserting a lack of democracy in El Salvador and Guatemala. The administration highlighted the nonparticipation of the armed opposition in the 1984 Nicaraguan elections (just as liberals pointed to the nonparticipation of the left in the 1984 Salvadoran elections). Administration officials also scrutinized the amount and quality of political participation in Nicaragua, giving a degree of attention to human rights in Nicaragua matched only by the human rights scrutiny given by U.S. liberals to El Salvador and Guatemala. The administration concluded that the limitations of the electoral process and of the general level of political participation rendered Nicaragua undemocratic despite its elected government.

It is important to go beyond simply identifying the fact that the Reagan administration maintained a formal, institution-oriented view of democracy in Latin America, which in itself is scarcely a novel conclusion, to explore the question of why such a view was held. In the case of some U.S. officials, primarily hard-liners preoccupied with anticommunist concerns, the explanation is cynicism. Their talk of promoting democracy was largely rhetoric adopted for public relations purposes. They had little interest in the reality of the political situation in Latin American countries other than in bare communist versus noncommunist terms and were content to utilize the most simplistic view of democracy available. The status of democracy in Latin America became a kind of scoreboard issue with them; they chalked up countries in the won-lost column in the most superficial fashion and broadcast a running score in which democracy's lead over tyranny and darkness was ever-lengthening.

Out-and-out cynics, however, were only a small proportion of the overall set of officials concerned with Latin America. Many, or even most officials involved in Latin American affairs, from the very senior to the very junior, were sincere when they referred to countries with elected governments as democracies. They were willing to concede, at least in private, that many of the newly elected governments in Latin America had serious shortcomings. But they did treat democracy as something like an off-on switch in which the holding of elections and the coming to power of an elected government was the crucial transition from off to on. They saw countries with extremely weak, even debilitated elected civilian governments and very limited forms of political participation, such as El Salvador and Guatemala in the late 1980s, as being fledgling democracies but democracies nonetheless.

This narrow view of democracy was not a peculiarity of U.S. officials. It is common among many Americans and has its roots in the national experience of democracy in the United States, or at least the popular historical notions (and myths) about U.S. democracy. The process of democratic development in the United States had at least two distinctive features relative to other Western developed countries. The first was that the process of democratic development was not a long, slow process of transformation from a monarchical, feudal society to a republican, democratic one. There was a transition from a monarchical to a representative government but this transition was a rebellion against the ruling colonial power, not an internal evolution from a centuries-old feudal system to a democratic one. In at least the public conception of U.S. history, the United States was from its very origins a democratic culture, a young democratic society (with the important exception of the existence of slavery) seeking to get away from oppressive English monarchical rule. The second distinctive feature is that the U.S. Constitution and the particular institutional arrangement of government it oversees has existed without major change since the creation of the United States of America in the eighteenth century.

Each of these distinctive features has consequences for how people in the United States tend to conceive of democracy and the process of democratization, and how they address these issues abroad. The unusual "democratic from the start" nature of U.S. society leads Americans not to have any intuitive sense of what a long-term, internal evolution from a nondemocratic society to a democratic society is like. The profound question facing most nondemocratic countries of how a society that has known only dictatorship, repression, injustice, and inequality can democratically transform the myriad antidemocratic habits, beliefs, and customs, as well as antidemocratic internal power structures, finds little resonance in the U.S. national experience. As a result, Americans tend to underemphasize the deep-rooted, evolutionary process of social, economic, and cultural change that goes into democratization and see the process as a matter of a nondemocratic society simply adopting the right institutional framework.

Second, the remarkable endurance of the institutional configuration of U.S. democracy leads Americans to reify that configuration. The institutions of U.S. democracy are equated with the ideas and principles behind them. Thus, for example, the idea of a representative government has become identified with a three-part government consisting of executive, legislative, and judiciary branches with the former two elective and the third not. The U.S. version of democracy has come to be thought of by Americans not merely as one of many possible versions, but the very essence of democracy itself. As a result, when the United States sets about to try to promote democracy in a foreign country, it tends not to think about how the general ideas and principles of democracy might take form in that society but to assume that the other country should devote itself to establishing the institutional configuration the United States associates with democracy.

The conception of democracy employed by the Reagan administration thus reflected a deeper pattern of U.S. thinking about democracy not limited to the 1980s. The Reagan administration's conception also reflected a long-standing U.S. attitude about political change in Latin America. Off and on during the twentieth century the United States has supported democratic political reforms in Latin America. That support has usually been promoted by the fear that stagnant, autocratic governments will foster political instability or pressures for radical political change and the belief that supporting democratic reforms is a way of avoiding that eventuality. The underlying U.S. goal is maintaining the basic societal orders of particular Latin American countries approximately as they are—ensuring that the economics are not drastically rearranged and that the power relations of the various social sectors are not turned upside down.

Thus, there is a built-in tension or even contradiction in the recurrent impulse to promote democracy. The impulse is to promote democratic change but the underlying objective is to maintain the basic order of what, historically at least, are quite undemocratic societies. The United States mitigates this tension by promoting very limited, controlled forms of democratic change. The deep fear in the United States government of populist-based change in Latin America—with all its implications for upsetting established economic and political orders and heading off in a leftist direction—leads to an emphasis on incremental change from the top down. Democratic development is interpreted as the strengthening or modification of existing governmental institutions. In other words, the United States works with the existing power structures and tries to teach or persuade them to be democratic rather than working from the bottom up to spread the ideas and principles of a democratic society among the citizenries.

## The Balance Sheet

An answer can now be given to the most fundamental question underlying this study: Did the Reagan administration's policies contribute significantly to the trend toward democracy in Latin America in the 1980s? The answer is a qualified no. The much-heralded resurgence of democracy was a mix of democratic transitions, primarily in South America, and civilianizing transitions in Central America. In almost all cases the democratic or civilianizing trend was the result of internal factors; it was not the result of external factors such as U.S. policy. The United States did play a clearly positive though not determinative role in some countries; in several countries U.S. policy was harmful to democracy or its prospects. Let us review the specific results of the policies examined in this book.

The United States did contribute to the establishment of elected civilian rule in El Salvador, Honduras, and Guatemala. The U.S. role was greatest in El Salvador. The Reagan administration's (and the Carter administration's before it) active support of the civilian-military juntas that emerged after the 1979 junior officers coup and of the creation of a viable electoral process was a crucial factor in the achievement of an elected civilian government in El Salvador. Similarly, the extensive U.S. support for the Duarte government was a major factor in Duarte's managing to last out a very difficult five-year term. The U.S. role in the Honduran electoral transition was less intense but still significant. The Carter administration's strong support for a civilian transition helped get the electoral process underway. The Reagan administration, after an initial period of uncertainty, helped see that process through to fruition in the 1981 elections. The Reagan administration's strong backing of the Suazo Cordova and Azcona Hoyo governments insured the continuation of civilian rule. In Guatemala, the United States had little influence on the transition from military to civilian rule. Once civilian rule was established in early 1986, the U.S. role increased. The economic and political support the United States gave to the Cerezo government was important in helping Cerezo stay in office, although it was of less weight than the U.S. role in El Salvador.

Although the United States contributed to the achievement of civilian rule in El Salvador, Honduras, and Guatemala, civilian rule in those countries did not constitute democracy. As detailed in chapters 1 and 2, the civilian governments of those countries exercised only very partial authority; the traditionally dominant sectors of the societies—the militaries and the business elite—maintained substantial authority and power. Moreover, the level and scope of political participation was not high. Political violence and intimidation by the security forces in all three countries, especially El Salvador and Guatemala, constituted a serious restraint on the exercise of political and civil rights.

Contrary to what the Reagan administration repeatedly said,

the civilian transitions in El Salvador, Honduras, and Guatemala were not broad-based political movements. The civilizing trend was a project of the militaries of those countries. The fall of Somoza in Nicaragua and the concomitant defeat of Somoza's National Guard prompted the militaries in neighboring countries to reconsider their direct political role and let civilian governments emerge. Civilian transitions were settled upon precisely as a means of insuring the military's long-term survival as well as permitting a large-scale U.S.-financed military expansion, not as means of reordering the traditional military dominance of the societies.

Furthermore, although the Reagan administration did help promote political reforms in El Salvador, Honduras, and Guatemala, its policies also had adverse effects with respect to promoting democracy. The huge quantities of military assistance to El Salvador and Honduras helped the Salvadoran and Honduran militaries expand dramatically and consolidate their dominant domestic position. The assistance also fanned corruption in the militaries, increasing their lawless tendencies. The Reagan administration never used its military assistance relationships with El Salvador, Honduras, or Guatemala to push hard for changes in the militaries' abiding disrespect for human rights and civilian authority. More generally, the intensive and often overbearing U.S. involvement in the economic, political, and military affairs of these countries inevitably weakened the legitimacy of these governments in their attempt to establish themselves as sovereign, representative authorities.

The Reagan administration's obsessive anti-Sandinista campaign had spillover negative effects on the rest of Central America. By fostering a civil war in Nicaragua and attempting to involve all the countries of the region in that war in different ways, the Reagan administration helped create an atmosphere of political tension and violence that contributed to the economic problems of the region by increasing the disruption of Central American economic interchanges and worsening the already bad climate for foreign investment. The anti-Sandinista policy also heightened the general militarization trend in the region, which worked against the democratic trend. Honduras was particularly hurt by the anti-Sandinista policy. The basing of the contras in Honduras was a continuous burden on its already weak social fabric and the Reagan administration's general treatment of Honduras as a mere tool of U.S. anti-

Sandinista policy reduced the Honduran government to the status of the United States's regional lapdog.

Costa Rica was a case somewhat apart. The Reagan administration's attempts to involve Costa Rica in the U.S. anti-Sandinista policy provoked political divisions in Costa Rica as well as sharp diplomatic tensions between Costa Rica and Nicaragua; for a time in the mid-1980s it appeared that the Reagan administration might be leading Costa Rica down a path of militarization and political polarization. In the end, however, Costa Rica's democratic institutions proved capable of withstanding the various strains imposed by the U.S.-Nicaraguan conflict and Costa Rican democracy emerged from the 1980s in relatively good health. The economic component of the Reagan administration's Costa Rica policy, the provision of massive amounts of economic assistance to Costa Rica, significantly contributed to Costa Rica's partial recovery from the crippling economic recession of the early 1980s. The positive economic component of the Reagan policy appears, in the final view, to have been more lasting and significant than the negative political and military components.

The Reagan administration's two invocations of military force in Latin America and the Caribbean, the invasion of Grenada and the contra war against Nicaragua, had different results. The invasion of Grenada succeeded in accomplishing the Reagan administration's main goal of ousting the leftist Grenadan rulers. The United States did oversee the restoration of elected rule in Grenada. The electoral process was compromised by U.S. covert efforts to shape the process but the newly elected government gradually established itself as a credible, representative authority and Grenada in the late 1980s was clearly far more democratic than in the early 1980s. The Grenada policy involved costs as well as benefits. The invasion resulted in several hundred deaths, mostly Grenadans, and put the United States in clear violation of the well-established international norm of nonintervention. Most Americans were willing to accept those costs in return for what they perceived to be a clear victory for the United States against the Soviet Union.

The political results of the Reagan administration's intensive, vast anti-Sandinista campaign were ambiguous. The contras never succeeded in ousting the Sandinistas. They also failed to gain consistent support from the U.S. Congress (and the U.S. public) and by the end of the Reagan years had accepted a cease-fire with the Sandinistas that left the Sandinistas firmly in power. The existence of the contras did, however, move the Sandinistas to enter into regional peace negotiations (that the Reagan administration opposed), which led to elections, which in turn resulted in the Sandinistas losing power. The Sandinistas agreed to hold elections not because the contras had the Sandinistas against the wall, but because the contras were weakened (owing to their loss of support in Washington) and because the Sandinistas were certain they would win. The elections appeared to be a low-risk means of getting rid of the contras once and for all and paving the way for a normalization of Nicaragua's regional and extraregional relationships. The Sandinistas unexpectedly lost the elections and a government led by Violeta Chamorro took power. The new Nicaraguan government is trying to make Nicaragua a working democracy but Nicaragua is profoundly polarized by ten years of civil war, rendering the achievement of a working democracy extremely difficult.

The ambiguous positive effects of the Reagan administration's contra policy were counterbalanced by its many negative aspects. Most importantly, the contra war resulted in the deaths of tens of thousands of Nicaraguans, scarring the country for decades to come. Together with the U.S. economic sanctions against Nicaragua, the war also inflicted serious economic harm and aggravated sociopolitical divisions in the society. The Reagan administration policy also had negative effects outside Nicaragua. As mentioned previously, it had a deleterious impact on the rest of Central America and on the United States itself. It harmed the tenor of U.S. democracy (through the Iran-contra activities), put the United States at odds with the international community, dissipated a great deal of the administration's political capital with Congress, and repelled a good portion of the U.S. public.

The Reagan administration's policies toward South America had little effect on the dramatic movement toward democracy that spread through that region in the 1980s. The early policy of rebuilding diplomatic and military ties with the military governments of Brazil, Argentina, Chile, and other countries worked against the democratic trend by politically bolstering undemocratic governments against growing domestic pressures to cede power. One exception was Bolivia, where, owing to the Bolivian military's involvement in drug trafficking, the Reagan administration did not attempt a rapprochement with the military government and the U.S. embassy in Bolivia vigorously and effectively supported a transition to elected rule.

The Reagan administration's later policy of diplomatic support for the new democratic governments of South America was a genuinely prodemocratic policy but had little real substance. The greatest threat to the survival of the nascent democratic rule in many South American countries was the continuing economic stagnation. The Reagan administration never developed a significant economic component to its policy of diplomatic support for democracy. In general, the democratic trend in South America was the result of domestic factors, such as the economic recession of the early 1980s, the decline or demise of many of the leftist guerrilla movements of the 1970s, public exhaustion with the military governments, and the sociopolitical effects (such as improved education, greater social mobility, and increased political participation by the middle and lower-middle classes) of the preceding two decades of economic growth.

Finally, the policy of the second Reagan administration to exert economic and diplomatic pressure against the remaining right-wing dictators in the region achieved very mixed results. The most favorable case was Chile. After following a pro-Pinochet line in the early 1980s, the administration shifted in 1984 and 1985 to a policy of firm support for the holding of the constitutionally mandated plebiscite on Pinochet's continued rule. The plebiscite was held in October 1988, instituting a successful return to elected rule. The U.S. prodemocratic policy was a boost to the democratic Chilean opposition but was only a minor factor in what was a thoroughly Chilean political transition. In Paraguay the administration similarly shifted to a policy of open support for a transition from the long-time dictatorship of General Stroessner to an elected government. The United States did not have strong economic or political leverage in Paraguay, however, and the U.S. role in the eventual transition although positive, was extremely modest.

The administration's policy of pressure worked out rather unfavorably in Haiti and Panama. In Haiti, the Reagan administration did weigh in during the final weeks of Jean-Claude Duvalier's rule to help speed what had already become his inevitable departure. During the post-Duvalier period, however, the Reagan administration's active attempts to steer the interim government toward an electoral transition ended in failure. In Panama, the Reagan administration reversed a long, close friendship with General Manuel Antonio Noriega, the de facto leader of Panama since the early 1980s, only when public revelations about his involvement in international drug trafficking and in other sordid activities made the friendship politically unfeasible. The administration's frantic, improvisatory effort to oust Noriega in the first half of 1988 was a humiliating failure. Prompted largely by the unending embarrassment of Noriega's successful defiance of the United States, the Bush administration invaded Panama in 1989, capturing Noriega and restoring civilian rule.

*Lessons*

As the United States enters into a new decade of relations with Latin America, it faces an unusual juncture. Since World War Two, the basis of U.S. policy in Latin America has been anticommunism, the desire to prevent the emergence of leftist or perceived Communist governments from coming to power. In recent years, however, the threat of communism in Latin America (whether perceived or real) has declined significantly and shows no sign of reviving. With the defeat of the Sandinistas in Nicaragua, Cuba is the only remaining leftist government in the region. Marxist-Leninist rebel groups are still active in El Salvador, Peru, Guatemala, and Colombia but they are isolated movements, not the harbingers of any regional trend. The decline of communism in Eastern Europe and the liberalization trend in the Soviet Union have undercut the U.S. perception that an expansionistic, international communist movement is trying to gain control of Latin America. The result of these trends is that the traditional anticommunist basis of U.S. policy toward Latin America is fading away, leaving the United States with no set script in Latin American affairs.

It is likely that as the United States assembles a new policy framework for Latin America, promoting democracy will figure as a primary, even dominant concern. The resurgence of democracy in Latin America in the 1980s is a fact that commands attention in the international community and almost inevitably leads the United

States to commit itself to protecting and promoting that trend. Furthermore, the democratic trend in Latin America has convinced many once-skeptical U.S. policymakers that democracy is possible in Latin America. In particular, the ability of elected governments to emerge and survive in countries caught in powerful left-right civil conflicts has persuaded many U.S. conservatives that democratic governments are a feasible alternative to anticommunist authoritarians and that democratic governments in Latin America are fully consistent with and even favorable to U.S. security interests.

Promoting democracy has appeal for more symbolic reasons as well. It is a sweeping, lofty policy theme. The United States is experiencing a relative decline in its global power but is not yet prone to give up universalistic, grandiose policy themes. Promoting democracy is a natural choice in this regard. It also has the advantage that it easily attracts bipartisan support. After the divisiveness of the Reagan years, the Bush administration is intent on building a bipartisan Latin America policy. Promoting democracy is an "apple pie" theme in Latin American affairs. It appeals to liberals because of its moralistic quality and its promise of addressing the problems of human rights and of socioeconomic injustice that dominate U.S. liberals' perception of Latin America. It appeals to conservatives because of its implicit stance in opposition to non-American political ideologies and in favor of promoting the U.S. way in Latin America. Furthermore, a democracy theme for Latin America policy corresponds with the direction of U.S. foreign policy generally. The perception of a worldwide trend toward democracy has seized policymakers in the United States, with the result that promoting democracy is becoming a dominant stated theme of the Bush administration's global foreign policy.

Given that promoting democracy is likely to be a focus of U.S. policy toward Latin America in the 1990s, and in fact of U.S. policy in many other parts of the world as well, it is important to draw some lessons from the experiences of the 1980s, a decade in which promoting democracy was almost always the stated theme of U.S. policy in Latin America and often a genuine concern as well. Numerous lessons are evident from the intense and turbulent U.S. involvement in Latin America's democratic resurgence of the 1980s. Almost all are cautionary.

Perhaps the most basic, and the most important, lesson is that the United States does not really have much influence over the political evolution of most Latin American countries. The main finding of the analysis in the previous chapters is that the United States had neither a significant positive role, nor for that matter a significant negative role, in the political evolution of most countries in Latin America in the 1980s, despite the high level of time, energy, and resources the U.S. government devoted to various parts of the region. Although this conclusion may seem surprising to those who saw the Reagan administration as a powerful actor, whether positive or negative, in Latin America, upon further reflection it should not be. The political evolution of a country in any given period involves the most fundamental elements of the country's social, economic, political, and cultural character. The notion that an external actor can have a profound and lasting effect on that political evolution through some set of relatively short-term diplomatic, economic, or even military means ignores the complexities and realities of how societies are made up and how they change.

A second lesson is that the traditional tension in U.S. policy toward Latin America between fighting communism and promoting democracy has not been resolved. Repeated attempts have been made from the late 1950s on to resolve the tension, usually by trying to enlist democracy promotion as a means of fighting communism. The Reagan administration's policies toward El Salvador, Honduras, and Guatemala were such efforts, at least in part, and drew significantly from the ideas of the Alliance for Progress. Yet the Reagan policies, like their predecessors, ran into the problem that they entailed large-scale assistance to antidemocratic militaries, strengthening the hold of those already dominant institutions over the political life of their societies. Efforts to change the political role and attitude of the military were weak and unsuccessful; they were dwarfed by the concrete fact of the hundreds of millions of dollars of U.S. military assistance pouring in.

In general, the Reagan administration tried to propagate the notion that communism was the main threat to democracy in Latin America and that therefore fighting communism was equivalent to promoting democracy. In reality, however, the main obstacles to democracy in Latin America have historically been a variety of structural domestic factors such as the extreme concentration of economic and political power in the hands of undemocratic elites, the sociopolitical marginalization of whole classes of citizens, and the lack of any underlying national consensus on basic democratic values. Leftist revolutionary movements have arisen in response to these various shortcomings; they are a symptom much more than a cause of the lack of democracy. Thus, fighting communism, at least in the manner which the United States has traditionally done so, tends to involve strengthening the forces of groups that constitute the primary obstacles to democracy. This is not at all to say that not fighting communism would necessarily promote democracy, but only that a deep-seated tension between anticommunist and pro-democracy policies exists in U.S. relations with Latin America and that the United States has not found a solution to it.

Although the decline of leftism in Latin America will reduce the number of U.S. anticommunist campaigns there, the same democracy-security contradictions are likely to exist with any U.S. policy explicitly based on security concerns that involves military assistance. The rise of the drug issue in U.S.-Latin American relations is a good example. The United States instinctively approaches the drug issue as a security problem that requires U.S. assistance to Latin American militaries and police. Such assistance may help alleviate the security problems but it is bound to raise problems of compatibility with the goals of democracy and human rights.

A third lesson is that the conception of democracy Americans tend to apply abroad is not well suited to generating effective policies of promoting democracy. As discussed earlier in this chapter, the U.S. national experience with democratic development, or at least the popular myths of the development of democracy in the United States, gives Americans a strongly institution-oriented view of democracy in which the process of democratic development is seen as the creation or improvement of a particular set of governing institutions, primarily through elections. The importance of bottom-up self-transformation of a society as the basis for democratic development is underemphasized or even feared. Instead, U.S. policies of promoting democracy concentrate on shaping the institutions of government in certain acceptable forms.

A fourth lesson is that the nature of the U.S. foreign policy-making process is at odds with the nature of the task of promoting democracy in other countries. Democratic development in most Latin American countries is a slow, precarious process, riddled with setbacks and uncertainties. A well-designed policy of promoting democracy should be both steadily funded and implemented over many years rather than called into question year by year and it should be planned in advance rather than simply improvised in response to a sudden crisis or turn of events. It should also be overt but quiet, carried out in a low-profile manner rather than trumpeting its own existence in a manner that will exacerbate the inevitable tension caused by one country involving itself in the internal affairs of another. And finally it should be a policy of low expectations that gives explicit recognition to the marginal role external actors generally have in the political evolution of societies.

Unfortunately, however, the U.S. foreign-policy-making process is not conducive of policies with those characteristics. Long-term, steady implementation and funding is rarely a feature of U.S. foreign policy for a variety of reasons, including the tendency for new administrations to try to reinvent the foreign policy wheel and the short attention span of the U.S. government and the U.S. public. A lack of advance planning and the tendency to make foreign policy in a reactive, crisis-oriented fashion is also characteristic of U.S. foreign policy. The global ambit of U.S. interests is so broad, and in a sense so unfocused, that U.S. foreign policymakers tend not to concentrate their attention systematically in a few regular areas but to respond to emergencies that are continually cropping up in scattered parts of the world.

With respect to the need for low-profile policies grounded in low expectations, the U.S. policy-making process also poses problems. The United States tends to launch itself into areas such as promoting democracy abroad with its moral sails fully rigged. Since the United States decides to try to promote democracy abroad in no small part to convince itself and others that it is doing good in the world, the United States tends to carry out such policies in a loud, even triumphal fashion. Similarly, such policies are usually invested with extremely high expectations. The United States confidently takes on the goal of altering other countries' political history and gives itself all of three to five years to accomplish that monumental task. The high expectations reflect the inveterate optimism characteristic of Americans as well as their chronic habit of overestimating the United States's ability to influence events in other countries.

A fifth lesson is that agreeing on promoting democracy as the core element of U.S. policy toward Latin America does not in fact mean that any significant agreement has been reached. Promoting democracy appeals as a natural basis for a bipartisan policy toward Latin America. Yet promoting democracy is such a general concept that it does not provide as solid a policy foundation as one might first think. One can take many approaches to promoting democracy, approaches which may be so drastically different from one another as to divide a policy community more than unify it.

The best example of this problem was Nicaragua. The Reagan administration claimed—and some Reagan administration officials believed—that it was promoting democracy in Nicaragua by supporting the contras. U.S. liberals and moderates, however, objected strongly to the contra policy, in part at least because the contras were an undemocratic force and the contra war was giving the Sandinistas an excuse to crack down on internal opposition. Conservatives and liberals agreed that the United States should promote democracy in Nicaragua but disagreed violently as to what the United States should actually do. Agreeing on promoting democracy as a policy objective solved little in terms of real policy concordance.

A sixth and final lesson is that making democracy the primary lens for viewing Latin America can distort our view of the region as much as focus it. This is not to say that democracy is unimportant to Latin America. It is to say, however, that Latin Americans do not judge the overall situation of their countries in terms of a simple formula of democracy versus nondemocracy. To begin with, Latin Americans experience the political life of their countries on a day-to-day basis, they confront the fine-grained reality of that life, they do not simply look at occasional snapshots of the overall form of the governing institutions. In the 1980s Latin Americans were faced every day with the complexities and ambiguities of transitions from dictatorships to democracy, with the many ways in which an elected government may still be unaccessible, unresponsive, and dishonest as well as dominated by antidemocratic forces brooding in the background. Moreover, they confront the totality of life in the country. They experience not just the political situation but the economic, cultural, and social features of the society. In the 1980s, economic problems were of particular importance. The unending economic crisis afflicting almost all Latin American countries imposed hardships and suffering that outweighed many of the gains derived from progress in the political domain.

If you asked a U.S. government official in the late 1980s to describe the situation of South America he would likely have por-trayed the situation in very positive terms, highlighting the many recent transitions to democracy and pointing to a two-colored map that pictured the victory of democracy over dictatorship in dra-matic, clear-cut terms. If you asked a South American the same question, chances are he would have emphasized the economic cri-sis of the region and the precariousness of the new elected govern-ments. Thus when U.S. officials in this period gave speeches on Latin America in which they talked of the region's "democratic revo-lution" in glowing terms and described Latin America as being on a profound upward climb, they were not describing the Latin Amer-ica that Latin Americans experienced or understood. A Latin Amer-ica policy that makes democracy, particularly a relatively narrow conception of democracy, its primary lens for viewing the region risks relying on a distorted view of the region.

In sum, the cautionary lessons regarding the relationship be-tween the United States and Latin American democracy are many and they are serious. Taken together they are not intended as an argument that the United States should refrain from making pro-moting democracy a goal of its policy toward Latin America. Rather they indicate that the United States should do so in a knowing, clear-minded fashion, explicitly recognizing the very limited influ-ence the United States has on the political evolution of Latin Amer-ica, the continuing tensions between U.S. anticommunist concerns and prodemocracy goals, the shortcomings of the narrow concep-tion of democracy the United States tends to employ abroad, the weaknesses of the U.S. foreign policy-making process for democracy policies, the fact that agreeing on promoting democracy as a foreign policy goal does not necessarily lead to agreement on specific poli-cies, and the limitations of democracy as a lens for understanding Latin America. Only if such limitations and uncertainties are ac-knowledged can the United States pursue the goal of promoting de-mocracy in a manner that will reflect a productive, realistic sense of the United States' proper role in Latin America and a genuine under-standing of Latin America itself. The goal of democracy in Latin America deserves no less.

# Notes

## A NOTE ON SOURCES

As noted in the Preface, much of the factual information in this book is drawn from numerous formal interviews and informal conversations with current or former officials involved in Latin American affairs during the 1980s at the State Department, Defense Department, White House, Agency for International Development, United States Information Agency, Justice Department, and Treasury Department. Some of these interviews were with former high-level officials such as Assistant Secretaries of State for Inter-American Affairs Thomas Enders, Langhorne Motley, and Elliott Abrams; National Security Council staff members Walter Raymond, Constantine Menges, and José Sorzano; and numerous U.S. ambassadors to Latin America. Most of the interviews, however, were with low- and mid-level officials; my own experience in the State Department convinced me that much of the most useful information about foreign policy-making and policy implementation resides in the lower levels of the policy bureaucracy. Unfortunately, very few low- and mid-level officials are willing to talk on the record to a researcher such as myself—they are generally career professionals who must be very cautious about what they say for attribution. My status as a former State Department official helped get me in the door to see many relevant officials; it did not, however, overcome their very understandable reluctance to speak on the record. As a result, with the exception of some on-the-record interviews with former high-level officials (who once out of office are almost always happy to speak on the record and to provide detailed accounts of the policy matters they were involved in), most of the interviews and conversations were conducted off the record and I am not able to attribute the information I gained from them to particular persons. In a few cases where the information I am presenting is new or somewhat controversial, I cite confidential interviews and at least identify which agency of government the information came from.

I did not conduct interviews with any CIA officers or other intelligence agency officials. All references in the book to CIA activities are drawn from public sources. I have undoubtedly missed a significant amount of relevant

CIA covert activity related to political change in Latin America in the 1980s, particularly in Central America. Although such activities were probably important in and of themselves, I believe they generally conformed to the policy framework presented in the book and did not constitute a policy apart or fundamentally different from that which I have described.

All economic and military figures cited are drawn from the Agency for International Development's annual report on foreign aid entitled *U.S. Overseas Loans and Grants*. The years cited are government fiscal years. Thus for example if I say that the United States gave $10 million to a particular country in 1984, the aid was obligated between October 1, 1983 and September 30, 1984. I have made extensive use of the annual compendiums of U.S. foreign policy documents and statements published by the State Department, entitled *American Foreign Policy Current Documents*. Citations to these volumes are abbreviated as *AFP*, with the relevant year noted.

## INTRODUCTION

1. See for example, Richard R. Fagen, *Forging Peace: The Challenge of Central America* (New York: Basil Blackwell, 1987); Walter LeFeber, *Inevitable Revolutions: The United States and Central America* (New York: W. W. Norton, 1984).

2. In his book *American Politics: The Promise of Disharmony* (Cambridge: Belknap Press, 1981), 250–251, Samuel Huntington argues that a direct causal relationship has held throughout the twentieth century between the exertion of U.S. influence in Latin America and the achievement of democracy there. For example:

> The interventions by United States Marines in Haiti, Nicaragua and the Dominican Republic, and elsewhere in those years often bore striking resemblances to the interventions by Federal marshals in the conduct of elections in the American South in the 1960s: registering voters, protecting against electoral violence, ensuring a free vote and an honest count. . . . When American intervention ended, democracy ended.

3. A recent comprehensive study of the development of democracy in Latin America in the twentieth century finds that the United States has generally not played a significant role:

> Those who assume that the source of Latin America's political turmoil and democratic failures is primarily external—U.S. intervention and manipulation; economic dependence—may be disappointed with the historical analyses in this volume. Without exception, each of our authors attributes the course of political development and regime change primarily to internal structures and actions, while acknowledging the way structures have been shaped historically by international factors, such as the struggle for independence against the metropolis and the relations with the former motherlands.

Larry Diamond, Juan J. Linz and Seymour Martin Lipset, eds., *Democracy in Developing Countries, Volume IV: Latin America* (Boulder, CO: Lynne

Rienner, 1989), 47. See also, Abraham Lowenthal, ed., *Exporting Democracy: The United States and Latin America* (Baltimore: Johns Hopkins University Press, 1991).

4. This quote comes from the title of a State Department report on El Salvador: "El Salvador: The Battle for Democracy," U.S. Department of State, Public Information Series, November 1988.

5. Address by President Reagan before the OAS Permanent Council, October 7, 1987, *AFP 1987*, 787.

6. Prepared statement by Assistant Secretary of State Elliott Abrams before a Subcommittee of the House Banking, Finance, and Urban Affairs Committee, December 5, 1985, *AFP 1985*, 1087.

7. Statement by Secretary of State George Shultz, Port-au-Prince, Haiti, August 15, 1986, *AFP 1986*, 815.

8. Prepared statement by Assistant Secretary of State Elliott Abrams, Hearing before a Subcommittee of the House Committee on Appropriations, April 22, 1988, *AFP 1988*, 683–694.

9. "The Reagan Legacy in Latin America: Active Support for Democracy," speech at the University of Oklahoma, Norman, Oklahoma, January 12, 1989, Current Policy No. 1144, Bureau of Public Affairs, U.S. Department of State.

10. Elliott Abrams, "Latin America in the Time of Reagan," *New York Times*, July 27, 1988.

11. Statement by Secretary of State George Shultz before the House Foreign Affairs Committee, Washington, D.C., October 13, 1987, Current Policy No. 1010, Bureau of Public Affairs, U.S. Department of State.

12. "No Delay for Democracy," address by Secretary of State George Shultz before the National Foreign Policy Conference for Young Political Leaders, Department of State, Washington, D.C., June 13, 1987, Current Policy No. 846, Bureau of Public Affairs, U.S. Department of State.

13. Elliott Abrams, "Latin America in the Time of Reagan," *New York Times*, July 27, 1988.

14. Press Interview with Elliott Abrams, August 7, 1985, La Paz, Bolivia, *AFP 1985*, 1077.

15. Juan J. Linz, *The Breakdown of Democratic Regimes: Crisis, Breakdown and Reequilibration* (Baltimore: Johns Hopkins University Press, 1978), 5.

16. John A. Booth and Mitchell A. Seligson, *Political Participation in Latin America. Volume I: Citizen and State* (New York: Holmes and Meier, 1978), 6–7.

## CHAPTER ONE

1. *New York Times*, March 19, 1981.

2. The assistance was a $5.7 million reprogramming of nonlethal military aid.

3. Transcript of a press briefing, February 27, 1981, *AFP 1981*, 1274.

4. See Jeane Kirkpatrick, "Dictators and Double Standards," *Commentary* (November 1979): 29–40, and "U.S. Security and Latin America," *Commentary* (January 1981): 34–45.

5. "Department of State Special Report No. 80," February 23, 1981, *AFP 1981*, 1230–1236. The report came under much criticism as being poorly researched and sensationalistic. See for example, *Wall Street Journal*, June 8, 1981; *Washington Post* June 9, 1981. The State Department responded to the many criticisms of the report in, "Response to Stories about Special Report No. 80," U.S. Department of State, June 17, 1981.

6. $20 million was approved under Section 506(a) of the Foreign Assistance Act (which permits the President to grant limited quantities of emergency military aid without congressional approval); $5 million was reprogrammed from existing military assistance programs.

7. From 1946 to 1980 the United States gave $22.5 million of military assistance to El Salvador. Total U.S. military assistance to Latin America and the Caribbean in 1981, excluding El Salvador, was $24.09 million. Note that these figures are in current, not constant dollars.

8. Address by Assistant Secretary of State for Inter-American Affairs Thomas Enders before the World Affairs Council, Washington, July 19, 1981, *AFP 1981*, 1326–1330.

9. In testimony before the House Foreign Affairs Committee, Haig stated that the churchwomen may have tried to run a roadblock and that there might have been an exchange of fire between the churchwomen and Salvadoran security personnel. U.S. Congress, House, Committee on Foreign Affairs, *Foreign Assistance Legislation for Fiscal Year 1982, Part I*, 97th Cong., 1st Sess., 1981 (Washington: U.S. Government Printing Office, 1981), 163. When these remarks prompted controversy, Haig tried to laugh the issue away. When asked directly if he was suggesting that the churchwomen may have run a roadblock, Haig replied: "Oh, not at all. No, not at all. My heavens. . . . The dear nuns who raised me in my parochial schooling would forever isolate me from their affections and respect." And when asked whether his supposition of an exchange of fire implied that the nuns had fired on the Salvadoran security forces, he said, "I have not met any pistol-packing nuns in my days, Senator." U.S. Congress, Senate, Committee on Foreign Relations, *Foreign Assistance Authorization for Fiscal Year 1982*," 97th Cong., 1st Sess., 1981 (Washington: U.S. Government Printing Office, 1981), 36.

10. International Security and Development Cooperation Act of 1981, PL 97–113.

11. Author interview with Department of Defense official involved in security assistance to El Salvador.

12. See "Caribbean Basin Initiative," address by President Reagan before the Permanent Council of the Organization of American States, February 24, 1982, *AFP 1982*, 1381–1387.

13. See Richard S. Newfarmer, "Economic Policy Toward the Carib-

bean Basin: The Balance Sheet," *Journal of Interamerican Studies and World Affairs*, 27 (February 1985): 63–90. See also, Abraham F. Lowenthal, "CBI: Misplaced Emphasis," *Foreign Policy* 47 (Summer 1982): 114–118; Sidney Weintraub, "CBI: A Flawed Model," *Foreign Policy* 47 (Summer 1982): 128–133.

14. In a speech on Central America given in 1987, for example, President Reagan included an anecdote about a Salvadoran grandmother resisting guerrilla pressure not to vote in the 1982 elections. "Promoting Freedom and Democracy in Central America," address before the American Newspaper Publishers Association," Ellis Island, New York, May 3, 1987, Current Policy No. 952, U.S. Department of State, Washington, D.C.

15. See for example, Piero Gleijeses, "The Case for Power Sharing in El Salvador," *Foreign Affairs* 61 (Summer 1983): 1048–1063; *Changing Course: Blueprint for Peace in Central America and the Caribbean*, Report by PACCA (Policy Alternatives for the Caribbean and Central America), (Washington: Institute for Policy Studies, 1984).

16. Enders did not actually propose negotiations between the government and the military leaders of the rebels but rather between the government and the leftist political parties allied with the FMLN. His idea was not that a peace settlement would likely result but that the political wing of the FMLN might be wooed away from the military leadership and that getting the leftist political parties into a dialogue with the government would moderate the public image of the U.S. policy and increase Congressional support. The hardliners just saw that Enders was backing away from the no negotiations policy and reacted furiously. Enders was also forced out because he had alienated many people in the administration, particularly hardliners in the White House, the Defense Department, and CIA, with his secretive, aloof style and his strong-willed attempts to keep the policy-making process directly in his hands. Roy Gutman, *Banana Diplomacy: The Making of American Policy in Nicaragua 1981–1987* (New York: Simon and Schuster, 1988), 126–133.

17. "It Isn't Nutmeg That's at Stake in the Caribbean and Central America. It is the U.S. National Security." Address by President Reagan before the Annual Meeting of the National Association of Manufacturers, March 10, 1983, *AFP 1983*, 1285–1290.

18. The decision to appoint the Kissinger Commission was also based on the lack of Congressional and public support for the administration's Nicaragua policy; nonetheless, securing a bipartisan base for the El Salvador policy was the administration's main concern.

19. See *Report of the National Bipartisan Commission on Central America* (Washington: U.S. Government Printing Office, January 1984).

20. Author interview with AID official.

21. Precise figures for the U.S. elections assistance to El Salvador are difficult to obtain because the funds were local currency assistance funds. When AID gives dollar grants to a country for balance-of-payments support, the funds go directly to the Central Bank of the country and the Cen-

tral Bank is required to generate one dollar's worth of local currency for every dollar of U.S. assistance and to use these local currency funds, which are referred to as local currency assistance, for development projects. Local currency funds are not technically U.S. assistance funds (but rather the product of U.S. dollar assistance), AID therefore is not required to report precise budget figures for specific local currency assistance projects. Estimates for the total amount of local currency that went to the Salvadoran electoral commission vary significantly among U.S. officials, and range from three to eight million dollars worth of local currency funds. A brief description of the U.S. election assistance program for the 1984 Salvadoran elections is given in Marilyn Anne Zak, "Assisting Elections in the Third World," *The Washington Quarterly* (Autumn 1987): 175–193.

22. Author interview with U.S. official involved in the elections assistance program to El Salvador.

23. *Washington Post*, April 10, 1984, May 13, 1984; *Boston Globe*, May 14, 1984; *Time*, May 21, 1984. The amounts of covert assistance may not have been high in absolute terms but given that El Salvador has a population approximately fifty times smaller than the United States, the per capita equivalent in the United States of the covert aid to Duarte would be a $50 million to $100 million donation to a presidential candidate.

24. Author interview with a senior State Department official who worked in the U.S. embassy in El Salvador in 1984.

25. *Washington Post*, October 16, 1984; *New York Times* October 17, 1984.

26. An outstanding study of U.S. military policy in El Salvador by four active duty U.S. army officers details the many shortcomings of the policy. See A. J. Bacevich, James P. Hallums, Richard H. White, and Thomas F. Young, *American Military Policy in Small Wars: The Case of El Salvador* (Washington: Pergamon-Brasseys's, 1988).

27. *El Salvador: "Death Squads"—a Government Strategy* (London: Amnesty International Publications, 1988); *Human Rights in El Salvador on the Eve of Elections* (Washington: Americas Watch, 1988).

28. *Washington Post*, May 25, 1986; *Christian Science Monitor*, August 10, 1987; *Wall Street Journal*, September 14, 1987.

29. "El Salvador: The Battle for Democracy," Public Information Series, U.S. Department of State, Washington, D.C., November 1988.

30. Some observers contend that the Democratic Convergence's low vote totals were not an accurate reflection of the left's popular support because the Convergence's campaign activities were very limited (owing to their recent entry into the process and the continuing fear of repression) and because the areas of the country most sympathetic to the left had the lowest areas of voter participation owing to the civil war.

31. "El Salvador: The Battle for Democracy," Public Information Series, U.S. Department of State, Washington, D.C., November 1988.

32. Bacevich, Hallums, White, and Young, *American Military Policy in Small Wars: The Case of El Salvador*.

33. "El Salvador: The Battle for Democracy," Public Information Series, U.S. Department of State, Washington, D.C., November 1988.

34. See Elliott Abrams, "The Reagan Legacy in Latin America: Active Support for Democracy," address given at the University of Oklahoma, January 12, 1989, Current Policy No. 1144, U.S. Department of State, Washington, D.C.

35. Joel Millman, "El Salvador's Army: A Force Unto Itself," *New York Times Magazine*, December 10, 1989, 47, 95–97.

## CHAPTER TWO

1. U.S. military assistance to Honduras varied between two and four million dollars per year from 1977 to 1980. Assistance in 1981 (which was requested and approved during the Carter period) rose to $8.9 million. Scholarly literature on the Carter administration's policy in Honduras is scarce. See Mark B. Rosenberg, "Honduran Scorecard—Military and Democrats in Central America," *Caribbean Review* 12, (Winter 1983): 12–15, 39–42; Philip L. Shepard, "Honduras," in Morris J. Blachman, William M. Leo-Grande and Kenneth Sharpe, eds., *Confronting Revolution: Security Through Diplomacy in Central America* (New York: Pantheon, 1986), 125–155; Thomas P. Anderson, *Politics in Central America* (New York: Praeger, 1988), chap. 11.

2. Prepared statement by Assistant Secretary of State Thomas Enders before a Subcommittee of the Senate Foreign Relations Committee, December 14, 1981, *AFP 1981*, 1366–1369.

3. Author interview with Jack Binns, U.S. Ambassador to Honduras, September 1980–September 1981.

4. Statement by Principal Deputy Assistant Secretary of State Stephen Bosworth, before the Subcommittee on Inter-American Affairs of the House Foreign Affairs Committee, September 21, 1982, *AFP 1982*, 1465.

5. *Washington Post*, February 18, 1986.

6. As with the El Salvador electoral assistance project, the Honduras project was primarily funded by local currency assistance and thus no budget figure for the project was reported by AID (see note 21, chap. 1 on local currency assistance projects). AID officials have different memories of the amount of funds spent on the electoral assistance project in Honduras in 1985, with estimates ranging from five to fifteen million dollars.

7. Author interview with State Department official who worked in the U.S. embassy in Honduras in the mid-1980s.

8. Anderson, *Politics in Central America*, 162.

9. Mark B. Rosenberg, "Can Democracy Survive the Democrats? From Transition to Consolidation in Honduras," in John A. Booth and Mitchell A. Seligson, eds., *Elections and Democracy in Central America* (Chapel Hill: University of North Carolina Press, 1989) 43, 50.

10. See *Honduras: Civilian Authority—Military Power. Human Rights Violations in the 1980s* (London: Amnesty International Publications, 1988).

11. Thomas P. Anderson, "Politics and the Military in Honduras," *Current History* (December 1988): 425−428, 431−432.

12. James LeMoyne, "Testifying to Torture," *New York Times Magazine,* June 5, 1988, 45−47, 62−66.

13. *Washington Post,* January 8, 1987; Gutman, *Banana Diplomacy,* 324−325.

14. *New York Times,* April 9, 1988; *Washington Post,* April 9, 1988.

15. *New York Times,* April 13, 1988; April 10, 1988. Another anti-U.S. demonstration of about 1,000 people took place later in April. *Washington Post,* April 22, 1988.

16. Statement by Deputy Assistant Secretary of State for Inter-American Affairs Stephen Bosworth before two subcommittees of the House Foreign Affairs Committee, July 30, 1981, *AFP 1981,* 1332−1334.

17. Caesar Sereseres, one of the few U.S. academic experts on the Guatemalan insurgency, and a political conservative or moderate, testified before Congress in 1983 that "the EGP [the main group of Guatemalan rebels] developed and evolved virtually independent of Cuba, the Soviet Union, and the communist support network." See "Guatemalan Politics, Internal War, and U.S. Policy Options," in *United States Policy Toward Guatemala,* Hearing before the Subcommittee on Western Hemisphere Affairs of the House Committee on Foreign Affairs, March 9, 1983, 98th Congress, 1st Session, 50.

18. Ibid., 50.

19. This account of the different ways of thinking about Guatemala policy in the early Reagan administration is based on interviews with State Department officials who worked in the Bureau of Inter-American Affairs during that period. A similar account is given in Piero Gleijeses, "Perspectives of a Regime Transformation in Guatemala," in Wolf Grabendorff, Heinrich-W. Krumwiede, and Jorg Todt, eds., *Political Change in Central America: Internal and External Dimensions* (Boulder, CO: Westview, 1984), 127−138, at 132−134.

20. Bosworth testimony, cited note 16, 1333.

21. *Washington Post,* May 5, 1981.

22. Bosworth testimony, cited note 16, 1333.

23. *New York Times,* December 16, 1981.

24. Gabriel Aguilera Peralta, "The Hidden War: Guatemala's Counterinsurgency Campaign," in Nora Hamilton, Jeffry A. Freiden, Linda Fuller, and Manuel Pastor, Jr., eds., *Crisis in Central America: Regional Dynamics and U.S. Policy in the 1980s* (Boulder, CO: Westview, 1988), 153−172.

25. *Miami Herald,* April 17, 1982.

26. An administration spokesperson discussing Reagan's meeting with Ríos Montt referred to the Guatemalan strongman as "a schoolteacher" whose "personal probity" was unchallengeable—a somewhat strained description of a lifelong Guatemalan military officer known primarily for his

megalomania and peculiar religious views. State Department press briefing, December 6, 1982, *AFP 1982*, 1293.

27. Being a sale rather than a grant or loan, this transaction did not need formal Congressional approval. The administration had nonetheless kept the Guatemalan request on hold until it thought it could make a plausible case on the human rights issue and not overly offend Congress.

28. *Guatemala: The Human Rights Record* (London: Amnesty International Publications, 1987), 113–127.

29. *New York Times*, March 3, 1984, February 3, 1985.

30. Statement by Vice President Bush in Guatemala City, January 14, 1986, *AFP 1986*, 721.

31. Prepared statement by Assistant Secretary of State Elliott Abrams, Hearings before a Subcommittee of the House Committee on Appropriations, April 22, 1988, *AFP 1988*, 688.

32. The license was for a sale of 20,000 M-16s by Colt Industries totaling $13.8 million, conveniently just below the $14 million threshold above which Congressional review of an export license is required. The license came to public attention soon after the May 11, 1988 coup attempt in Guatemala and was thought by some observers to be a bone thrown by the administration to the disgruntled Guatemalan military.

33. *Closing the Space: Human Rights in Guatemala, May 1987–October 1988* (Washington: Americas Watch, 1988).

34. Ken Anderson and Jean-Marie Simon, "Permanent Counterinsurgency in Guatemala," *Telos* 73 (Fall 1987): 9–46.

35. On the causes of the Guatemalan military's decision to permit a transition to civilian rule, see Richard Millet, "Guatemala's Painful Progress," *Current History* (December 1986): 413–416, 430–431.

36. The House Foreign Affairs Committee made its recommendation of additional assistance for Costa Rica as part of its review of the Economic Support Funds portion of the administration's foreign aid budget for 1982.

37. U.S. military assistance to Costa Rica in the first half of the 1980s was almost all Military Assistance Program grants. From 1982 to 1986 U.S. military assistance totaled $27 million. Previous military aid to Costa Rica totaled $6.9 million (mostly loans rather than grants) in the 1960s and 1970s and $100,000 in the 1950s.

38. See for example, Morris J. Blachman and Ronald G. Hellman, "Costa Rica," in Blachman, LeoGrande, and Sharpe, *Confronting Revolution*, 156–182.


## CHAPTER THREE

1. On U.S. policy and the fall of Somoza, see Robert Pastor, *Condemned to Repetition: The United States and Nicaragua* (Princeton: Princeton University Press, 1987); Anthony Lake, *Somoza Falling* (Boston: Houghton Mifflin, 1989); Jeane Kirkpatrick, "U.S. Security and Latin America," *Commentary*,

(January 1981): 29–40; William LeoGrande, "The Revolution in Nicaragua: Another Cuba?" *Foreign Affairs* 58 (Fall 1979): 28–50; Shirley Christian, *Nicaragua: Revolution in the Family* (New York: Random House, 1985).

2. Cynthia Arnson, *Crossroads: Congress, the Reagan Administration, and Central America* (New York: Pantheon, 1989), 35–51.

3. This account of the Reagan administration's Nicaragua policy is drawn from interviews with U.S. policymakers, including Elliott Abrams, Langhorne Motley, José Sorzano, Constantine Menges, Lawrence Pezzulo, and a number of officials who requested anonymity. It also draws heavily on Roy Gutman's excellent book *Banana Diplomacy: The Making of American Policy in Nicaragua 1981–1987* (New York: Simon and Schuster, 1988). Other secondary sources consulted include: Robert Pastor, *Condemned to Repetition. The United States and Nicaragua*, chaps. 12–13; Viron P. Vaky, "Positive Containment in Nicaragua," *Foreign Policy* 68 (Fall 1987): 42–58; Wayne Smith, "Lies about Nicaragua," *Foreign Policy* 67 (Summer 1987): 87–103; Forrest D. Colburn, "Embattled Nicaragua," *Current History* (December 1987): 405–408, 431; Dario Moreno, "Peace and the Nicaraguan Revolution," *Current History* (December 1988): 405–408, 431–432; Joshua Muravchik, "The Nicaraguan Debate," *Foreign Affairs* 65 (Winter 1986/87): 366–382; Robert Woodward, *Veil: The Secret Wars of the CIA 1981–1987* (New York: Pocket Books, 1987); Arnson, *Crossroads: Congress, the Reagan Administration, and Central America*; William LeoGrande, "Rollback or Containment? The United States, Nicaragua, and the Search for Peace in Central America," in Bruce M. Bagley, ed., *Contadora and the Diplomacy of Peace in Central America. Vol. 1: The United States, Central America, and Contadora* (Boulder: Westview Press, 1987), 83–112.

4. Statement issued by the Department of State, April 1, 1981, *AFP 1981*, 1298.

5. The *Wall Street Journal* was first with the story in its April 6, 1984 edition.

6. *Congressional Record*, October 10, 1984, H 11980 and H 11884.

7. Author interview with senior State Department official directly involved in the Nicaragua policy.

8. The extremely tense and mistrustful relations between the hard-liners and the moderates in these negotiations, and in the Nicaragua policy process generally, is vividly conveyed by Constantine Menges, a devout hard-liner, in his book *Inside the National Security Council: The True Story of the Making and Unmaking of Reagan's Foreign Policy* (New York: Simon and Schuster, 1988).

9. *Washington Post*, November 5, 1984; Department of State daily press briefing, November 5, 1984, *AFP 1984*, 1107.

10. Literature on the secret supply network is vast. The central source is the material produced by the Congressional committees investigating the Iran-contra scandal. See *Report of the Congressional Committees Investigating the Iran-Contra Affair*, S. Rept. No. 100–216, H. Rept. No. 100–433, 100th Cong., 1st. sess. (Washington: U.S. Government Printing Office, 1987) and the numerous annexes to the report.

11. The Esquipulas II accord is reprinted in *Current History* (December 1987): 430, 436–437.

12. Address to the nation by President Reagan, May 9, 1984, *AFP 1984*, 1067; Address by President Reagan before the White House Outreach Group, July 18, 1984, *AFP 1984*, 1079.

13. Address to the nation by President Reagan, March 16, 1986, *AFP 1986*, 753.

14. Remarks by President Reagan, April 14, 1983, *AFP 1983*, 1309.

15. Press interview with President Reagan, March 28, 1984, *AFP 1984*, 1048.

16. Address by President Reagan before the OAS Permanent Council, October 7, 1987, *AFP 1987*, 787.

17. Remarks to the press by President Reagan, April 14, 1983, *AFP 1983*, 1309.

18. Transcript of a press conference by President Reagan, February 21, 1985, *AFP 1985*, 966.

19.. Ibid., 966.

20. Address to the nation by President Reagan, June 24, 1986, *AFP 1986*, 767.

21. Press interview with President Reagan, March 28, 1984, *AFP 1984*, 1048.

22. Press interview with President Reagan, August 1, 1984, *AFP 1984*, 1081.

23. Press interview with President Reagan, March 4, 1985, *AFP 1985*, 977.

24. Address by President Reagan at the Conservative Political Action Conference's 12th Annual Dinner, March 1, 1985, *AFP 1985*, 973.

25. State Department press briefing, April 8, 1982, *AFP 1982*, 1438.

26. "Areas of Challenge in the Americas," Address by Assistant Secretary of State for Inter-American Affairs Thomas Enders before the Inter-American Press Association, Chicago, September 30, 1982, *AFP 1982*, 1274.

27. Rep. Bill Richardson (D-N.M.), for example, switched from a no to a yes vote on contra aid (nonlethal aid) in 1985 with the explanation, "What I had hoped to do with my vote was signal the Sandinistas . . . that progressive democrats like myself were eager for them to mend their undemocratic ways." *New York Times*, November 26, 1985.

28. War deaths as a percentage of the total population of the United States (the population at the time the war took place) are the following: the Civil War—0.4 percent, World War I—0.05 percent, World War II—0.2 percent, the Korean War—0.02 percent, and the Vietnam War—0.02 percent, for a total of 0.69 percent of the U.S. population. The 30,000 Nicaraguans killed in the contra war represented 0.83 percent of the Nicaraguan population. All U.S. casualty and population figures are drawn from *Information Please Almanac 1989* (Boston: Houghton Mifflin, 1989)

29. The international legal basis of the administration's Nicaragua policy was tested when Nicaragua brought suit against the United States before the International Court of Justice in 1984, charging the United States

with having violated international law in mining Nicaragua's harbors and taking other hostile acts against Nicaragua. To the extent that the United States did defend itself before the Court (the United States hastily withdrew its acceptance of the Court's jurisdiction just before Nicaragua filed suit and participated only in the jurisdictional phase of the case), it argued self-defense. The administration contended that its actions against Nicaragua were part of a set of collective self-defense measures taken to defend El Salvador against Nicaragua. The Court rejected this argument, finding that Nicaragua had not been supporting the Salvadoran rebels since early 1981 and that even if it had been, the provision of arms and equipment would not have constituted an "armed attack" necessary to trigger the right of individual or collective self-defense. See "Case Concerning Military and Para-military Activities in and against Nicaragua, Nicaragua v. United States of America, Merits, Judgment of June 27, 1986," *Reports of Judgments, Advisory Opinions and Orders 1986*, International Court of Justice, 14.

30. On Grenada and the U.S. invasion generally see Jiri Valenta and Herbert J. Ellison, eds., *Grenada and Soviet/Cuban Policy: Internal Crisis and U.S./OECS Intervention* (Boulder, CO: Westview, 1986); Kai P. Schoenhals and Richard A. Melanson, *Revolution and Intervention in Grenada: The New Jewel Movement, the United States, and the Caribbean* (Boulder, CO: Westview, 1985).

31. *New York Times*, April 9, 1982.

32. The Grenadan army was enlarged to about 1,000 men, a large number relative to Grenada's small population (110,000) and to the size of other armies in the Eastern Caribbean. Although the army was expanded, Grenada remained without an air force or navy.

33. Anthony Payne, Paul Sutton, and Tony Thorndike, *Grenada: Revolution and Invasion* (New York: St. Martin's Press, 1984), chap. 6.

34. Bishop did get a short meeting with National Security Adviser William Clark and Deputy Secretary of State Kenneth Dam.

35. Payne, Sutton, and Thorndike, *Grenada*, chap. 6.

36. Woodward, *Veil*, 322–326.

37. Ibid., 326.

38. Richard Gabriel, "Scenes from an Invasion: How the U.S. Military Stumbled to Victory in Grenada," *The Washington Monthly* (February 1986): 34–41; *U.S. News and World Report*, November 3, 1986, 42. The Pentagon awarded 8,633 medals to the 7,000 participants in the invasion (by contrast, Great Britain awarded 679 medals to the 28,000 participants in the Falklands War).

39. Woodward, *Veil*, 337.

40. Statement by President Reagan, October 25, 1983, *AFP 1983*, 1398.

41. *New York Times*, October 27, 1983.

42. Address to the nation by President Reagan, October 27, 1983, *AFP 1983*, 1411.

43. Ibid., 1411.

44. *The Grenada Documents: An Overview and Selection* (Washington: U.S. Department of State and U.S. Department of Defense, 1984).

45. President Reagan was probably also influenced to strike against Grenada because of the feelings of anger and helplessness provoked by the October 23 bombing of the U.S. marine barracks in Lebanon. Nonetheless, the decision to invade had been informally reached the day before; only the formal presidential approval remained. Given the consensus of his advisers and the October 23 request from the OECS, Reagan would almost certainly have given the formal approval even if the Lebanon bombing had not occurred.

46. A concise analysis of the international law problems with the invasion of Grenada is given in William C. Gilmore, *The Grenada Intervention* (New York: Facts on File, 1984). The argument that the invasion was compatible with international law is made by John Norton Moore in *Law and the Grenada Mission* (Charlottesville, N.C.: Center for Law and National Security, 1984).

## CHAPTER FOUR

1. Brazil gained a civilian government in 1985, not through direct presidential elections but through indirect electoral college elections.

2. Prepared Statement by Assistant Secretary of State Thomas Enders before Subcommittees of the House Foreign Affairs Committee, October 22, 1981, *AFP 1981*, 1201. The four largest suppliers were West Germany, France, Israel, and Italy.

3. *AFP 1981*, 1207−1223.

4. Susan Kaufman Purcell, "War and Debt in South America," *Foreign Affairs* 61 (America and the World 1982): 660−674.

5. "Three Tasks for U.S. Policy in the Hemisphere," Address by Assistant Secretary Designate Thomas Enders before the Council of the Americas, Washington, D.C., June 3, 1981, *AFP 1981*, 1194.

6. Department of Defense responses to additional questions submitted by the chairman of the Senate Foreign Relations Committee, May 4, 1981, *AFP 1981*, 1189.

7. For an analysis of the place of the South Atlantic in U.S. national security, see Lars Schoultz, *National Security and United States Policy Toward Latin America* (Princeton: Princeton University Press, 1987), 195−199.

8. Letter from the Assistant Secretary of the Treasury for Legislative Affairs to the chairman of a subcommittee of the House Banking, Finance, and Urban Affairs Committee, July 1, 1981, *AFP 1981*, 1371−1372. The Carter administration had abstained on loans to Argentina, Paraguay, and Uruguay and opposed loans to Chile, on the basis of human rights legislation passed in 1977.

9. The most comprehensive and well-argued conservative critique of Carter's human rights policy is Joshua Muravchik, *The Uncertain Crusade: Jimmy Carter and the Dilemmas of Human Rights Policy* (Lanham, MD: Hamilton Press, 1986).

10. Response by Assistant Secretary of State for Congressional Rela-

tions Fairbanks to a question submitted by the chairman of a subcommittee of the House Banking, Finance, and Urban Affairs Committee, September 10, 1981, *AFP 1981*, 1372–1373.

11. Jacobo Timerman, *Prisoner Without a Name, Cell Without a Number* (New York: Knopf, 1981).

12. *New York Times*, May 7, 1981, May 11, 1981, and May 29, 1981; *Washington Post*, May 21, 1981, May 22, 1981, and May 24, 1981.

13. Paul Sigmund, "Latin America: Change or Continuity?" *Foreign Affairs* 60 (America and the World 1981): 629–657.

14. Prepared statement by Assistant Secretary Enders before subcommittees of the House Foreign Affairs Committee, October 22, 1981, *AFP 1981*, 1201.

15. The repeal of the ban was contained in Section 725 of the International Security and Development Cooperation Act of 1981, PL 97–113.

16. Section 726 of the International Security and Development Cooperation Act of 1981, PL 97–113. The certification requirement has three parts. The president must certify that the Chilean Government has made significant improvement in human rights, is taking steps to bring the perpetrators of the 1976 killing of Orlando Letelier to justice, and is openly opposed to international terrorism.

17. Albert Fishlow, "The United States and Brazil: The Case of the Missing Relationship," *Foreign Affairs* 60 (Spring 1982): 904–23; Abraham Lowenthal, *Partners in Conflict* (Baltimore: Johns Hopkins University Press, 1988), chap. 5; Eul-Soo Pang, "Brazil's New Democracy," *Current History* (February 1983): 54–57, 87–89; Robert M. Levine, "Brazil: The Dimensions of Democratization," *Current History* (February 1982): 60–63, 86–87; Riordan Roett, "Staying the Course," *The Wilson Quarterly* 7 (Summer 1983): 46–61.

18. "Brazil and the United States Today," Address by Assistant Secretary Enders before the Chamber of Commerce, Sao Paulo, Brazil, August 19, 1981, *State Department Bulletin* (November 1981): 87–89; Dinner toast by Vice President Bush, *State Department Bulletin* (January 1982): 14–15.

19. Enders, "Brazil and the United States Today."

20. Gary Wynia, "Argentina: Rebuilding the Relationship," in Richard S. Newfarmer, ed., *From Gunboats to Diplomacy: New U.S. Policies for Latin America* (Baltimore: Johns Hopkins University Press, 1984), 162–75; Carlos Moneta, "The United States and Argentina," in Robert Wesson and Heraldo Muñoz, eds., *Latin American Views of U.S. Policy* (New York: Praeger, 1986), 106–121; Joseph S. Tulchin, *Argentina and the United States: A Conflicted Relationship* (Boston: Twayne, 1990), chaps. 8, 9.

21. *New York Times*, August 22, 1981. See chapter 5 for a more complete analysis of U.S.-Chilean relations in the early 1980s.

22. The description of Ambassador Corr's activities in Bolivia are drawn from an author interview with Corr.

23. Ibid.

24. James Malloy and Eduardo Gamarra, for example, conclude the following:

The United States was an important influence during the Siles period, although it by no means had the capacity to determine specific political outcomes. Under Ambassador Corr, the U.S. embassy maintained a high profile. The United States was openly supportive of the democratization process.

James M. Malloy and Eduardo Gamarra, *Revolution and Reaction: Bolivia 1964–1985* (New Brunswick, N.J.: Transaction Press, 1988), 176.

25. Author interview with Ambassador Edwin Corr.

26. Langhorne Motley, "Letting Off Steam," in Hans Binnendijk, ed., *Authoritarian Regimes in Transition* (Washington: Foreign Service Institute, 1987), 248–253.

27. Author interview with State Department official involved in South American affairs.

28. Howard Wiarda, "United States Policy in South America: A Maturing Relationship?" *Current History* (February 1985): 49–52, 86–87.

29. Interview with Assistant Secretary Abrams, La Paz, August 7, 1985, *AFP 1985*, 1077.

30. Author interview with Department of Defense official involved in Latin American affairs. The *New York Times* reported in January 1989 that the U.S. Ambassador to Peru, Alexander Watson, had warned senior Peruvian military officers that Peru could face international isolation if they seized power. *New York Times*, January 15, 1989.

31. There is a large literature on the debt crisis and U.S. debt policy. See, for example, Riordan Roett, "Democracy and Debt in South America: A Continent's Dilemma," *Foreign Affairs* 62 (America and the World 1983): 695–720; Pedro-Pablo Kuczynski, *Latin American Debt* (Baltimore: Johns Hopkins University Press, 1987); William D. Rogers, "The United States and Latin America," *Foreign Affairs* 63 (America and the World 1984): 560–580; Esperanza Durán, ed., *Latin America and the World Recession* (Cambridge: Cambridge University Press, 1985); Benjamin J. Cohen, "International Debt and Linkage Strategies: Some Foreign-Policy Implications for the United States," *International Organization* 39 (Autumn 1985): 699–727; "The Latin American Debt Problem," Office of the Assistant Secretary, International Affairs, Department of the Treasury, November 13, 1984, in *Dealing with the Debt Problem of Latin America*, Proceedings of a Conference, Joint Economic Committee Print, 98th Congress, 2d Session, S. Rpt. 98–284.

32. See, for example, P. Lernoux, "Beggaring our Latin Neighbors," *Nation*, December 12, 1987, 709–710; J. Amuzegar, "Dealing with Debt," *Foreign Policy* 68 (Fall 1987): 140–58; *The Americas in 1988: A Time for Change*, Report of the Inter-American Dialogue (Lanham, MD: University Press of America, 1988); Robert Rothstein, "Give Them a Break," *The New Republic* February 1, 1988, 20; Richard Feinberg, "Latin Blood Money," *New York Times*, September 22, 1988.

33. Author interview with member of the State Department Bureau of Inter-American Affairs.

34. The administration was also somewhat influenced by its fear of the

precedential effect on U.S. borrowers, such as farmers, of any debt forgiveness policy for foreign debtors.

35. Lamentations from the U.S. academic and policy community about the Reagan administration's low level of interest in South America appeared regularly in the 1980s. A typical example is Richard Millet, "The United States and Latin America," *Current History* (February 1984): 49–53, 84–85.

36. "Democracy and the Path to Economic Growth," Address by Secretary of State George Shultz before the 8th Annual Conference on Trade, Investment and Development in the Caribbean Basin, Miami, Florida, December 6, 1984, *AFP 1984*, 1116.

37. For an analysis of the historical association of democracy and capitalism, see Charles Lindbloom, *Politics and Markets* (New York: Basic Books, 1977), part V.

38. John Sheahan, *Patterns of Development in Latin America: Poverty, Repression, and Economic Strategy* (Princeton: Princeton University Press, 1987), 313.

39. Interview with Assistant Secretary Abrams, La Paz, Bolivia, August 7, 1985, *AFP 1985*, 1077.

40. The rapidly growing literature on the causes of the reemergence of democracy in South America uniformly emphasizes the importance of internal political and economic factors. None of the studies finds any great role of U.S. policy. See for example, Philip O'Brien and Paul Cammack, eds., *Generals in Retreat: The Crisis of Military Rule in Latin America* (Manchester: Manchester University Press, 1985); Guillermo O'Donnell, Philippe C. Schmitter, and Laurence Whitehead, eds., *Transitions from Authoritarian Rule in Latin America* (Baltimore: Johns Hopkins University Press, 1986); Larry Diamond, Juan J. Linz, and Seymour Martin Lipset, eds., *Democracy in Developing Countries, Volume IV: Latin America* (Boulder, CO: Lynne Rienner, 1989); James M. Malloy and Mitchell Seligson, eds., *Authoritarians and Democrats: Regime Transition in Latin America* (Pittsburgh: University of Pittsburgh Press, 1987); George A. Lopez and Michael Stohl, eds., *Liberalization and Redemocratization in Latin America* (Westport, CT: Greenwood Press, 1987).

## CHAPTER FIVE

1. Export-Import Bank financing for Chile was suspended in 1979 because of the Chilean government's failure to make a serious effort to investigate and prosecute three Chilean military officers indicted by a U.S. court for the 1976 murder in Washington, D.C., of two Chileans, Orlando Letelier (who had been Ambassador to the United States under Allende) and Ronni Moffitt. The administration's decision to lift the suspension in 1981 was not based on any progress in the case, only on the administration's desire to improve relations with Pinochet. The State Department explained the removal of the suspension as follows:

Our willingness to take steps [such as the suspension of Exim financing], which affected U.S. interests as well as those of the Government of Chile, demonstrated the seriousness with which we viewed this matter. The actions were not intended to be permanent. We continue to hope the government of Chile will move to prosecute those implicated in the Letelier/ Moffitt case but unlike the 1978–1979 request for extradition, we are not an active party to the investigation.

Statement issued by the U.S. Department of State, February 20, 1981, *AFP 1981*, 1387.

2. See note 8, chap. 4.

3. In February 1981, for example, the United States voted against a resolution authorizing the U.N. Human Rights Commission to give special attention to the human rights situation in Chile. *New York Times*, February 21, 1981, and February 27, 1981.

4. *New York Times*, August 22, 1981.

5. The State Department annual human rights report of 1981 stated that "the human rights situation in Chile has improved significantly since 1977." *Country Reports on Human Rights for 1981* (Washington: U.S. Government Printing Office, 1982), 369. The report also praised Pinochet's economic policies for their free market orientation and their little-known progressive qualities: "Social spending is now more carefully focused on the poorer segments of the population." Ibid., 370.

6. Chile was not invited to participate in the 1980 UNITAS exercises as one element of a package of punitive measures the Carter administration imposed in response to the Letelier case. The Reagan administration's explanation of its decision to reinvite Chile conveys the generally pro-Pinochet attitude behind the policy shift:                                          `

Concerning the UNITAS exercises, the fact that Chile was not invited last year does not determine policy for this year. Chile has an important navy in South America and its participation enhances the value of the UNITAS exercises and strengthens overall hemispheric defense. In addition, Chile is important to our ability to maintain control of the southern sea-lanes of communication.

Prepared statement by Acting Assistant Secretary of State for Inter-American Affairs John Bushnell, before two subcommittees of the House Foreign Affairs Committee, March 10, 1981, *AFP 1981*, 1389.

7. Prepared Statement by Lt. Gen. Ernest Graves, Director, Defense Security Assistance Agency, Department of Defense, before the Senate Foreign Relations Committee, May 14, 1981, *AFP 1981*, 1189.

8. The certification requirement has three parts. The President must certify that the Government of Chile has made significant progress in complying with international human rights, that the provisions of military assistance would be in the national interest of the United States, and that the Government of Chile has taken appropriate steps to cooperate to bring to justice those indicted in the United States in connection with the murders of Orlando Letelier and Ronni Moffitt. Section 726(b) of the International Security and Development Cooperation Act of 1981.

9. Elliott Abrams, who was then Assistant Secretary for Human Rights and Humanitarian Affairs, strongly opposed certifying Chile on human rights and has said he was ready to resign if the State Department and the president decided to go ahead with a certification. Author interview with Abrams.

10. The communiques, although very mild, did annoy the Chilean government, which regarded all such messages as unwarranted interference in Chile's internal affairs. In November 1983, Chilean Foreign Minister Miguel Schweitzer complained that "fourteen communiques from the State Department about political dialogue seems excessive to me." *Washington Post*, November 24, 1983.

11. Theberge attended the tenth anniversary celebration in Chile of the 1973 military coup. He also largely ignored the Chilean opposition and Chilean human rights groups. In 1983 he sent strongly worded cables to the State Department advising against pressuring Pinochet on human rights or democracy.

12. Author interview with Langhorne Motley.

13. Author interview with Elliott Abrams and Langhorne Motley.

14. Unnamed administration official, quoted in, *New York Times*, February 6, 1985.

15. See Genaro Arriagada, *The Politics of Power* (Boston: Unwin Hyman, 1988), 75–76.

16. Not too much should be made of the fact that the administration initiated rather than just supported the resolution. It initiated the resolution in large part to head off a more strongly worded resolution by Mexico.

17. Barnes's activities were praised even by liberal critics of the administration's Latin America policies. See for the example the glowing account by the International Human Rights Law Group in its report on the plebiscite, *Chile: The Plebiscite and Beyond* (Washington: International Human Rights Law Group, February 1989).

18. See for example, Peter Hakim, "Forging an Effective U.S. Policy Toward Chile," *Christian Science Monitor*, June 3, 1986; Cynthia Brown, "No Pinochet, No Pinochetism," *New York Times*, July 18, 1987.

19. Abrams declared in July 1987 for example that "Chile remains a special target for foreign Communists." Prepared statement by Assistant Secretary for Inter-American Affairs Elliott Abrams, July 21, 1987, *AFP 1987*, 825.

20. Author interviews with National Security Council staff members Jacqueline Tillman and José Sorzano.

21. Author interview with Elliott Abrams.

22. Author interview with José Sorzano, who was present at the meeting.

23. Statement issued by the Department of State, *AFP 1987*, 829.

24. *Washington Post*, January 5, 1988.

25. The National Endowment for Democracy had also spent $630,000 in 1987 on democracy assistance in Chile, more money than it spent on any other Latin American country that year.

26. *Chile: The Plebiscite and Beyond,* report by the International Human Rights Law Group, February 1989; *NDI Reports* (National Democratic Institute for International Affairs newsletter), Fall 1988, 3; *New York Times,* November 18, 1988.

27. Author interview with AID official, October 1988.

28. Abrams says the intelligence clearly showed that Pinochet was seriously considering calling off the plebiscite. Author interview with Abrams.

29. Author interview with Abrams.

30. Author interview with Abrams.

31. Assistant Secretary Abrams stated before Congress in 1986, for example:

> We have very limited real influence [in Chile]. We have few carrots and few sticks available. We have no security assistance program; no military training relationship; no bilateral economic assistance program to speak of except for a small amount of humanitarian food aid. Because of legislative restrictions imposed on the Executive by the Congress, we have very limited channels of communication to the Chilean Armed Forces, who must play a key role in assuring a peaceful transition to democracy.

Prepared statement before the Subcommittee on International Development Institutions and Finance of the Committee on Banking, Finance, and Urban Affairs, U.S. House of Representatives, July 30, 1986, *AFP 1986,* 830.

32. A close observer of the U.S. assistance effort in the Chilean plebiscite concurs with this modest assessment. See Peter Winn, "U.S. Electoral Aid in Chile: Reflections on a Success Story," Paper presented at Washington Office on Latin America conference "U.S. Electoral Assistance and Democratic Development: Chile, Nicaragua, Panama," January 19, 1990, Washington, D.C.

33. "Latin America and the Caribbean: The Paths to Democracy," Speech by Elliott Abrams to the Washington World Affairs Council, June 30, 1987, Current Policy No. 982, Bureau of Public Affairs, U.S. Department of State. On September 21, 1987 Abrams met with the Paraguayan Foreign Minister "to express the U.S. Government's increasing concern about the deteriorating human rights situation in Paraguay." State Department press statement, September 22, 1987, *AFP 1987,* 834.

34. The incident occurred on February 9, 1987. *New York Times,* March 24, 1987. The State Department called in the Paraguayan Ambassador to protest the incident.

35. Author interviews with State Department officials involved in U.S. policy toward Paraguay 1986–1988.

36. "Latin America and the Caribbean: The Paths to Democracy," Speech before the Washington World Affairs Council, June 30, 1987.

37. *New York Times,* March 24, 1987.

38. Riordan Roett, "Paraguay After Stroessner," *Foreign Affairs* 68 (Spring 1989): 124–142.

39. Those eager to believe that the Reagan administration's policy of verbal pressure for democracy contributed significantly to the fall of Stroessner would be well-advised to keep in mind that this was not the first

time a conservative U.S. administration pursued such a policy. The *Christian Science Monitor* reported on April 24, 1959, for example, on critical remarks made by the U.S. Ambassador to Paraguay regarding Stroessner's dictatorial rule:

> The [U.S.] Ambassador encouraged all Paraguayans to think more of their membership of the Western democratic family. . . . Reports from this upriver republic spoke of the deep impression the ambassadorial remarks had created, the significance of the speech having been quickly appreciated in official quarters, where there is increasing sensitiveness—and embarrassment—over the Paraguayan reputation of being the last remaining dictatorship in South America.

The resemblance to the situation in the 1980s, both the policy of verbal pressure and Paraguay's status as one of the last holdouts against democracy, is striking.

40. This account of the Reagan administration's policy toward Panama is drawn from interviews and informal conversations with numerous U.S. officials, the extensive newspaper accounts of the policy in 1987 and 1988, and two key secondary sources, Frederick Kempe, *Divorcing the Dictator: America's Bungled Affair with Noriega* (New York: G. P. Putnam's Sons, 1990) and John Dinges, *Our Man in Panama: How General Noriega Used the United States—and Made Millions in Drugs and Arms* (New York: Random House, 1990). Frank McNeil, *War and Peace in Central America* (New York: Charles Scribner's Sons, 1988) also contains much useful information.

41. *New York Times*, June 24, 1986.

42. McNeil, *War and Peace in Central America*, 286.

43. From McNeil's written deposition to the Senate Foreign Relations Committee, March 15, 1988, McNeil, *War and Peace in Central America*, 281–290.

44. McNeil, *War and Peace in Central America*, Appendix A.

45. *New York Times*, June 12, and June 13, 1986. The stories were written by Seymour Hersh, who had collected an array of information from U.S. intelligence sources.

46. Assistant Secretary Elliott Abrams met with Delvalle in Miami a week or two before Delvalle split with Noriega. Delvalle was considering announcing the firing of Noriega at the OAS in Washington. Abrams supported the firing but counseled Delvalle not to do it at the OAS. Abrams believed at the time that Delvalle was insufficiently courageous to go through with the firing. Author interview with Abrams.

47. *New York Times*, March 30, 1988.

48. *New York Times*, May 30, 1988.

49. In mid-1988 the State Department developed a covert action plan for CIA support to dissident Panamanian military officers seeking to oust Noriega. The Senate Intelligence Committee, fed up with the administration's desperation tactics in Panama and concerned that the plan could end up in the assassination of Noriega, rejected the proposal.

50. Very little has been written about U.S. policy toward Haiti in the

crucial 1985–1987 period. Some accounts of Haitian politics do cover aspects of U.S. policy in the period during and after Duvalier's fall but they are impressionistic. See Elizabeth Abbott, *Haiti: The Duvaliers and Their Legacy* (New York: McGraw Hill, 1988); Amy Wilentz, *The Rainy Season: Haiti Since Duvalier* (New York: Touchstone, 1989); Mark Danner, "Beyond the Mountains," *The New Yorker,* November 27, December 4, and December 11, 1989.

51. The certifications also had to establish that Haiti was cooperating with the United States in stopping the flow of illegal migration and improving the performance of aid programs.

52. For a more thorough analysis of the 1981–1985 period, see Georges Fauriol, "The Duvaliers and Haiti," *Orbis* 32 (Fall 1988): 587–607.

53. Author interview with Elliott Abrams.

54. *New York Times,* February 11, 1986.

55. *New York Times,* April 4, and April 11, 1986.

56. For a critical view of NDI's program in Haiti, see Michael Massey, "While Democrats Dither," *The New Republic,* November 16, 1987, 14–16.

57. *New York Times,* November 30, 1987.

58. *New York Times,* February 11, 1986.

59. *New York Times,* June 21, 1988.

60. *New York Times,* February 12, 1986.

61. For example, Arthur Schlesinger Jr. called for "a multinational rescue mission undertaken through the Organization of the American States or the United Nations," in "Yes, Washington, There is a Haiti," *New York Times,* September 8, 1987.

62. Author interview with Elliott Abrams.

63. See Raymond Bonner, *Waltzing with a Dictator: The Marcoses and the Making of American Policy* (New York: Times Books, 1987), chaps. 14–17.


## CHAPTER SIX

1. On the relation between the prodemocracy and anticommunist purposes of the Alliance for Progress, see Howard J. Wiarda, "Did the Alliance Lose its Way, or Were its Assumptions All Wrong from the Beginning and Are Those Assumptions Still with Us?" in L. Ronald Scheman, ed., *The Alliance for Progress: A Retrospective* (New York: Praeger, 1988), 95–120.

2. Section 281(a) of the 1961 Foreign Assistance Act as amended.

3. Robert Packenham, *Liberal America and the Third World* (Princeton: Princeton University Press, 1973), 100–101.

4. "A Retrospective of A.I.D.'s Experience in Strengthening Democratic Institutions in Latin America 1961–1981," Report produced for AID by Creative Associates International, September 1987. Some of these programs predated Title IX and were simply brought under the Title IX umbrella; others were created as efforts to respond to the Title IX directive.

5. Ibid., V–2.

6. Author interviews with AID officials involved in the human rights projects of the late 1970s.

7. "Promoting Democracy and Peace," Address by President Reagan to the British Parliament, London, June 8, 1982, *AFP 1982*, 18.

8. "The Democratic Revolution and its Future," Address before the Berlin Press Association, Berlin, September 13, 1981, *AFP 1981*, 60.

9. Summary of Project Democracy submitted to the U.S. Congress in 1983. Reprinted in "Authorizing Appropriations for Fiscal Years 1984–1985 for the Department of State, the U.S. Information Agency, the Board for International Broadcasting, the Inter-American Foundation, the Asia Foundation, to Establish the National Endowment for Democracy," Hearings and Markup before the Committee on Foreign Affairs and its Subcommittee on International Operations, House of Representatives, 98th Congress, 1st Session on H.R. 2915 (Washington: U.S. Government Printing Office, 1984), Appendix 6.

10. The American Political Foundation's feasibility study was carried out from December 1, 1982, to November 30, 1983. AID contributed $150,000 for the study in late 1982. Another $150,000 from the President's Unanticipated Needs Account was added in early 1983 and then another $100,000 in mid-1983. "Events Leading to the Establishment of the National Endowment for Democracy; Report to Senator Malcolm Wallop," U.S. General Accounting Office, July 6, 1984. On the early planning for NED, see also Christopher Madison, "Selling Democracy," *National Journal* (June 28, 1986): 1603–1608; Howard Wiarda, *The Democratic Revolution in Latin America: History, Politics and U.S. Policy* (New York: Holmes and Meier, 1990), chap. 6.

11. The proposal was a $20 million request for the rest of fiscal year 1983 and a $65 million request for fiscal year 1984.

12. Secretary of State Shultz, USIA Director Wick, and some other USIA officials testified on Project Democracy in early 1983. The hearings reveal some of Congress's doubts about the project. See hearings cited note 9.

13. Rep. Kostameyer used that phrase to describe Project Democracy in the hearings on the project. Ibid., 41.

14. Joel M. Woldman, "The National Endowment for Democracy," Congressional Research Service Issue Brief, April 2, 1987, 5.

15. Congress authorized $31.3 million for the NED for fiscal year 1984. It only appropriated $18 million, however, and the $18 million figure became the NED's approximate annual budget for the rest of the 1980s despite early attempts by the NED to increase its annual appropriation up to the $31.3 million authorization level.

16. Robert Parry and Peter Kornbluh, "Iran-Contra's Untold Story," *Foreign Policy* 72 (Fall 1988): 3–30.

17. "Section 116(e) Projects and Obligations FY 1978 to FY 1983," AID report (undated).

18. "Section 116(e): Projects and Obligations Fiscal Year 1984," AID report (undated), 4.

19. "Summary of Human Rights and Democracy Program Fiscal Year 1987," AID report (undated), 1.

20. See note 21, chap. 1 on the funding levels of the El Salvador electoral assistance project and the difficulty of obtaining definite figures for local currency aid projects.

21. See note 6, chap. 2 on the funding of the Honduran electoral assistance project.

22. Author interview with State Department official who served in Honduras in 1985.

23. "Summary of Human Rights Funding FY 1985," AID Report, undated.

24. The only published overview of the administration of justice program is a workship report, *Elusive Justice: The U.S. Administration of Justice Program in Latin America*, issued by the Washington Office on Latin America in May 1990. The Lawyers Committee for Human Rights has done studies of the El Salvador Judicial Reform Program, which is one part of the administration of justice program. See *From the Ashes: A Report on the Effort to Rebuild El Salvador's System of Justice* (1987) and *Underwriting Injustice: AID and El Salvador's Judicial Reform Program* (1989).

25. The interagency working group used James Gardner's study of the Law and Development program, *Legal Imperialism: American Lawyers and Foreign Aid in Latin America* (Madison: University of Wisconsin Press, 1980), as its main source of historical analysis.

26. Section 712 of the 1985 International Security and Cooperation Development Act, creating Section 534 of the Foreign Assistance Act.

27. Author interview with AID official.

28. Author interview with AID official.

29. *National Endowment for Democracy Annual Report 1986*, 32.

30. The Free Trade Union Institute predates the National Endowment; it was founded in 1977 and then brought under the Endowment umbrella in 1983.

31. *National Endowment for Democracy Annual Report 1986*, 44.

32. Paul Buchanan, "U.S. Labor and Latin American Democracy," in Abraham F. Lowenthal, ed., *Exporting Democracy: The United States and Latin America* (Baltimore: Johns Hopkins University Press, 1991).

33. A useful analysis of the contrasting methodologies of the Democratic and Republican Institutes is provided in Joshua Muravchik, "U.S. Political Parties Abroad," *The Washington Quarterly* (Summer 1989): 91-100.

34. Keith Schuette, President of the National Republican Institute, quoted in Joshua Muravchik, "U.S. Political Parties Abroad," 97.

35. National Republican Institute for International Affairs, pamphlet on current activities, 1989.

36. Memorandum from Brian Atwood, NDI President, to the Chairman, Board of Directors and Senior Advisory Committee of the National Democratic Institute, September 23, 1988, 5-6.

37. *National Endowment for Democracy Annual Report 1986,* 40–41.

38. In 1986, 1987, and 1988, the Republican Institute gave grants of $75,000, $100,000 and $145,000 respectively to the Asociación para la Defensa de la Libertad y Democracia en Costa Rica, a conservative political foundation. The Republican Institute's use of funds in a country that did not appear to have a pressing need for democracy assistance generated some controversy in the United States.

# Bibliography

Abbott, Elizabeth. *Haiti: The Duvaliers and Their Legacy.* New York: McGraw Hill, 1988.

Agency for International Development. *A Retrospective of A.I.D.'s Experience in Strengthening Democratic Institutions in Latin America 1961–1981.* Report produced by Creative Associates International for the Agency for International Development. September 1987.

———. *Annual Reports of Section 116(e) Human Rights Programs.*

Americas Watch. *Human Rights in El Salvador on the Eve of Elections.* Washington: Americas Watch, 1988.

———. *Closing the Space: Human Rights in Guatemala, May 1987–October 1988.* Washington: Americas Watch. 1988.

Americas Watch, and National Coalition for Haitian Refugees. *Duvalierism Since Duvalier.* Washington: Americas Watch and National Coalition for Haitian Refugees, 1986.

Amnesty International. *El Salvador: "Death Squads"—a Government Strategy.* London: Amnesty International Publications, 1988.

———. *Honduras: Civilian Authority-Military Power. Human Rights Violations in the 1980s.* London: Amnesty International Publications. 1988.

———. *Guatemala: The Human Rights Record.* London: Amnesty International Publications, 1987.

Amuzegar, Jahangir. "Dealing with Debt." *Foreign Policy* 68 (Fall 1987): 140–158.

Andersen, Martin E. "The Military Obstacle to Latin Democracy," *Foreign Policy* 73 (Winter 1988/89): 94–113.

Anderson, Ken, and Jean-Marie Simon. "Permanent Counterinsurgency in Guatemala," *Telos* 73 (Fall 1987): 9–46.

Anderson, Thomas P. *Politics in Central America.* New York: Praeger, 1988.

———. "Politics and the Military in Honduras," *Current History* (December 1988): 425–428, 431–432.

Arnson, Cynthia. *Crossroads: Congress, the Reagan Administration, and Central America.* New York: Pantheon, 1989.

Arriagada, Genaro. *The Politics of Power.* Boston: Unwin Hyman, 1988.

Bacevich, A. J., James P. Hallums, Richard H. White, and Thomas F. Young.

*American Military Policy in Small Wars: The Case of El Salvador.* Washington: Pergamon-Brassey's, 1988.

Bagley, Bruce M. "Contadora: The Failure of Diplomacy," *Journal of Interamerican Studies and World Affairs* 28 (Fall 1986): 1–32.

——, ed. *Contadora and the Diplomacy of Peace in Central America. Volume I: The United States, Central America, and Contadora.* Boulder, CO: Westview, 1987.

Baloyra, Enrique A. *El Salvador in Transition.* Chapel Hill: University of North Carolina, 1982.

——. "Dilemmas of Political Transition in El Salvador," *Journal of International Affairs* 38 (Winter 1985): 221–242.

——. "The Seven Plagues of El Salvador," *Current History* (December 1987): 413–416, 433–434.

Bellegarde-Smith, Patrick. *Haiti: The Besieged Citidel.* Boulder, CO: Westview Press, 1990.

Best, Edward. *U.S. Policy and Regional Security.* Hants, Great Britain: Gower, 1987.

Blachman, Morris J., and Ronald G. Hellman. "Costa Rica." In Morris J. Blachman, William M. LeoGrande, and Kenneth Sharpe, eds., *Confronting Revolution: Security Through Diplomacy in Central America.* New York: Pantheon, 1986, 156–182.

Blachman, Morris J., William M. LeoGrande, and Kenneth Sharpe, eds. *Confronting Revolution: Security Through Diplomacy in Central America.* New York: Pantheon, 1986.

Boeninger, Edgardo. "The Chilean Road to Democracy," *Foreign Affairs* 64 (Spring 1986): 812–832.

Bonner, Raymond. *Weakness and Deceit.* New York: Times Books, 1984.

——. *Waltzing with a Dictator: The Marcoses and the Making of American Policy.* New York: Times Books, 1987.

Booth, John A. *The End and the Beginning: The Nicaraguan Revolution.* Boulder, CO: Westview, 1985.

Booth, John A., and Mitchell A. Seligson. *Political Participation in Latin America. Volume I: Citizen and State.* New York: Holmes and Meier, 1978.

——. *Elections and Democracy in Central America.* Chapel Hill: University of North Carolina Press, 1989.

Brown, Cynthia, ed. *With Friends Like These: The Americas Watch Report on Human Rights and U.S. Policy in Latin America.* New York: Pantheon Books, 1985.

Buchanan, Paul. "U.S. Labor and Latin American Democracy." In Abraham F. Lowenthal, ed., *Exporting Democracy: The United States and Latin America.* Baltimore: Johns Hopkins University Press, 1991.

Burns, Bradford. *At War in Nicaragua: The Reagan Doctrine and the Politics of Nostalgia.* New York: Harper & Row, 1987.

Calvert, Peter. *Guatemala: A Nation in Turmoil.* Boulder, CO: Westview Press, 1985.

Chace, James. *Endless War: How We Got Involved in Central America—and What Can Be Done.* New York: Vintage, 1984.

Child, Jack, ed. *Conflict in Central America: Approaches to Peace and Security.* New York: St. Martin's Press, 1984.

Christian, Shirley. *Nicaragua: Revolution in the Family.* New York: Random House, 1985.

Cirincione, Joseph, ed. *Central America and the Western Alliance.* New York: Holmes and Meier, 1985.

Cohen, Benjamin J. "International Debt and Linkage Strategies: Some Foreign-Policy Implications for the United States," *International Organization* 39 (Autumn 1985): 699–727.

Colburn, Forrest D. "Embattled Nicaragua," *Current History* (December 1987): 405–408, 431.

Coleman, Kenneth M, and George C. Herring, eds. *The Central American Crisis.* Wilmington, DE: Scholarly Resources, 1985.

Dahl, Robert A. *Polyarchy: Participation and Opposition.* New Haven: Yale University Press, 1971.

Danner, Mark. "Beyond the Mountains," *The New Yorker,* November 27, December 4, and December 11, 1989.

Diamond, Larry. "Beyond Authoritarianism and Totalitarianism: Strategies for Democratization," *The Washington Quarterly* (Winter 1989): 141–163.

Diamond, Larry, Juan J. Linz, and Seymour Martin Lipset, eds. *Democracy in Developing Countries, Volume IV: Latin America.* Boulder, CO: Lynne Rienner, 1989.

Dickey, Christopher. "Central America: From Quagmire to Cauldron," *Foreign Affairs* 62 (America and the World 1983): 659–694.

———. *With the Contras: A Reporter in the Wilds of Nicaragua.* New York: Simon and Schuster, 1985.

Dillon, Sam. "Dateline El Salvador: Crisis Renewed." *Foreign Policy* 73 (Winter 1988/89): 153–170.

Dinges, John. *Our Man in Panama: How General Noriega Used the United States—and Made Millions in Drugs and Arms* (New York: Random House, 1990).

Di Palma, Giuseppe, and Laurence Whitehead. *The Central American Impasse.* New York: St. Martin's Press, 1986.

Diskin, Martin. *Trouble in Our Backyard: Central America and the United States in the Eighties.* New York: Pantheon, 1983.

Drake, Paul, and Eduardo Silva, eds. *Elections and Democratization in Latin America, 1980–1985.* La Jolla, CA: Center for Iberian and Latin American Studies, 1986.

Dunkerly, James. *The Long War: Dictatorship and Revolution in El Salvador.* London: Junction Books, 1982.

———. *Power in the Isthmus: A Political History of Central America.* New York: Verso, 1988.

Durán, Esperanza, ed. *Latin America and the World Recession*. Cambridge: Cambridge University Press, 1985.

Fagen, Richard R. "The Carter Administration and Latin America: Business as Usual?" *Foreign Affairs* 57 (America and the World 1978): 652–669.

———. *Forging Peace: The Challenge of Central America*. New York: Basil Blackwell, 1987.

Fagen, Richard R., and Olga Pellicer. *The Future of Central America: Policy Choices for the U.S. and Mexico*. Stanford: Stanford Univeristy Press, 1983.

Falcoff, Mark, and Robert Royal. *The Continuing Crisis: U.S. Policy in Central America and the Caribbean*. Washington: Ethics and Public Policy Center, 1987.

Falcoff, Mark, Arturo Valenzuela, and Susan Kaufman Purcell. *Chile: Prospects for Democracy*. New York: Council on Foreign Relations, 1988.

Farer, Tom J. "Manage the Revolution?" *Foreign Policy* 52 (Fall 1983): 96–117.

Fauriol, Georges. "The Duvaliers and Haiti," *Orbis* 32 (Fall 1988): 587–607.

———. "The Shadow of Latin American Affairs," *Foreign Affairs* 69 (America and the World 1989/90): 116–134.

Fauriol, Georges, and Eva Loser. *Guatemala's Political Puzzle*. New Brunswick, N.J.: Transaction Books, 1988.

Findling, John E. *Close Neighbors, Distant Friends: United States—Central American Relations*. New York: Greenwood Press, 1987.

Fishlow, Albert. "The United States and Brazil: The Case of the Missing Relationship," *Foreign Affairs* 60 (Spring 1982): 904–923.

Gabriel, Richard. "Scenes from an Invasion: How the U.S. Military Stumbled to Victory in Grenada," *The Washington Monthly* (February 1986): 34–41.

García, José Z. "El Salvador: A Glimmer of Hope." *Current History* (December 1986): 409–412.

Gardner, James. *Legal Imperialism: American Lawyers and Foreign Aid in Latin America*. Madison: University of Wisconsin Press, 1980.

Gedda, George. "A Dangerous Region," *Foreign Service Journal* 60 (February 1983): 18–21, 34.

Gershman, Carl. "The United States and the World Democratic Revolution." *The Washington Quarterly* (Winter 1989): 127–139.

Gilmore, William C. *The Grenada Intervention*. New York: Facts on File, 1984.

Gleijeses, Piero. "The Case for Power Sharing in El Salvador," *Foreign Affairs* 61 (Summer 1983): 1048–1063.

———. "Perspectives of a Regime Transformation in Guatemala." In Wolf Grabendorff, Heinrich-W. Krumwiede and Jorg Todt, eds., *Political Change in Central America: Internal and External Dimensions*. Boulder, CO: Westview, 1984, 127–138.

Goodman, Louis, Johanna Mendelson, and Juan Rial, eds. *The Military and Democracy: The Future of Civil-Military Relations in Latin America*. Lexington, MA: Lexington Books, 1990.

Gutman, Roy. *Banana Diplomacy: The Making of American Policy in Nicaragua 1981–1987.* New York: Simon and Schuster, 1988.

Hahn, Walter, F., ed. *Central America and the Reagan Doctrine.* Lanham, MD: University Press of America, 1987.

Hamilton, Nora, Jeffry A. Freidan, Linda Fuller, and Manuel Pastor, Jr., eds. *Crisis in Central America: Regional Dynamics and U.S. Policy in the 1980s.* Boulder, CO: Westview, 1988.

Herman, Edward S., and Frank Brodhead. *Demonstration Elections: U.S.-Staged Elections in the Dominican Republic, Vietnam, and El Salvador.* Boston: South End Press, 1984.

Huntington, Samuel. *American Politics: The Promise of Disharmony.* Cambridge: Belknap Press, 1981.

Inter-American Dialogue. *The Americas in 1988: A Time for Choices.* Lanham, MD: University Press of America, 1988.

International Court of Justice. "Case Concerning Military and Paramilitary Activities in and against Nicaragua, Nicaragua v. United States of America, Merits, Judgment of June 27, 1986," *Reports of Judgments, Advisory Opinions and Order 1986.* The Hague: International Court of Justice, 1986.

International Human Rights Law Group. *Chile: The Plebiscite and Beyond.* Washington: International Human Rights Law Group, February 1989.

International Human Rights Law Group, and Washington Office on Latin America. *Political Transition and the Rule of Law in Guatemala.* Washington, D.C., 1988.

Jacoby, Tamar. "The Reagan Turnaround on Human Rights." *Foreign Affairs* 64 (Summer 1986): 1066–1086.

Karl, Terry. "Exporting Democracy: The Unanticipated Effects of U.S. Electoral Policy in El Salvador." In Nora Hamilton, Jeffry A. Freiden, Linda Fuller, and Manuel Pastor, Jr., eds., *Crisis in Central America: Regional Dynamics and U.S. Policy in the 1980s.* Boulder, CO: Westview, 1988, 173–192.

Kassebaum, Nancy L. *Report of the U.S. Official Observer Mission to the El Salvador Constituent Assembly Elections of March 28, 1982.* Washington: U.S. Government Printing Office, 1982.

Kempe, Frederick. *Divorcing the Dictator: America's Bungled Affair with Noriega.* New York: G. P. Putnam's Sons, 1990.

Kirkpatrick, Jeane. "Dictators and Double Standards," *Commentary* (November 1979): 29–40.

———. "U.S. Security and Latin America," *Commentary* (January 1981): 34–45.

Kryzanek, Michael J. *U.S.-Latin American Relations.* New York: Praeger, 1985.

Kuczynski, Pedro-Pablo. *Latin American Debt.* Baltimore: Johns Hopkins University Press, 1987.

Lake, Anthony. *Somoza Falling.* Boston: Houghton Mifflin, 1989.

Lawyers Committee for Human Rights. *From the Ashes: A Report on the*

*Effort to Rebuild El Salvador's System of Justice*. New York: Lawyers Committee for Human Rights, 1987.

———. *Underwriting Injustice: AID and El Salvador's Judicial Reform Program*. New York: Lawyers Committee for Human Rights, 1989.

LeFeber, Walter. *Inevitable Revolutions: The United States and Central America*. New York: W.W. Norton, 1984.

———. *The Panama Canal: The Crisis in Historical Perspective*. New York: Oxford University Press, 1989.

Leiken, Robert S., ed. *Central America: Anatomy of Conflict*. New York: Pergamon Press, 1984.

LeMoyne, James. "Testifying to Torture," *New York Times Magazine* (June 5, 1988): 45–47, 62–66.

———. "El Salvador's Forgotten War," *Foreign Affairs* 68 (Summer 1989): 105–125.

LeoGrande, William M. "The Revolution in Nicaragua: Another Cuba?" *Foreign Affairs* 58 (Fall 1979): 28–50.

———. "Rollback or Containment? The United States, Nicaragua, and the Search for Peace in Central America." In Bruce M. Bagley, ed., *Contadora and the Diplomacy of Peace in Central America. Vol. 1: The United States, Central America, and Contadora*. Boulder: Westview Press, 1987, 83–112.

Levine, Robert M. "Brazil: The Dimensions of Democratization," *Current History* (February 1982): 60–63, 86–87.

Levinson, Jerome. *The Alliance that Lost Its Way*. Chicago: Quadrangle Books, 1970.

Lewis, Gordon K. *Grenada: The Jewel Despoiled*. Baltimore: Johns Hopkins University Press, 1987.

Linz, Juan J. *The Breakdown of Democratic Regimes: Crisis, Breakdown and Reequilibration*. Baltimore: Johns Hopkins University Press, 1978.

Lopez, George A., and Michael Stohl, eds. *Liberalization and Redemocratization in Latin America*. Westport, CT: Greenwood Press, 1987.

Lowenthal, Abraham F. "CBI: Misplaced Emphasis," *Foreign Policy*, 47 (Summer 1982): 114–118.

———. "Ronald Reagan and Latin America: Coping with Hegemony in Decline." In Kenneth A. Oye, Robert J. Lieber, Donald Rothchild, eds., *Eagle Defiant: United States Foreign Policy in the 1980s*. Boston: Little Brown, 1983, 311–337.

———. *Partners in Conflict*. Baltimore: Johns Hopkins University Press, 1988, chap. 5.

———. "The United States and South America," *Current History* (January 1988): 1–4, 42–43.

———, ed. *Exporting Democracy: The United States and Latin America*. Baltimore: Johns Hopkins University Press, 1991.

Madison, Christopher. "Selling Democracy," *National Journal* (June 28, 1986): 1603–1608.

Maechling, Charles Jr. "Human Rights Dehumanized," *Foreign Policy* 52 (Fall 1983): 118–135.

Mainwaring, Scott. "The Transition to Democracy in Brazil," *Journal of Interamerican Studies and World Affairs* 28 (Spring 1986): 149–179.

Malloy, James M., and Eduardo Gamarra. *Revolution and Reaction: Bolivia 1964–1985.* New Brunswick, N.J.: Transaction Press, 1988.

Malloy, James M., and Mitchell Seligson, eds. *Authoritarians and Democrats: Regime Transition in Latin America.* Pittsburgh: University of Pittsburgh Press, 1987.

Manwaring, Max G., and Court Prisk, eds. *El Salvador at War.* Washington: National Defense University Press, 1988.

McDonald, Ronald. "Confrontation and Transition in Uruguay," *Current History* (February 1985): 57–60, 87–88.

McNeil, Frank. *War and Peace in Central America.* New York: Charles Scribner's Sons, 1988.

Menges, Constantine. *Inside the National Security Council: The True Story of the Making and Unmaking of Reagan's Foreign Policy.* New York: Simon and Schuster, 1988.

Middlebrook, Kevin J., and Carlos Rico, eds. *The United States and Latin America in the 1980s: Contending Perspectives on a Decade of Crisis.* Pittsburgh: University of Pittsburgh Press, 1986.

Millet, Richard. "The Politics of Violence: Guatemala and El Salvador," *Current History* (Fall 1981): 70–74.

———. "The United States and Latin America," *Current History* (February 1984): 49–53, 84–85.

———. "Guatemala: Progress and Paralysis," *Current History* (March 1985): 109–113, 136.

———. "Guatemala's Painful Progress," *Current History* (December 1986): 413–416, 430–431.

Millman, Joel. "El Salvador's Army: A Force Unto Itself," *New York Times Magazine* (December 10, 1989): 47, 95–97.

Molineu, Harold. *U.S. Policy Toward Latin America: From Regionalism to Globalism.* Boulder, CO: Westview, 1986.

Moneta, Carlos. "The United States and Argentina." In Robert Wesson and Heraldo Muñoz, eds., *Latin American Views of U.S. Policy.* New York: Praeger, 1986, 106–121.

Montgomery, Tommie Sue. *Revolution in El Salvador: Origins and Evolution.* Boulder, CO: Westview, 1982.

Moore, John Norton. *Law and the Grenada Mission.* Charlottesville, NC: Center for Law and National Security, 1984.

Moreno, Dario. "Peace and the Nicaraguan Revolution," *Current History* (December 1988): 405–408, 431–432.

Morris, James A. *Honduras: Caudillo Politics and Military Rulers.* Boulder, CO: Westview Press, 1984.

Motley, Langhorne. "Letting Off Steam." In Hans Binnendijk, ed., *Authori-*

*tarian Regimes in Transition.* Washington: Foreign Service Institute, 1987, 248–253.

Muravchik, Joshua. "The Nicaraguan Debate," *Foreign Affairs* 65 (Winter 1986/87): 366–382.

———. *The Uncertain Crusade: Jimmy Carter and the Dilemmas of Human Rights Policy.* Lanham, MD: Hamilton Press, 1986.

———. "U.S. Political Parties Abroad," *The Washington Quarterly* (Summer 1989): 91–100.

National Endowment for Democracy. *Annual Report* (1984–1989).

Needler, Martin. *The Problem of Democracy in Latin America.* Lexington, MA: D.C. Heath, 1987.

Newfarmer, Richard S. "Economic Policy Toward the Caribbean Basin: The Balance Sheet," *Journal of Interamerican Studies and World Affairs* 27 (February 1985): 63–90.

———, ed. *From Gunboats to Diplomacy: New U.S. Policies for Latin America.* Baltimore: Johns Hopkins University Press, 1984.

O'Brien, Philip, and Paul Cammack, eds. *Generals in Retreat: The Crisis of Military Rule in Latin America.* Manchester: Manchester University Press, 1985.

O'Donnell, Guillermo, Philippe C. Schmitter, and Laurence Whitehead, eds. *Transitions from Authoritarian Rule in Latin America.* Baltimore: Johns Hopkins University Press, 1986.

Pang, Eul-Soo. "Brazil's New Democracy," *Current History* (February 1983): 54–57, 87–89.

Packenham, Robert. *Liberal America and the Third World.* Princeton: Princeton University Press, 1973.

Parry, Robert, and Peter Kornbluh. "Iran-Contra's Untold Story," *Foreign Policy* 72 (Fall 1988): 3–30.

Pastor, Robert. *Condemned to Repetition: The United States and Nicaragua.* Princeton: Princeton University Press, 1987.

———. "The Reagan Administration and Latin America: Eagle Insurgent." In Kenneth A. Oye, Robert J. Lieber, and Donald Rothchild, eds., *Eagle Resurgent? The Reagan Era in American Foreign Policy.* Boston: Little Brown, 1987.

———. "Securing a Democratic Hemisphere," *Foreign Policy* 73 (Winter 1988–89): 41–59.

———, ed. *Democracy in the Americas: Stopping the Pendulum.* New York: Holmes and Meier, 1989.

Payne, Anthony, Paul Sutton, and Tony Thorndike. *Grenada: Revolution and Invasion.* New York: St. Martin's Press, 1984, chap. 6.

Peeler, John. *Latin American Democracies: Colombia, Costa Rica, Venezuela.* Chapel Hill: University of North Carolina Press, 1985.

Peralta, Gabriel Aguilera. "The Hidden War: Guatemala's Counterinsurgency Campaign." In Nora Hamilton, Jeffry A. Freiden, Linda Fuller, and Manuel Pastor, Jr., eds., *Crisis in Central America: Regional Dynamics and U.S. Policy in the 1980s.* Boulder, CO: Westview, 1988, 153–172.

Perloff, Harvey S. *Alliance for Progress, A Social Invention in the Making*. Baltimore: Johns Hopkins University Press, 1969.

Perry, William. "In Search of a Latin America Policy: The Elusive Quest. *The Washington Quarterly* (Spring 1990): 125–134.

Policy Alternatives for the Caribbean and Central America (PACCA). *Changing Course: Blueprint for Peace in Central America and the Caribbean*, Washington: Institute for Policy Studies, 1984.

Purcell, Susan Kaufman. "War and Debt in South America," *Foreign Affairs* 61 (America and the World 1982): 660–674.

———. "The Choice in Central America," *Foreign Affairs* 66 (Fall 1987): 109–128.

Remmer, Karen L. "Redemocratization and the Impact of Authoritarian Rule in Latin America," *Comparative Politics* 17 (April 1985): 253–276.

*Report of the National Bipartisan Commission on Central America*. Washington: U.S. Government Printing Office, January 1984.

Robinson, Linda. "Peace in Central America?" *Foreign Affairs* 66 (America and the World 1987/88): 591–613.

———. "Dwindling Options in Panama," *Foreign Affairs* 68 (Winter 1988/89): 187–205.

———. *Congress and U.S. Policy Toward Nicaragua in 1987*. Washington: Congressional Research Service, January 13, 1989.

———. "Hanging in the Balance: El Salvador's Future and the Limits of U.S. Power," *Commonweal* (April 21, 1989): 242–245.

Roett, Riordan. "Staying the Course," *The Wilson Quarterly* 73 (Summer 1983): 46–61.

———. "Democracy and Debt in South America: A Continent's Dilemma," *Foreign Affairs* 62 (America and the World 1983): 695–720.

———. "Paraguay After Stroessner," *Foreign Affairs* 68 (Spring 1989): 124–142.

Rogers, William D. "The United States and Latin America," *Foreign Affairs* 63 (America and the World 1984): 560–580.

Ropp, Steve C. "Panama's Defiant Noriega," *Current History* (December 1988): 417–420.

Ropp, Steve C., and James A. Morris. *Central America: Crisis and Adaptation*. Albuquerque: University of New Mexico Press, 1984.

Rosenberg, Mark B. "Honduran Scorecard—Military and Democrats in Central America," *Caribbean Review* 12 (Winter 1983): 12–15, 39–42.

———. "Can Democracy Survive the Democrats? From Transition to Consolidation in Honduras." In John A. Booth and Mitchell A. Seligson, eds., *Elections and Democracy in Central America*. Chapel Hill: University of North Carolina Press, 1989, 40–59.

Rosenberg, Mark and Philip Shepard. *Honduras Confronts its Future: Contending Perspectives on Critical Issues*. Boulder, CO: Lynne Rienner, 1986.

Rotberg, Robert I. "Haiti's Past Mortgages its Future," *Foreign Affairs* 67 (Fall 1988): 93–109.

Sanchez, Nestor. "The Communist Threat," *Foreign Policy* 52 (Fall 1983): 43–50.

Sanford, Jonathan E. *Central America: Major Trends in U.S. Foreign Assistance Fiscal 1978 to Fiscal 1990.* Washington: Congressional Research Service, June 19, 1990.

Schoenhals, Kai P., and Richard A. Melanson. *Revolution and Intervention in Grenada: The New Jewel Movement, the United States, and the Caribbean.* Boulder, CO: Westview, 1985.

Schoultz, Lars. *National Security and United States Policy Toward Latin America.* Princeton: Princeton University Press, 1987.

Schulz, Donald E., and Douglas H. Graham. *Revolution and Counterrevolution in Central America and the Caribbean.* Boulder, CO: Westview, 1984.

Serafino, Nina. "Dateline Managua: Defining Democracy," *Foreign Policy* 70 (Spring 1988): 166–182.

Sereseres, Caesar, D. "Guatemalan Politics, Internal War, and U.S. Policy Options." In *United States Policy Toward Guatemala,* Hearing before the Subcommittee on Western Hemisphere Affairs, U.S. Congress, House of Representatives, Committee on Foreign Affairs, 98th Cong., 1st Sess., March 9, 1983. Washington: U.S. Government Printing Office, 1983, 20–59.

Sheahan, John. *Patterns of Development in Latin America: Poverty, Repression, and Economic Strategy.* Princeton: Princeton University Press, 1987.

Shepard, Philip L. "Honduras." In Morris J. Blachman, William M. LeoGrande, and Kenneth Sharpe, eds., *Confronting Revolution: Security Through Diplomacy in Central America.* New York: Pantheon, 1986, 125–155.

Sigmund, Paul. "Latin America: Change or Continuity?" *Foreign Affairs* 60 (America and the World 1981): 629–657.

Smith, Wayne. "Lies about Nicaragua," *Foreign Policy* 67 (Summer 1987): 87–103.

Timerman, Jacobo. *Prisoner Without a Name, Cell Without a Number.* New York: Knopf, 1981.

Torres-Rivas, Edelberto. *Repression and Resistance: The Struggle for Democracy in Central America.* Boulder, CO: Westview, 1989.

Tulchin, Joseph S. *Argentina and the United States: A Conflicted Relationship.* Boston: Twayne, 1990.

Turner, Robert F. *Nicaragua v. United States: A Look at the Facts.* Washington: Pergamon-Brassey's, 1987.

U.S. Congress. *Report on the Congressional Committees Investigating the Iran-Contra Affair.* S. Rept. No. 100–216, H. Rept. No 100–433, 100th Cong., 1st. Sess. Washington: U.S. Government Printing Office, 1987.

U.S. Congress. House of Representatives. Committee on Foreign Affairs and Subcommittee on International Operations. *Hearings and Markup on*

*Authorizing Appropriations for Fiscal Years 1984–85 for the Department of State, the U.S. Information Agency, the Board for International Broadcasting, the Inter-American Foundation, the Asia Foundation, to Establish the National Endowment for Democracy.* Washington: U.S. Government Printing Office, 1984.

U.S. Department of State. *American Foreign Policy Current Documents 1981.* Washington: U.S. Department of State, 1984.

———. *American Foreign Policy Current Documents 1982.* Washington: U.S. Department of State, 1985.

———. *American Foreign Policy Current Documents 1983.* Washington: U.S. Department of State, 1985.

———. *American Foreign Policy Current Documents 1984.* Washington: U.S. Department of State, 1986.

———. *American Foreign Policy Current Documents 1985.* Washington: U.S. Department of State, 1986.

———. *American Foreign Policy Current Documents 1986.* Washington: U.S. Department of State, 1987.

———. *American Foreign Policy Current Documents 1987.* Washington: U.S. Department of State, 1988.

———. *American Foreign Policy Current Documents 1988.* Washington: U.S. Department of State, 1989.

———. *Country Reports on Human Rights* (1981–1989).

U.S. Department of State, and U.S. Department of Defense. *The Grenada Documents: An Overview and Selection.* Washington: U.S. Department of State and U.S. Department of Defense, 1984.

U.S. Department of the Treasury. "The Latin American Debt Problem," Office of the Assistant Secretary, International Affairs, Department of the Treasury, November 13, 1984 in *Dealing with the Debt Problem of Latin America*, Proceedings of a Conference, Joint Economic Committee Print, 98th Congress, 2d Session, S. Rpt. 98–284. Washington: U.S. Government Printing Office 1985.

U.S. General Accounting Office. *Events Leading to the Establishment of the National Endowment for Democracy. Report to Senator Malcolm Wallop.* Washington: U.S. General Accounting Office, July 6, 1984.

———. *Central America: Impact of U.S. Assistance in the 1980s.* Washington: U.S. General Accounting Office, 1989.

U.S. Library of Congress. Congressional Research Service. *El Salvador, 1979–1989: A Briefing Book on U.S. Aid and the Situation in El Salvador.* Washington: Congressional Research Service, April 28, 1989.

Vaky, Viron P. "Positive Containment in Nicaragua," *Foreign Policy* 68 (Fall 1987): 42–58.

Valenta, Jiri, and Esperanza Durán, eds. *Conflict in Nicaragua: A Multidimensional Perspective.* Boston: Allen and Unwin, 1987.

Valenta, Jiri, and Herbert J. Ellison, eds. *Grenada and Soviet/Cuban Policy: Internal Crisis and U.S./OECS Intervention.* Boulder, CO: Westview, 1986.

Washington Office on Latin America. *Police Aid and Political Will.* Washington: Washington Office on Latin America, 1987.

———. *Elusive Justice: The U.S. Administration of Justice Program in Latin America.* Washington: Washington Office on Latin America, 1990.

———. *U.S. Electoral Assistance and Democratic Development: Chile, Nicaragua and Panama.* Washington: Washington Office on Latin America, 1990.

Weeks, John. "An Interpretation of the Central America Crisis," *Latin American Research Review* 21 (1986): 31–54.

Weinstein, Martin. *Uruguay: Democracy at the Crossroads.* Boulder, CO: Westview Press, 1988.

Weintraub, Sidney. "CBI: A Flawed Model," *Foreign Policy* 47 (Summer 1982): 128–133.

Wesson, Robert, and Heraldo Muñoz, eds. *Latin American Views of U.S. Policy.* New York: Praeger, 1986.

Whelan, James R. *Out of the Ashes: Life, Death and Transfiguration of Democracy in Chile.* Washington: Rengery Gateway, 1989.

White, Richard Alan. *The Morass: United States Intervention in Central America.* New York: Harper & Row, 1984.

Wiarda, Howard J. "Is Latin America Democratic and Does It Want to Be? The Crisis and Quest of Democracy in the Hemisphere." In Howard J. Wiarda, ed., *The Continuing Struggle for Democracy in Latin America.* Boulder, CO: Westview, 1980, 3–24.

———. *In Search of Policy: The United States and Latin America.* Washington: American Enterprise Institute, 1984.

———. "United States Policy in South America: A Maturing Relationship? *Current History* (February 1985): 49–52, 86–87.

———. "Can Democracy Be Exported? The Quest for Democracy in U.S. Policy toward Latin America." In Howard J. Wiarda. *Finding Our Way? Toward Maturity in U.S.-Latin American Relations.* Washington: American Enterprise Institute, 1987, chap. 5.

———. "Did the Alliance Lose its Way, or Were its Assumptions All Wrong from the Beginning and Are Those Assumptions Still with Us?" In L. Ronald Scheman, ed., *The Alliance for Progress: A Retrospective.* New York: Praeger, 1988, 95–120.

———. *The Democratic Revolution in Latin America: History, Politics and U.S. Policy.* New York: Holmes and Meier, 1990.

———, ed. *Rift and Revolution: The Central American Imbroglio.* Washington: American Enterprise Institute, 1984.

Wilentz, Amy. *The Rainy Season: Haiti Since Duvalier.* New York: Touchstone, 1989.

Winn, Peter. "U.S. Electoral Aid in Chile: Reflections on a Success Story," Paper presented at Washington Office on Latin America conference "U.S. Electoral Assistance and Democratic Development: Chile, Nicaragua, Panama," January 19, 1990, Washington, D.C.

Woldman, Joel M. *The National Endowment for Democracy.* Washington: Congressional Research Service Issue Brief, April 2, 1987.

Woodward, Robert. *Veil: The Secret Wars of the CIA 1981–1987,* New York: Pocket Books, 1987.

Wynia, Gary. "Argentina: Rebuilding the Relationship." In Richard S. Newfarmer, ed., *From Gunboats to Diplomacy: New U.S. Policies for Latin America.* Baltimore: Johns Hopkins University Press, 1984, 162–175.

———. *Argentina: Illusions and Reality.* New York: Holmes and Meier, 1986.

———. "Readjusting to Democracy in Argentina," *Current History* (January 1987): 5–8, 34.

Zak, Marilyn Anne. "Assisting Elections in the Third World," *The Washington Quarterly* (Autumn 1987): 175–193.

# INDEX

Designer: Sandy Drooker
Compositor: G&S Typesetters
Text: Zapf Book Light
Display: Eurostile Bold
Printer: Bookcrafters, Inc.
Binder: Bookcrafters, Inc.